# Understanding
# **Substance Abuse**
# & Treatment

**Edited by**
George Pratsinak, Ph.D.,
and
Robert Alexander, Ph.D.

**Contributors:**
Dr. Robert Alexander
Dr. Brian Grover
Dr. Lee Lederer
Dr. Don Murray
Dr. George Pratsinak
Dr. Dennis Schimmel
Dr. Michael Sharp
Dr. Mark Simpson
Dr. Vickie Verdeyen
Dr. Gary Whittenberger

This manual was originally produced by the Federal Bureau of Prisons to establish standards for the Comprehensive Drug Education Program offered in Federal Bureau of Prisons facilities and to provide accurate information regarding drugs, addiction, and treatment.

Special thanks to Dr. Curt Toler, Chief of Psychological Services, and Dr. Don Murray, National Drug Abuse Program Coordinator, Federal Bureau of Prisons, for their leadership and support. We are indebted to Bureau of Prisons Director J. Michael Quinlan for his strong leadership in this area, which affects correctional systems nationwide.

This publication may be ordered from:

**American Correctional Association**
**8025 Laurel Lakes Court**
**Laurel, MD 20707-5075**

This manual will continue to be revised in the future. Please send comments to:

Dr. Robert Alexander      or      Dr. Don Murray
Psychology Services                           National Drug Abuse Program Coordinator
Federal Correctional Institution            Federal Bureau of Prisons
Petersburg, VA 23804-1000                320 First Street, NW
                                           NALC Room 301
                                           Washington, DC 20534

President: Helen G. Corrothers
Executive Director: James A. Gondles, Jr.
Publications Director: Patricia L. Poupore
Managing Editor: Elizabeth Watts
Editor: Alexandra Rockey
Inside Design: Mary Beth Mason
Cover Design: Kristen Mosbaek
Cover Illustration: Sherrell Medbery

Printed in the United States of America in 1992 by Goodway Graphics, Springfield, Va.

ISBN 0-929310-73-X

# CONTENTS

# FOREWORD

Substance abuse treatment has become one of corrections' most important program services. More and more offenders who pass through the criminal justice system have a problem with alcohol or drugs. In 1990, the National Institute of Justice's Drug Use Forecasting program found the percentage of male arrestees testing positive for an illicit drug at the time of arrest ranged from 30 percent in Omaha to 78 percent in San Diego. The 1989 Bureau of Justice Statistics *Survey of Inmates in Local Jails* reported that more than half of convicted inmates reported being under the influence of drugs or alcohol at the time of offense. Overall, 13 percent of convicted jail inmates reported they had committed their current offense to obtain money for drugs.

It is clear that alcohol and drug abuse are a major problem in society—a contributing factor to many crimes. Many offenders simply don't know the facts about substance abuse and its potential harmful effects. This manual was designed to train those who conduct treatment programs to teach offenders basic information about substance abuse—the different types of drugs and their effects on the body and mind, treatment methods, HIV infection and AIDS, and how substance abuse affects family relationships. It is also a valuable tool to help line staff better understand and recognize substance abuse.

Besides basic information about all classes of drugs—alcohol, barbiturates, amphetamines, etc.—this manual contains extensive resource lists of recommended organizations and helpful films and publications. Lesson plan outlines are also provided to assist the trainer. And, true/false tests with answer keys are included.

In the coming decade, it will be one of corrections' mandates to better serve the large number of substance abusers under our care. This manual will facilitate this process and help these offenders move toward a socially productive, drug-free life.

We are indebted to Federal Bureau of Prisons Director J. Michael Quinlan for allowing the American Correctional Association to share this valuable work with corrections systems nationwide.

*James A. Gondles, Jr.*
*Executive Director*

# I.
# DESIGNING A TREATMENT PROGRAM

*In the long run, I think an offender's value system is the key element in determining his or her future life. While programs such as education and vocational training are important, they alone cannot succeed in changing values. A person's values are internal—they come from within.*

Norman Carlson
Former Director
Federal Bureau of Prisons

Drug abuse programs can be designed to assist inmates in restructuring their values. This change in values ultimately can change the way an inmate thinks, feels, and views the world. The ultimate task of any program, be it educational or therapeutic, is to change and improve behavior. Drug abuse programs can be effective in this change process. A key element in the change process is for an inmate to understand that a problem exists, that treatment is available for that problem, and that with a positive attitude and consistent motivation, success can be achieved.

No program can exist separate from the client. In our case, the client is the inmate. Based on our experience, three general categories of referrals to drug abuse programs will be seen. These three types of inmates can be called (1) the primary addict, (2) the primary criminal (secondary addict), and (3) the cultural addict.

The primary addict actually might be relieved to be in prison. Prison might have saved this individual from the terminal stages of addiction and death. The client might make statements like, "If I weren't locked up, I would be dead by now," or "When I committed my crime I didn't care about anything but getting high." These peoples' lives were destroyed by their compulsion to use drugs. They might be tearful and remorseful during their interview. They also might have had a high social and financial position in the community. Basically, crime was a means for getting drugs. The primary addict can be a master of manipulation, and corrections staff should be careful to maintain professional demeanor at all times.

The next type of inmate, the primary criminal, is capable of acting the part of the true addict to gain special consideration. Care should be taken to evaluate the sincerity of the client. Primary criminals sometimes use their drug abuse problems to obtain more favorable treatment. They might project the blame for selfishness and criminal activities onto drugs when in reality they probably would have committed crimes even if they never had used drugs. For these inmates, drugs and crime were simply a means of satisfying their selfish pleasure-seeking desires and intense craving for excitement and stimulation. As correctional workers, we are well aware of this type of inmate. This type of client might try to "blame" drugs for his or her own selfish behavior. This person might attempt to use drug abuse as an excuse to try to avoid a stiffer sentence. Sometimes, primary criminals truthfully admit that they never used drugs. In order to avoid treatment, more often these inmates falsely will deny they ever had a drug problem. Once their drug problem is treated, their selfish manner of thinking might remain.

The cultural addict uses the excuse of poverty and environment to explain his or her behavior. These individuals might not be interested in change because any behavior change would involve learning a different way of life. Consequently, many have resigned themselves to continue using drugs because they do not want to change their lifestyle, their environment, or the people with whom they associate. The cultural addict might argue that the drug laws are unjust, that drugs don't hurt anyone, and that everyone they know uses drugs. These inmates might not seek assistance unless they can be helped to expand their horizons and develop more positive attitudes toward their own lives and value systems.

## TREATMENT GOALS

The goal of a comprehensive drug education program is to instigate a positive change in the attitudes and lives of all inmates. Internal change is the key to success. Consequently, the motivation of an inmate and decisions he or she makes while in treatment are important elements of the change process. The first objective of treatment might be to understand how and why people become psychologically and physically addicted to drugs. A lecture/discussion presents the role of peer influence, chosen role models, the environment, the importance of having goals, the role of the familial link, the personality, and finally the role of drugs as a positive reinforcer (a desire to feel high) and an avoidance mechanism (to suppress negative feelings). Physical addiction to certain drugs can occur and can be explained by the concept of an altered chemical equilibrium in the body. Personal examples of physical addiction can be elicited from group members to illustrate these reasons.

The second objective is to help each participant understand the effects drugs have on his or her psychological, social, and physical well-being. Most group participants respond well to a film presentation followed by a group discussion replete with personal examples. An overview film followed in subsequent sessions by films on specific drugs has worked well.

The third objective of this first phase of treatment is to impart the idea that an addiction is not cured, but only arrested. This means that treatment must be a daily process in which a personal inventory is made. Illogical reasons for failing to quit can be brought up in discussion. Films such as *Angel Death* can be helpful to illustrate how an addict sometimes is his or her own worst enemy.

The final objective of treatment is to impart the message that help is available. Each participant needs to understand that relapse is common, but that help always is available, both in the institutions and in the community. A discussion of self-help groups such as NA or AA might be appropriate at this point, and the film *Twelve Steps* could introduce participants to the philosophy of the self-help groups. A national directory of treatment resources (published by the National Institute of

Drug Abuse and available at no cost) could be made available to the group. Sometimes group members return just prior to release to obtain specific names and phone numbers of community programs. Relapse prevention is covered in more detail in Chapter XIV.

## TREATMENT TECHNIQUES

Several treatment techniques can be used effectively to increase the intensity of each participant's self-evaluation. Self-evaluation tasks can be given as homework assignments to help each person examine his or her past behavior and lifestyle. The first assignment is to have each client write an autobiography. This autobiography can be used in or out of group to help inmates gain an overall sense of where they have been so they can better determine their past errors and future goals.

The second exercise that has proved helpful is to ask each participant to list those elements, such as events, times, and places where they commonly used drugs that now trigger their drug cravings. Each client should rank his or her most common "triggers" to help identify areas of vulnerability and to gain better insight into personal addiction.

Finally, ask students to rank and examine the three most important elements in their lives (for example, God, country, family, health, education, self, money, children, crime, drugs). Ask students whether or not their behavior in the community was consistent with the values they now have listed.

Bibliotherapy can be offered to expand existing services. Inmates could be asked to read specific books and either complete a structured self-help workbook on the material or write a paper on information presented in the book. Bibliotherapy programs, including the "Bradshaw Series on the Family," the Claudia Black video series, and an expanded cocaine education series also can be added to expand the education component. Clients can be asked to complete a structured psychoeducational series on specific books or to write a paper on what the book was about and how the information contained therein can apply to improving the individual's coping strategies.

### Counseling/Self-help and Specialized Services

In many institutions, further programming will be available. Self-help groups have been a strong part of the additional services offered at institutions. Self-help volunteers often are willing to come into institutions and provide services free of charge.

Finally, contract professionals or volunteers who can provide specific specialized and independent services (such as family therapy, Adult Children of Alcoholics counseling, psychopharmacology education, Vietnam veterans counseling, and AIDS education) can be recruited as needed to broaden the education programs.

## TREATMENT FORMATS

### Small Group Format

For security reasons, small groups might be the preferred way to conduct drug education and counseling in a medium or maximum security facility. Of course, circumstances differ at each facility; therefore, these decisions must be made at the local level.

Inmates usually are enrolled in a group comprising eight to twelve participants. Each session lasts from one to two hours each meeting. Introductions are made and the course overview is presented. Typically, concepts of addiction and the effects of each type of drug are discussed. Videotapes and other audiovisual aids help stimulate interest and involvement. Photocopied material often is useful. It is important to allow each inmate to express his or her program expectations, and it also is useful to ask willing participants to offer a brief description of their experiences with drugs. These personal observations can be elicited and elaborated on following each film or presentation in successive sessions.

At the beginning of the program, it is important to announce a firm rule: What is said within a group is not told to inmates or staff outside of the group. The only limit to confidentiality is if a major security breach, such as threats of harm to self or others, is made. Rules may vary, but it is usually a good idea to uphold a policy of expelling group members who violate the code of confidentiality.

### Large Group Formats

In a minimum security setting or in an especially secure medium security setting, drug education groups can be larger. In those cases, the size of a group simply can be based on the number of inmates who request service. Where possible, small groups usually are preferred over larger ones. The formal "classroom" approach can be effective in relaying drug information to large groups of up to forty students. However, such a large class usually is difficult to control unless minimum security inmates compose the group. Structure is more important in these larger groups, and less opportunity exists for personal disclosure. In fact, it is helpful to discourage personal disclosure in large groups because confidentiality cannot be enforced and because domineering inmates might occupy too much class time talking about themselves.

If the class is large, instructors should offer a follow-up therapy group for those who are assessed with severe drug problems. This therapy group, available to inmates who have completed the drug education class, would allow personal disclosure in a small-group setting.

### Frequency of Groups

Frequency of group meetings is another consideration. Groups with a focus on attitude change usually work better if they meet more frequently—even daily—as opposed to weekly or monthly, as the participants' motivation usually is high. Due to a number of restrictions, most institutions hold weekly group sessions, which still can be considered effective.

Daytime groups in which participants attend on a "call out" basis report a lower dropout rate than evening groups. Evening groups have the added advantage, however, of proving the degree of commitment of each participant, since individuals are more likely to be responsible for their own attendance.

## CRITERIA FOR COMPLETION

Participants in every group may be required to sign a treatment contract. This contract outlines the purpose and methods of each group as well as any conditions or requirements that a participant should understand before beginning treatment within the group. It also must state that confidentiality ends when major breaches of security such as threats of harm to self or others are brought to the attention of the staff.

The following page can be modified for use as a treatment contract (with your institution's program name substituted). A standard treatment plan also could be used.

A student is allowed to miss no more than three classes (six of the forty hours) regardless of the reasons, or he or she must take the course over again. For every class missed within this limit, a make-up paper will be required for each class missed so that all inmates put in equivalent work for their certificate of completion. A two-page minimum length for these papers has been a workable criteria. The following are suggested topics:

- "Alcohol and My Life"
- "My History of Cocaine Use"
- "How Alcohol and Other Drugs have Affected my Family"
- "What I Learned from my Experience With Drugs"
- "What I have Seen on the Street in the Drug Trade"

Any topic concerning personal or observational experience with drugs and drug abuse is acceptable. Research papers would also be acceptable, with books or chapters being read and a brief report written. However, most students find it easier and more beneficial to write about themselves. Having students write about their experiences concerning drugs has often been found to be useful in changing attitudes. Additional readings and papers may be required at the discretion of the instructor. These papers must be considered as confidential, and the content may vary widely based on their own personal opinions or feelings.

### Final Exam

Each class ends with a final examination testing each student's mastery of knowledge concerning drugs and their effects. Students must obtain a score of at least 70 percent correct to earn a certificate of completion. The criteria of 70 percent is a

## DRUG EDUCATION PROGRAM TREATMENT CONTRACT

Student's name _____ Reg. No. _____

Instructor's name _____ Position _____

The Drug Education Program is a forty-hour education program followed by a final examination to test each student's knowledge of drugs and the effects of abuse. The final examination must by passed at the 70 percent level or higher. The course will focus on the concepts of physical and psychological addiction, information on alcohol and other drugs, effects on families, the danger of infections, ways to avoid relapse, and healthier lifestyle options. A student can miss no more than three classes regardless of the reason, or the entire course must be retaken. Students must complete a two-page make-up paper for each class missed, so all students who earn a certificate of completion will have put equivalent work into the program. The paper can be on any aspect of drugs and drug abuse.

If a student attends all classes but does not pass the final examination, a letter verifying attendance will be written. However, the student will be expected to attend the next available course. Most students do pass.

What is said in the classes or written in make-up papers is confidential except in the event of a major breach of security such as threats of harm to self or others. Your counselor or case manager will be informed whether you are participating and whether you successfully have completed the program.

Informed Consent to Participate in the Drug Education Program:

*The purposes, goals, and methods of the Drug Education Program have been explained to me. I understand that confidentiality will be maintained except in matters involving major breaches of security such as threats to self or others.*

Signature:_____ Date course began:_____

minimum standard, as scores higher than 80 percent usually indicate a more substantial mastery of the material. However, the major purpose of a drug education program is to introduce inmates to drug treatment, and because the educational level of many inmates is low, the 70 percent score is the minimum standard for completion. All group disclosures and papers will remain confidential except in cases in which a breach of security or threats of harm to self or others has occurred.

If a student is psychologically, physically, or learning disabled to such a degree that he or she is unable to pass the final examination, the program coordinator is authorized to grant an exemption. This exemption should be written. However, the student must show good motivation and attend at least one entire course.

Before a student is exempted, the staff should attempt to individualize educational material and procedures to compensate for deficits. For example, inmates who cannot read or even who totally are dyslexic successfully have passed a final examination when it has been administered orally.

The program instructor should review the final examination before the last class of the session, and any test material that has not been covered should be explained at this time. The instructor also might wish to summarize all the material covered during the course. Instructors should ensure they don't word their review in such a way that it parallels exactly the wording on the examinations.

The final examination should not be designed to serve as a test of reading skill. Many students might be familiar with words when presented orally but will not recognize the same words on paper. For this reason, instructors should remind students at the beginning of each final examination that if requested any question will be read aloud.

Inmates should not be permitted to review final examinations prior to completing the program. Even if pretests are administered for research purposes, students must complete the entire program. Only final examinations will serve to verify knowledge.

If a student has attended all classes but has not passed the final examination at the 70 percent level, a letter verifying the student's attendance should be placed in the central file. This letter should recommend a course of continuing education for the student and commend the individual for participating.

### Record-keeping

A sign-in roster should be passed around during each class to verify attendance and for permanent records. Records of participation, final examinations, and program-related material that could require verification should be stored in a secure location. All confidential materials should be maintained in locked file cabinets.

At the end of each program, a permanent summary of attendance and scores should be recorded for audit and verification purposes. All group activity summaries should be placed in a file.

### Participant Recognition

At each program end, inmates can receive the original copy of a certificate of completion. A copy is held for his or her file, and a copy is sent to the inmate's central file. Be sure to type on the certificate the name of the group or program as well as the number of completed course hours. Some programs also offer incentives such as a graduation photograph or T-shirts emblazoned with slogans—"Just Say No to Drugs" or baseball caps. Social reinforcers encourage group pride and can include sponsoring an intrainstitutional basketball team or an art show related to drug abuse. Institutional "town hall" meetings are a good place to make these award and certificate presentations. In some cases, the Education Department might be willing to allow graduates to receive certificates during the yearly education graduation program. Innovation and enthusiasm make the education and therapy groups much more enjoyable for both inmates and staff. Flexibility and experimentation are encouraged; successful methods are communicated to other programs.

## AFTERCARE

Aftercare is an important element of each person's treatment. It is vitally important to offer transitional services to inmates who must face the same environment in which they originally had problems related to drug abuse. Aftercare can be as simple as referring members to self-help or twelve-step programs or can be more elaborate and specific referrals. A free publication titled the *National Directory of Drug Abuse and Alcoholism Treatment Programs* is available from the National Institute on Drug Abuse, P.O. Box 2345, Rockville, MD; 301/468-2600. This directory can assist staff with referrals and aftercare placements. Other key organizations in the recovery field are mentioned in Appendix C. Commercially published directories and referral lists are available, but many are expensive duplicates of the free NIDA material.

## SUMMARY

A number of treatment levels and services are provided to incarcerated drug abusers in prison. The minimum level of treatment in the BOP is a forty-hour Comprehensive Drug Abuse Education Program, which is based on this treatment manual or equivalent material. The basic-level program can be expanded by adding individual or group counseling and by using some of the material referenced in this manual. Good resources include bibliotherapy programs, which are structured self-help programs based on psychology texts, and twelve-step programs cultivated at each facility.

Expanded treatment programs will offer more elaborate treatment plans based on behavioral and cognitive strategies, a relapse prevention component, individual and group therapy, and an aftercare component. The research and comprehensive treatment programs will include a higher staff-to-client ratio, including treatment specialists.

# II.
# THEORETICAL PERSPECTIVES IN DRUG ABUSE TREATMENT: MODELS OF ADDICTION

There are several theories as to how addiction is caused. Through the years, several models of addiction have been developed. What follows is a review of these models that might be helpful in understanding the process of addiction.

## THE MORAL/LEGAL MODEL

The moral model of drug dependence is the oldest. According to this model, drug abuse results from a moral weakness or a lack of willpower. The addict is viewed as someone with a weak, bad, or evil character. The goal of rehabilitation is to increase the willpower of addicts by instilling moral convictions against substance abuse and also to protect them from their weakness by threatening punishment. The drug abuser then will change from evil to good or from weak to strong. Specific avenues of change have included religious conversion, public condemnation by the clergy, physical punishment, and/or incarceration.

Preventive measures under this model rely on personal willpower, the ability of society to foster moral and religious convictions, or the threat of punishment. In order for this model to prove successful, a minority of a specific population must be the transgressors, and punishment must be swift, certain, and severe. Countries that advocate the death penalty for those suspected of drug use, for example, experience few drug abuse problems.

The model appears to work best with those with borderline or situational drug abuse problems. Heavily addicted people also have been known to find relief through religious conversion or the fear of punishment after they successfully have been detoxified. This model holds people accountable for their behavior and is useful in overcoming denial and/or rationalization. The moral model contrasts the disease model, which tells people they are "powerless" over their addictions.

## THE MEDICAL MODEL

Medical personnel have attempted, sometimes successfully, to treat addictions with other drugs. In the 1800s, alcohol addiction was treated with opium, opium addiction was treated with morphine, and morphine addiction has been treated with heroin. Now, heroin addiction is being treated with an even stronger drug: methadone. Methadone successfully has detoxified many addicts, and maintenance programs offer an alternative to street heroin to ward off withdrawal pains.

## Jellinek's Influence

The medical model has been the most common and popular explanation of drug abuse for the past several decades. In the 1950s, E. M. Jellinek developed the famous curve of addiction describing symptoms of early, middle, and late addiction. He was able to show how this "illness" was progressive and predictable. Jellinek identified four types of alcoholism: alpha, beta, gamma, and delta. Although Jellinek identified only the gamma type as a disease, eventually the public and the scientific community grouped together all the types. In 1956, the American Medical Association formally pronounced alcoholism a disease. Jellinek also developed the "Jellinek Curve," which described the gradual progression of alcoholism as a unidimensional process involving four phases.

Phase I, the prealcoholic phase, is characterized by using alcohol to relax and to deal with the everyday tensions and hassles of life. Continued drinking for these purposes leads to a gradual increase in physiological tolerance, and the individual must drink larger quantities more frequently to achieve the same subjective effects.

Phase II, the early alcoholic phase, begins with the experience of a blackout, a brief period of amnesia that occurs during or directly after a drinking episode. Early alcoholism is characterized by the following experiences: continued blackouts; sneaking drinks; growing preoccupation with drinking and drinking situations; increased defensiveness about drinking; and feelings of guilt about drinking, resulting in increased use of defense mechanisms (primarily denial and rationalization).

In Phase III, the crucial phase, addiction occurs. Physiological dependence now clearly is evident, and the individual displays loss of control over his or her drinking. Marital conflict, interpersonal difficulties, job difficulties and loss, and increased aggressive behavior characterize this phase. The individual becomes willing to risk everything to continue drinking.

Phase IV is characterized as the chronic phase of the illness. Cirrhosis of the liver, pancreatitis, hypertension, cardiomyopathy, tachycardia, polyneuropathy, central nervous system damage, anemia, muscle and bone disease, skin disease, and oral cancers might occur either singly or in varying combinations.

With abrupt termination of drinking or other drug-abusing behavior during Phase IV, the individual might experience frightening hallucinations, violent tremors, severe agitation, paranoid episodes, and a host of other psychiatric symptoms. Manic acting-out, severe depression, a pervasive sense of hopelessness, suicidal thoughts, panic episodes, and self-loathing commonly are encountered during this late phase of the illness.

Jellinek's theory was based on questionnaire information obtained from a sample of Alcoholics Anonymous (AA) members. Of the 158 questionnaires he sent out, ninety-eight (62 percent) were used. Because Jellinek's model was consistent with the philosophies of AA, this group strongly embraced and supported the disease concept of alcoholism.

## The Disease Concept

Since that time, medical authorities all over the world, including the Public Health Service, have identified alcoholism as a disease. Proponents of the medical model describe the disease of drug dependency with the following characteristics:

1. Drug dependency is a PRIMARY DISEASE. It is not a secondary symptom of an underlying emotional problem.

2. Drug dependency is a PROGRESSIVE DISEASE. It gets progressively worse. The chemically dependent person becomes physically, spiritually, emotionally, and psychologically ill.

3. Drug dependency is a CHRONIC DISEASE. There is no cure. Relapsing is common. There is no way to drink in moderation or use other drugs again, or a return to total dependency is certain.

4. Drug dependency is a FATAL DISEASE. The disease only can be arrested. If it is not arrested, the chemically dependent person will die from it. Much emphasis is put on the importance of the abuser's body chemistry, brain functioning, or metabolism. The reason for the abuse is that the abuser has an illness or sickness.

## Intervention Using the Medical/Disease Model

Treatment under the disease model usually involves inpatient hospitalization, detoxification using drugs like Librium or Xanax for alcoholics, antidepressants for stimulant withdrawal, and methadone for heroin withdrawal. A final component to treatment under the medical/disease model is medical education for prevention/inoculation. Family/genetic predisposition is shown.

Treatment involves addressing the physical addiction to drugs—considered a "primary disease"—and inoculating the abuser by explaining what will happen to his or her body if drug use continues. Medical education is an important component of this model, and many addicts do stop using alcohol after they learn about the condition of their liver or are told what shape it will be in if they don't stop. The model does not view addiction as a psychological process, but as a physical one.

## Positive Changes Resulting from the Disease Model

1. The disease model helped to deemphasize the moral model and to remove the stigma aimed at drug abusers of a "weak character." Consequently, abusers were less likely to be seen as "evil" or as "bad" people and were more likely to seek help.

2. Public funds were made more readily available to support research and treatment programs.

# THE TWELVE-STEP MODEL

When the professional community or institutions fail to address a problem effectively, social responses develop. Such a model developed in 1935 and is closely aligned with the medical/disease models.

The roots of Alcoholics Anonymous, Narcotics Anonymous, and other twelve-step programs are planted firmly in parts of the moral and disease models of drug addiction. AA, the oldest of the twelve-step programs, was founded in 1935 in Akron, Ohio. Two alcoholics—one a salesman and the other a physician—came together to get sober by helping others get sober. They formulated the twelve steps as a guide to help other alcoholics recover from their addiction.

Because of the success of AA, many other groups since have been modeled along the same format, focusing on the addiction as the problem. Narcotics Anonymous (NA), for example, adapted the twelve steps to help drug addicts recover from narcotics and other illicit substances. More than fifty different groups, including Overeaters, Gamblers, and Sex and Love Addicts Anonymous, now use the twelve-step approach as the basis for treatment. A recent *Newsweek* article estimates fifteen million Americans seek help for addictive disorders through twelve-step-based programs.

The twelve steps used in NA (see Appendix E) underlie most of these nondirective support groups. Robert Dupont (1989), a psychiatrist and former director of the National Institute on Drug Abuse, lists five basic principles that form the basis of the twelve steps:

1. Admitting powerlessness or a lack of control over the particular substance or behavior.
2. Forming some type of reliance on a power outside of yourself.
3. Taking a personal inventory of yourself to see what you need to change about yourself.
4. Making amends for past wrongs.
5. Helping others who have similar problems.

According to the twelve-step model, acceptance of personal powerlessness is a crucial first step in the process of recovery. Many addicts enter treatment believing they are "weak" and simply need to learn how to control their drug usage. The first principle teaches addicts that they have no control and must remove themselves from settings or people likely to tempt them. This model upholds total abstinence as a necessary element for complete recovery—an impossible task for overeaters—and relies on the addict to transfer control to a higher power. The higher power can be God, nature, self, or anything else in which the addict has faith.

The second principle teaches addicts to become open-minded and focused on others as opposed to focused entirely on themselves.

The third step encourages the addict to make a thorough self-evaluation or personal inventory to assess the damage from the addictive behavior. This exercise fosters introspection and insight development.

The fourth principle encourages personal responsibility and restitution (a notion central in Reality Therapy), which begins to empower the addict. A person must correct past and any future wrongs in order to "work" the program. Finally, the last phase of treatment teaches the addict that he or she is responsible for carrying this message to others—an action that simultaneously will reinforce the convictions of the addict. In this manner, addicts can overcome their own feelings of social isolation and sense of being misunderstood—which characterizes the addiction cycle.

## Advantages of the Twelve-step Model

The twelve-step model offers drug treatment providers several advantages. It is neither punitive nor blaming, since people are encouraged to seek help as they would for any other disease. Guilt and shame are alleviated because people are not viewed as responsible for developing an addiction any more than they are responsible for developing cancer or high blood pressure. However, people are considered accountable for managing their disease through abstinence and twelve-step work.

A second advantage to the twelve-step approach is that it does not rely on professional assistance. These programs have proliferated worldwide and easily can be found in any community in this country. Released inmates can join these self-help groups nationwide, and the groups readily accept new members willing to pursue recovery. The groups reduce shame and guilt and also reduce the level of isolation a released inmate might feel.

Finally, these self-help groups are free of charge. Members help to support the groups by donating a nominal amount of money—large donations and donations from outsiders are discouraged—and meeting rooms usually are borrowed from churches or hospitals.

## Disadvantages of the Twelve-step Model

Not all addicts respond to the twelve-step model. These groups place special emphasis on spiritual growth and total abstinence from all drugs. Some addicts/alcoholics cannot relate to a spiritual higher power, and this often inhibits participation abilities. Other individuals, for whatever reason, are not willing to remain abstinent. Some people wish to return to controlled or nonproblematic drinking or drugging (Shaffer 1986). The number of drug and alcohol abusers who successfully have moderated their substance use is 5 to 15 percent, by some estimates (Brower et al. 1989). This counters the AA notion of being "one drink from a drunk."

Another disadvantage of the twelve-step model—although in some cases it serves as an advantage—is the degree of flexibility. The twelve steps are presented in broadly defined terms, which allows for a wide degree of variability and increases the likelihood of personal interpretations that don't parallel recovery. Some members, for example, use the steps to advance a specific religious rather than spiritual orientation. Moreover, twelve-step approaches offer little guidance in how to specifically implement these steps, leaving the addict at his or her own level of insight and application. As will be outlined in a later section, however, this disadvantage can be overcome by combining the twelve steps with relapse-prevention strategies.

Finally, some addicts are afflicted with specific mood disorders (for example, bipolar affective), dysthymia, or personality disorders (antisocial, borderline, or narcissistic, for example). Such problems impede an accurate self-evaluation, which is essential to the twelve-step recovery process. Drug and alcohol abuse also might be a form of self-medication for more serious psychiatric and psychological problems.

## THE ADDICTIVE BEHAVIOR MODEL

Over the last several years, many psychological models of addiction have emerged. G. A. Marlatt has been a leading figure in developing psychological models for understanding drug abuse and other addictions. Marlatt developed the addictive behavior model in the early 1980s from the principles of social-learning theory, cognitive psychology, and experimental social psychology. The addictive behavior model of addiction makes a number of assumptions that differ markedly from the medical model.

### Habit Disorders

Addictive behaviors are presumed to lie along a continuum of use rather than being defined in terms of discrete categories such as excessive use or total abstinence. All points along this continuum of use—from abstinence, to moderate, to excessive use—are assumed to be governed by similar processes of learning.

Addictive behaviors are viewed as overlearned habits that can be understood and modified in the same manner as other habits. This does not imply that continued excessive involvement in an addictive habit doesn't have negative physical consequences. Excessive habits can and often do lead to disease end-states, such as lung cancer in smokers and cirrhosis of the liver in alcohol abusers. The fact that a disease state is the product of a long-term addictive cycle does not necessarily imply that the behavior itself is a disease or is caused by an underlying physiological disorder.

Proponents of the addictive behavior model study the determinants of addictive habits, including situational and environmental antecedents, beliefs and expectations, the individual's family history, and prior learning experiences with the drug or activity. An equal interest lies in discovering the consequences of these behaviors so as to better understand both the reinforcing effects that might contribute to increased use and the negative consequences that might serve to inhibit the behavior.

### Conditioned Behavior

Besides the effects of the drug or activity itself, attention is paid to the social and interpersonal reactions the individual experiences before, during, and after engaging in an addictive behavior. Initially learning an addictive habit and subsequently performing the activity once the habit firmly is established involve social factors.

As mentioned earlier, one of the central underlying assumptions of this approach is that addictive behaviors consist of overlearned, maladaptive habit patterns.

These behaviors usually are followed by some form of immediate gratification—the "high" state of pleasure or arousal or the reduction in tension.

Addictive behaviors often are performed in situations perceived as stressful; an individual might drink in an attempt to reduce social anxiety or smoke to "calm the nerves." To the extent that these activities are performed during or prior to stressful or unpleasant situations, they represent maladaptive coping mechanisms. Addictive behaviors are maladaptive because they lead to delayed negative consequences in relation to health, social status, and self-esteem.

Habitual behaviors characterized by immediate gratification and delayed negative consequences have been identified as "social traps." These behaviors are not limited to using drugs, since they include nondrug-related activities such as compulsive gambling, compulsive work patterns ("workaholism"), certain sexual problems (exhibitionism, for example), compulsive overeating, and some manifestations of interpersonal relationships such as "addictive love."

### Internal Chemistry versus Learning

The source of the compulsion to engage in addictive behavior often is considered to be rooted in internal body chemistry— especially in circumstances in which a person experiences a "physical" craving for a particular drug. Overemphasizing internal physiological factors neglects the possibility that these behaviors are strongly influenced by the individual's expectations or anticipation of the desired effects of the activity. Recent research suggests that cognitive and environmental factors often exert greater influence in determining drug effects than the actual pharmacological or physical effects of the drug itself.

Marlatt and other researchers have performed experiments to determine what differences exist between how alcohol affects behavior based on our expectations versus the actual chemical effects. First, Marlatt determined that even people who have severe drinking problems reliably cannot distinguish between drinks containing tonic water, lime juice, and ice and the same drinks with an ounce of vodka added.

After establishing this fact, Marlatt used a large group of diagnosed alcoholics in the following way: One half of the group (Group A) were told they were engaging in an experiment to determine which of three brands of vodka tasted best. The other half of the group (Group B) were told they were to determine the best tasting of three brands of tonic water. Without the subject's knowledge, both Group A and Group B were subdivided into two more groups for a total of four groups. Thus, one half of the subjects who were expecting vodka got tonic water only, and one half of the subjects who expected tonic water only actually received vodka in their drinks. The experimenters then gave the subjects all the drinks they wanted.

The results of this study and other research using a similar design shows that abusers are more likely to experience cravings and loss of control when they are TOLD they are consuming alcohol—whether or not they actually are consuming alcohol. If abusers are TOLD they are NOT consuming alcohol, they do not report experiencing cravings and loss of control—whether or not they are consuming alcohol.

Researchers have also examined commonly held expectations regarding alcohol usage, including the belief that alcohol will reduce anxiety, increase aggressiveness, and lead to sexual enhancement. In all studies, the groups that reported experiencing anxiety reduction, increased aggressiveness, and sexual enhancement were the ones led to believe or expect that they were getting alcohol regardless of what substance they actually received.

The major implication of this research is that cognitive processes such as expectation and attribution are learned and thereby more accessible to modification and change than are relatively fixed physiological processes.

### Free Will

Some individuals argue that to accept the fact that addictive behaviors are learned is equivalent to "blaming the victim," because the addicted individual thereby is held personally responsible for his or her condition. Viewed from this perspective, the psychological model represents a regression to the earlier moral model of addiction.

This argument is based on the false assumption that individuals are responsible for their past learning experiences—that they "choose" to engage in these activities because of some lack of willpower or moral weakness. On the contrary, behavioral theorists define addiction as a powerful habit pattern, an acquired vicious cycle of self-destructive behavior that is locked in by the collective effects of complex learning principles. An individual who acquires an addictive habit is no more to be held responsible for this behavior than one of Pavlov's dogs would be held responsible for salivating at the sound of a ringing bell.

In addition to classical and operant conditioning factors, human drug use also is determined to a large extent by acquired expectancies and beliefs about drugs as an antidote to stress and anxiety. Social learning and modeling also exert a strong influence: drug use in the family and peer environment along with the pervasive portrayal of drugs in advertising and the media. Just because a behavioral problem can be described as a learned habit pattern does not imply that the person should be considered responsible for acquiring the habit or that the individual is capable of exercising voluntary control over the behavior.

It is important to note, however, that even though an individual's particular habit has been shaped and determined by past learning experiences (for which he or she is not to be held responsible), the process of changing habits does involve active participation and responsibility. By becoming involved in a self-management program, an individual can acquire new skills and cognitive strategies. Habits then can be transformed into behaviors that are controlled by the processes of awareness and responsible decision making.

## *Therapeutic Intervention*

As the individual undergoes deconditioning and cognitive restructuring and acquires new behavioral skills, he or she can begin to accept greater responsibility for positive change much as one does when acquiring or mastering any new skill or task. This approach supports the habit-changing process, which contrasts the position of personal powerlessness inherent in the disease model.

## *Disadvantages and Advantages of the Addictive Behavior Model*

This model is sound in that it is based on empirical evidence, sound psychological approaches, and an individualized treatment plan. However, not everyone has access to professionals with this type of expertise; this type of treatment also can be very expensive. Individuals with serious personality problems eventually might disregard new skills unless proper transitional services are available in the community. While this model poses much hope for the future, additional long-term longitudinal studies would help verify the strength of this approach to prevent relapse.

# RELAPSE

## *A Self-Fulfilling Prophecy*

It has been standard practice in the drug abuse treatment field to view any use of drugs following an abstinence-oriented treatment program as indicative of failure. This all-or-nothing outlook is reflected in most of the traditional treatment-outcome literature, where cases are reported either as successes (maintaining abstinence) or failures (any use).

This rigid approach to relapse has resulted in a number of problems. An individual in treatment who learns the black-white dichotomy of abstinence-relapse could become the victim of a self-fulfilling prophecy. In other words, the individual comes to believe that if he or she violates the abstinence expectation, this surely will result in an extreme relapse. On one side is absolute control or total restraint; the other extreme is loss of control or total indulgence.

Another problem with the traditional definition of relapse is its association with the return of the disease state. The cause of the relapse is attributed to internal factors related to the disease condition. Behaviors associated with relapse come to be equated with symptoms signaling reactivation of the underlying disease, much as experiencing fever and chills serves to signal relapse in malaria. This emphasis on internal causation carries the implicit message that people can't prevent the outbreak of symptoms: How does one prevent a fever from breaking out? This theory tends to overlook the influence of situational and psychological factors as potential determinants in the relapse process. It also reinforces the notion that the individual who experiences a relapse is a helpless victim of circumstances.

### Relapse Prevention and the Addictive Behavior Model

A primary assumption related to the addictive behavior model is that the cognitive and affective reactions to the first lapse after a period of abstinence (especially the attribution for the cause of the lapse) exert a significant influence that might determine whether or not the lapse will be followed by a full relapse.

### The Disease Model and Loss of Control

Although Jellinek's four-phase disease model of progression widely has been accepted, no compelling evidence exists to prove this model. In a truly representative sample of the total population of people who meet the criteria for alcoholism or chemical dependency, a uniform and unidimensional progression is the exception rather than the rule. Jellinek's studies were conducted with members of Alcoholics Anonymous, a highly selected sample of the alcoholic population. Although a number of alcoholics unquestionably fit the Jellinek model, research suggests that the majority do not conform to it at all.

A major belief of the disease model is that abusers experience loss of control and irresistible cravings. However, little empirical evidence supports this belief; in fact, evidence exists to disconfirm it, such as Marlatt and his research group's series of experiments described earlier with real and placebo drinks.

The disease model might be successful insofar as it convinces the alcoholic that he or she is sick, suffering from a medically recognized illness, and no longer is capable of drinking or using other drugs without losing control. If the individual accepts this diagnosis and agrees to never take another drink and does not, all is well. Unfortunately, the ability to maintain total abstinence is rare. A recent comprehensive study conducted by the Rand Corporation evaluated the outcome of more than 700 alcoholic patients following their participation in several typical treatment programs. It was found that less than 10 percent of the patients were able to maintain abstinence over a period of two years following discharge from the treatment program. This data demonstrates that relapse is the most common outcome of alcoholism treatment.

Relapse is the turning point at which the disease model is likely to backfire. If an alcoholic has accepted the belief that alcohol consumption is impossible to control once it has begun (as embodied in the AA slogan that one is always "one drink away from a drunk"), then he or she is likely to believe that even a single slip may precipitate a total, uncontrolled relapse. Since drinking under these circumstances is equated with a symptom signifying the reemergence of the disease, one is likely to feel as powerless to control this behavior as one would with any other disease symptom. Thus, the disease model establishes a self-fulfilling prophecy. The limitations of the medical model have prompted in recent years the development of several new models of addiction.

## A Relapse-prevention Model

Relapse is viewed as a transitional process, a series of events that might or might not be followed by a return to original levels of the drug-taking behavior. Rather than adopting a pessimistic view in which relapse is viewed as a treatment failure or a return of the disease state, a lapse is viewed as a fork in the road, with one path returning to the former problem level (relapse or total collapse) and the other continuing in the direction of positive change (prolapse). Whether or not a lapse is followed by a relapse or, in some cases, a prolapse, depends to a large extent on the individual's personal expectations and underlying model of the habit-change process. Rather than an indication of failure, a relapse more optimistically can be viewed as a challenge or an opportunity for new learning to occur.

It is assumed that the individual experiences a sense of perceived control or self-efficacy while abstaining. The behavior is "under control" as long as it does not occur; the longer the period of successful abstinence, the greater the individual's perception of self-efficacy. This perceived control will continue until the person encounters a high-risk situation.

A high-risk situation broadly is defined as any situation that poses a threat to the individual's sense of control and increases the risk of potential relapse.

In a recent study of several hundred relapse episodes obtained from clients with a variety of problem behaviors (problem drinking, smoking, heroin addiction, compulsive gambling, and overeating), researchers identified three primary high-risk situations that were associated with almost three-quarters of all the relapses reported.

- Negative Emotional States (35 percent of all relapses in the sample): situations prior to or at the time at which the first lapse occurs in which the individual experiences a negative or unpleasant emotional state, mood, or feeling such as frustration, anger, anxiety, depression, or boredom.

- Interpersonal Conflict (16 percent of the relapses): situations involving an ongoing or relatively recent conflict associated with any interpersonal relationship, such as marriage, friendship, family members, or employer-employee relations. Arguments and interpersonal confrontations occur frequently in this category.

- Social Pressure (20 percent of the relapses): situations in which the individual responds to the influence of another person or group of people exerting pressure on the individual to engage in the prohibited behavior. Social pressure either might be direct (direct interpersonal contact with verbal persuasion) or indirect (being in the company of others who are engaging in the same target behavior even though no direct pressure is involved, for example).

## Relapse Prevention Strategies

If the individual is able to execute an effective cognitive or behavioral coping response in the high-risk situation (he or she is assertive in counteracting social pressures, for example), the probability of relapse decreases significantly. The individual who copes successfully with the situation is likely to experience a sense of mastery or perception of control. Successful mastery of one problem situation often is associated with expecting to be able to cope successfully with the next challenging event. As the individual is able to cope effectively in more and more high-risk situations, perception of control increases in a cumulative fashion, and the probability of relapse decreases accordingly.

What happens if an individual is not able to cope successfully in a high-risk situation? It might be that the person never has acquired the coping skills involved or that the appropriate response has been inhibited by fear or anxiety. Or, perhaps the individual fails to recognize and respond to the risk involved before it is too late. Whatever the reason, if the individual doesn't cope, he or she is likely to experience a decrease in self-efficacy frequently coupled with a sense of helplessness and a tendency to passively give in to the situation. As self-efficacy decreases in the precipitating high-risk situation, one's expectations for coping successfully with subsequent problem situations also begin to drop. If the situation also involves temptation to engage in the prohibited behavior as a means of attempting to cope with the stress involved, the stage is set for a probable relapse.

The probability that an initial relapse will occur is increased greatly by the combined responses of being unable to cope effectively in a high-risk situation and the positive expectancies of the effects of the drug. At this point, unless a last-minute coping response or sudden change of circumstance occurs, the individual might cross over the border from abstinence to lapse. Whether or not this first lapse is followed by a total relapse depends to a large extent on the individual's perceptions of the "cause" of the lapse and the reactions associated with its occurrence.

## The Abstinence Violation Effect

The requirement of abstinence is an absolute dictum. Once someone has crossed over the line, there is no going back. From this all-or-nothing perspective, a single drink or cigarette is sufficient to violate the rule of abstinence: Once committed, the deed cannot be undone. Unfortunately, most people who attempt to stop an old habit such as smoking or drinking perceive quitting in this "once and for all" manner. To account for the reaction to transgressing an absolute rule, Marlatt has postulated a mechanism called the Abstinence Violation Effect (AVE).

According to Marlatt, the AVE occurs when an individual personally is committed to an extended or indefinite period of abstinence. The intensity of the AVE will vary as a function of several factors, including the degree of external justification, the strength of prior commitment or effort expended to maintain abstinence, the duration of the abstinence period, the presence of significant others, the perception of the initial lapse as a voluntary choice or preplanned activity, and the subjective value or importance to the individual of the prohibited behavior. The intensity of the AVE is augmented by the influence of two key cognitive-affective elements: cognitive dissonance (conflict and guilt) and a personal attribution effect (blaming the self as the cause of the relapse).

According to Festingers's original theory (1964), cognitive dissonance is assumed to develop out of a disparity between the individual's cognition or beliefs about the self (as an abstainer) and the occurrence of a behavior that directly is incongruent with this self-image (engaging in the forbidden act). The resulting dissonance is experienced as conflict or guilt ("I shouldn't have, but I did"). This internal conflict acts as a source of motivation to engage in behaviors (or cognition) designed to reduce the dissonant reaction.

To the extent that the problem behavior has been used as a coping response to deal with conflict and guilt in the past, it is likely that the individual will continue to engage in the previously prohibited behavior in an attempt to reduce the unpleasant reactions. An alcoholic, for example, who "falls off the wagon" for the first time might continue to drink after the first lapse in an attempt to relieve the conflict and guilt associated with the transgression itself—especially if the person used to drink when feeling guilty or conflicted. Thus, continued drinking in an attempt to reduce feelings of guilt might be mediated by negative reinforcement, such as in the case of drinking to escape from unpleasant emotional states.

It also is possible that the individual will attempt to reduce the dissonance associated with the first slip by intuitively altering the self-image to bring this in line with the new behavior. Someone who takes the first drink, for example, might reject the former self-image of an abstainer in favor of a new image that is consistent with the emergence of the prohibited behavior: "This just goes to show that I am an alcoholic after all and that I can't control my drinking once it starts." In either case the result is the same: The probability increases that the lapse will escalate into a full relapse.

The second component of the AVE is a self-attribution effect, wherein the individual attributes the cause of the relapse to personal failure. Rather than viewing the lapse as a unique response to a particularly difficult situation, the person is likely to blame the cause of the act on such factors as lack of willpower or internal weakness in the face of temptation.

To the extent that the person feels responsible for "giving in," attribution theory predicts that the person will attribute this failure to internal or personal causes. If the lapse is viewed as a personal failure in this manner, the individual's expectancy for continued failure will increase. If one feels weak-willed or powerless for giving in to the temptation of the first cigarette, for example, the expectation of resisting the second or third cigarette is correspondingly lower. Again, the bottom line is the same: an increased probability that the lapse will soon snowball into a full-blown relapse.

### Summary of Relapse Prevention Strategies

In summary, the medical model views the relapse process as a movement or transition between two extremes: The addicted individual is either in absolute control (therefore maintaining faultless abstinence) or has violated this control and, hence, experiences "loss of control." A single slip is taken as evidence that control has been violated; if this violation is attributed to the self—and perceived as evidence that one has no willpower—the behavior will go "out of control," beyond the limits of personal controllability. Recovery from loss of control, from the traditional perspective, only can be achieved through the influence of external pressures such as "hitting bottom," then relinquishing control to a "higher power."

The addictive behavior model provides an alternative to this dichotomy of total control and total loss of control. The model proposes the concept of a "balance point" or middle-way position between the extremes of restraint and indulgence. Through a combination of increased awareness, coping skills, and the acceptance of personal responsibility and choice, it might be possible to escape from the seesaw of relapse.

In the book *Assessment of Addictive Behaviors*, Donovan and Marlatt state: "Consistent with this model, our treatment approach combines the recovery-based principles derived from the twelve steps of Alcoholics Anonymous (AA) with professional treatment interventions using cognitive, behavioral, supportive, and insight-oriented techniques. . . ."

## A NEW APPROACH: THE BIOPSYCHOSOCIAL MODEL

A major criticism of addiction models has been their "reductionistic" and "mechanistic" approaches to addictions. The tendency is to reduce the focus of addiction to a single, unidimensional causative factor. The models reviewed above, as well as a variety of additional models, have merit and support. However, the apparent independence of such models might be less reflective of addictive behaviors than it is of the nature of the disciplines involved in developing the models. Many models and theories are overly narrow and restrictive and fail to account for the total addictive experience.

A new model of addiction, the biopsychosocial model, began to emerge in the late 1980s. D. M. Donovan has been a major proponent of this theory. Addiction is seen as a complex, progressive behavior pattern with biological, psychological, and environmental components. What sets this behavior pattern apart from others is the individual's overwhelmingly pathological involvement in it, subjective compulsion to continue it, and reduced personal control over it.

The behavior pattern continues despite its negative impact on the physical, psychological, and social functioning of the individual. The individual maintains his or her involvement with the addictive behavior even when other, more gratifying sources of reinforcement are present.

An apparent dependence exists that can lead to withdrawal distress when an individual is prevented from engaging in a forbidden behavior. He or she might experience an increasingly strong need for a given experience or behavior representing a form of tolerance. Craving with both physiological and cognitive underpinnings might be experienced as the powerfully strong desire and perceived need to engage in the behavior. The strength of the craving might be gauged by how willing the person is to sacrifice other sources of reward or well-being in life to pursue the addictive behavior. Finally, the power of the addictive experience promotes a tendency for rapid reinstatement of the behavior pattern following a period of abstinence.

This formulation is consistent with a biopsychosocial model of health. Such a model provides a metatheoretical framework in which biological, psychological, and social factors are seen as interacting to determine a given individual's health status. This approach assumes that the individual's status emerges as a result of the interaction of multiple causes. Consistent with this perspective, addiction is seen as a total experience involving physiological changes that are interpreted and given meaning by the individual within the environmental context in which the addictive behavior occurs.

It increasingly is becoming evident that a successful model of addiction must weave biological, pharmacological, psychological, situational, and social components in an intricate web of interrelated and interdependent causal agents to account for the total addictive experience. The emerging biopsychosocial model appears to be moving the addictions field in the needed direction.

An example of a move toward a biopsychosocial approach is the possible integration of the twelve-step approach and the addictive behavior model. This combined effort strengthens relapse-prevention efforts by using both strategies in concert. For example, the statement that "our lives had become unmanageable" can be interpreted as meaning that drug and alcohol abuse involves a number of personal and social deficiencies. The addictive model could help one discover these deficiencies by assisting people with their "moral inventory" rather than leaving their discovery to the personal limitations of each individual. Finally, the addictive behavior model helps the addict "make amends" by allowing for progress that is incompatible with substance abuse.

Whichever model you align yourself with, remember the strengths and weaknesses. The model of treatment and addiction you choose will shape your program, and hence is an important decision. Take care not to insult adherents loyal to a particular model, as all of these models have their strong points and have a place in helping people to recover.

## REFERENCES

Brower, K. J., F. C. Blow, and T. P. Beresford. 1989. Treatment implications of chemical dependency models: An integrative approach. *Journal of Substance Abuse Treatment* 6:147-57.

Donovan, D. M., and G. A. Marlatt, eds. 1988. *Assessment of addictive behaviors*. New York: Guilford Press.

Dupont, R. L. 1989. *Getting unhooked: A guide to the twelve-step programs*. Rockville, Md.: Dupont Publications.

Estes, N., and M. Heineman, eds. 1982. *Alcoholism: Development, consequences, and interventions*. New York: Mosby.

Jellinek, E. M. 1952. Phases of alcohol addiction. *Quarterly Journal of Studies on Alcohol* 13:673-84.

Jellinek, E. M. 1960. *Disease concept of alcoholism*. New Haven, Conn.: United Printing Service.

Marlatt, G. A., and J. R. Gordon, eds. 1985. *Relapse prevention: Maintenance strategies in the treatment of addictive behaviors*. New York: Guilford Press.

Peele, S. 1985. *The meaning of addiction: Compulsive experience and its interpretation*. Lexington, Ky.: D.C. Heath and Company.

Shaffer, H. J. 1986. Conceptual crisis and the addictions: A philosophy of science perspective. *Journal of Substance Abuse Treatment* 3:285-96.

Shedler, J., and J. Block. 1990. Adolescent drug use and psychological health: A longitudinal inquiry. *American Psychologist* 45 (May): 612-30.

Sobell, L. C., and M. B. Sobell. 1988. Behavioral assessment and treatment planning with alcohol and drug abusers: A review with an emphasis on clinical application. *Clinical Psychology Review* 8: 19-54.

Vaillant, G., and E. Milofsky. 1982. The etiology of alcoholism: A prospective viewpoint. *American Psychologist* 37:494-503.

Vaillant, G. 1984. *The natural history of alcoholism*. Cambridge: Harvard University Press.

Zucker, R., and E. Gomberg. 1986. Etiology of alcoholism reconsidered: The case for a biopsychosocial process. *American Psychologist* 41:783-93.

# III.
# EXPLAINING ADDICTION

The word "addiction" comes from the Latin term *addictus,* which means to be "given over" or "owned" as a slave might have been in ancient Rome. The dictionary defines addiction as a habitual or compulsive act. The central question is: How do drugs cause addiction?

There are two general categories of drugs: psychoactive and nonpsychoactive. Nonpsychoactive drugs, like antibiotics and blood pressure medicines, usually at normal dosages do not affect the brain and behavior. Psychoactive drugs are drugs that change thoughts, feelings, perceptions, and behavior. Most of the drugs taken illegally are psychoactive drugs.

The pharmacological characteristics of these drugs result in "pleasurable" changes in the user's state of mind and feelings. Drug users usually seek to change their feelings, moods, perceptions, and orientation to self and their environment. Consequently, drug use is an escape from self and surroundings. The use of psychoactive drugs is only one of the many ways in which feelings can be changed. Unfortunately for these users, drugs only temporarily can produce a synthetic version of desirable moods. In the long run, drug use is ineffective and produces additional problems. It has been said that an addict is in constant pursuit of that first high that never again can be found. Nevertheless, drug use has persisted throughout the ages and throughout all nations.

## WHY DO PEOPLE GET HIGH?

- To reduce pain

- To reduce uncomfortable or unwanted levels of activity or feelings of anxiety or nervousness

- To increase level of activity and feelings of energy and power and correspondingly reduce feelings of fatigue, depression, and sleepiness

- To gain social acceptance and change one's perception of the physical and social environment

- To achieve pleasurable feelings

- To achieve various levels of intoxication in order to forget problems

- To relieve boredom

From the psychological perspective, people might abuse psychoactive drugs for seven reasons. All involve changes in thoughts, feelings, behavior, or perception. These changes include the following:

• Relief of physical pain. Opiates like heroin, morphine, or methadone are still the preferred drugs.

• Reduction of uncomfortable or unwanted levels of activity or feelings such as anxiety, nervousness, hyperactivity, sleeplessness, overstimulation, or unwanted or unmanageable levels of basic drives such as sex or aggression. For most people, any central nervous system depressant can serve this function. Alcohol, barbiturates like Seconal, minor tranquilizers like Valium, and hypnotics like Quaaludes are all central nervous system depressants, also known as sedative/hypnotics. Opiates like heroin, Dilaudid, Demerol, Tylox, Talwin, and Percodan also have a sedating action in addition to their pain-killing aspects.

• To stay awake, feel stimulated, or powerful. A reduction in feelings of fatigue, depression, sleepiness. To increase confidence levels. Any central nervous system stimulant such as caffeine, amphetamines, cocaine, or a variety of synthetic drugs are used widely for these purposes.

• To change social status and gain acceptance. Users have a normal desire to belong to a group. The drug culture offers acceptance and recognition from peers. Drugs offer a common language and topic of conversation. Rituals surround use that involve social gatherings and traditions. Many users begin when a friend or relative offers or sometimes pressures them into trying a drug. Drug users want to be around other drug users, and often everyone feels pressure to use. This pressure to use usually begins during adolescence or even earlier. Users tend to discredit evidence about the damaging effects of drugs and generally feel capable of using their drug of choice safely. Many alcoholics claim they are more sociable when drunk.

• To experience feelings of pleasure (euphoria). People sometimes describe being high as feeling full of energy, floating, sensuous—like having sex or being in a dream-like state. Any psychoactive drug can produce some form of high if taken in sufficient quantity. The type of high that is sought might depend on what's available, peer pressure, personality factors, and one's first experience while under the influence of the drug.

• Some people are disturbed by social or emotional problems and use drugs to interfere with brain function to such a degree that memory is disrupted. Chronic alcoholics and those who use PCP often fit in this category. They actually try to "mess up" their brain to escape unpleasant memories. This is very dangerous, as large amounts of alcohol or other drugs are needed to induce this level of intoxication.

• Boredom is a problem for many people and is in part due to a lack of athletic, cultural, and goal-oriented stimulation. Young people often turn to drugs for something to do in order to relieve the boredom of their lives. In some areas, few positive alternatives to drugs exist. Finding interesting diversion is essential to prevent drug abuse.

### The Difference between Medical and Nonmedical Use of Drugs

Some medical drugs, like antibiotics and heart pills, are nonpsychoactive and are used to repair or help the body. Medicine tries to restore the natural balance of the body. This normal balance is called *homeostasis*. The body only can survive within narrow limits. The body's temperature, blood pressure, and sugar levels have to fall within narrow limits or death results. Even the psychoactive drugs like morphine are administered to restore a balance within the body. Painkillers are administered to help cancer patients and people recovering from surgery feel normal. The proper use of drugs under the direction of a physician is intended to help the patient reach homeostasis, most often in terms of pain relief, relieving excessive anxiety, and restoring the energy level for those who are depressed.

A doctor gives the patient a drug to restore the body's natural balance, while a drug user disrupts the body's natural balance. Medical uses of drug help repair damage to the body and help the body regain homeostasis. Abuse of drugs disrupts the delicate balance within the body.

## SOME DEFINITIONS

*Regular Social Use*—Less intense than an addiction; describes the majority of drug users. In other words, a person who feels that he or she cannot have fun without a drug would be considered psychologically dependent and in danger of progressing to an addiction.

*Psychological Addiction*—Irritability, craving, and looking for drugs. Emotional discomfort when drugs are not available. Believing that one cannot function effectively unless under the influence. Placing drugs before family, job, and health. Cocaine is known to cause the intense craving of psychological addiction in more than one-third of users when snorted and in the majority of users if they smoke it.

*Physical Addiction*—A change in the body's balance so marked that the drug is needed or the user will develop withdrawal symptoms. Withdrawal, and hence physical dependence, is present when seizures, convulsions, hallucinations, paranoia, pain, nausea, diarrhea, or other physical symptoms develop after a drug is withdrawn.

### Tolerance

Tolerance is the loss or reduction in effect from the same amount of drug used over a period of time or the increase in the amount of drug used over a period of time for the purpose of gaining a desired effect—an increase in dosage required to produce an effect. Sometimes tolerance is used to describe the amount of a drug an individual is able to consume before he or she is unable to handle the effects.

Because of the way that psychoactive drugs affect the body at the chemical level, repeated and frequent use of almost any drug eventually will not produce the same effects (high) produced originally by a similar dose. This phenomenon is known as tolerance, or a change in tolerance.

Eventually, the body needs the drug to feel normal and to counteract pain or depression. Users have to take more of the drug in progressively higher doses to obtain the same effect. Eventually the drug can produce paranoia (cocaine) or simply a feeling of being normal again (heroin). Some alcoholics have claimed they have drunk themselves "sober" because alcohol eventually came to have no positive effect on their mood.

Certain drugs, notably opiates (morphine) and their derivatives (heroin), the barbiturates, tranquilizers, alcohol, and cocaine, when used in sufficient amounts and frequencies over a period of time, produce chemical changes in the user that prohibits him or her from functioning "normally" without the drug.

The amount and frequency of the dosage required vary from drug to drug. Soon the drug is needed just to maintain a normal state. If the drug is withdrawn, physical pain, sweating, chills, diarrhea, hallucinations, paranoia, depression, stomach cramps, seizures, convulsions, and even death can occur. The presence of these symptoms indicates that the person is physically addicted to these drugs.

Psychological addiction is a compulsion to use the drug to feel better emotionally. A psychologically addicted person will feel irritable and uncomfortable without the drug, crave it intensely, and do almost anything to obtain it.

## Dosage

Dosage dictates the effects of drugs used legally and for medical reasons. A physician uses drugs to restore a natural balance to the body. For each drug prescribed exists an ineffective dose, an effective dose, a toxic dose, and for most, a lethal dose. The effects of drugs used illegally or for nonmedical reasons are a function of dose. For each exists also an ineffective dose, an effective dose, a toxic dose, and for most, a lethal dose.

Some drugs have multiple side effects. The side effects of drugs used legally often are critically important, and a physician's job is to weigh the potential benefits against the potential risks. Again, the ultimate goal is to recapture the body's natural balance (the word "disease" means "not at ease" or unbalanced).

Most of the drugs sold illegally are impure and often are not what they are supposed to be. They are contaminated with other substances, and accurate information regarding the purity seldom is available. For example, PCP sometimes is sold as THC or LSD; rat poison has been used to "cut" drugs.

Reports from laboratories that analyze street drugs verify the impurity of non-pharmaceutical street drugs. The imagination of the dealers of these drugs apparently is endless. At one time when mescaline widely was reported to be a popular drug, analyses of samples sold indicated that the predominant property was lysergic acid diethylamide (LSD). Taking an unknown substance in an unknown amount (alone or in combination with another drug) increases the risks involved, especially when the individual has little knowledge or understanding of drug action.

# THE PROGRESSIVE NATURE OF ADDICTION

When we use terms such as drug use, drug abuse, and drug addiction, we need to keep in mind that using drugs is a progressive disorder. Different stages of abuse result in different levels of addiction. The majority of people who use drugs believe they are in control of their habits. Under normal circumstances, addiction only becomes evident to users when their lives and feelings grow out of control. Even then, some people still believe they can control their use, and some addicts need to fail several times before they will accept their addiction as a fact.

In the beginning, drug use might not seem to affect a person's way of life. Users don't always see the dangers that lie ahead nor do they always see the legal problems they could face. Initially, users have an "it can't happen to me" mentality that seduces them into incorporating drugs into their lifestyle. This denial grows stronger as the drug satisfies needs for friendship, love, warmth, sex, and even food. In many cases their addiction gradually develops so that in the end, the users become slaves to the drug and the drug becomes their master. Some can last longer than others. Some realize what is happening and get out of the drug-use cycle before it is too late. Just like with quicksand, the deeper a person gets into drugs the harder it is to pull out. In the end, few can resist the seduction of hard drugs.

When we use the term "drug addict," we need to keep in mind that we are observing a progressive state of dependence on a drug that ultimately will affect several major life areas. Addiction is a behavioral and physical syndrome characterized by an inability to function without the drug.

It is useful to look at addiction as a process in which a person withdraws from family, job, self, and all those things that produce "natural high" and becomes dependent on the artificial mood produced by a chemical. It is estimated that 97 percent of drug abusers hold regular jobs. These people can be anyone in any walk of life.

Addiction, which is the ultimate form of dependence and that might be considered an illness, is a syndrome showing four main features:

1. It is progressive and usually gets worse if not treated.
2. There are stages that can be called mild, moderate, and severe or early, middle, and late.
3. It is often lethal if not treated.
4. A familial link is evident—children of alcoholics or drug users also tend to become alcoholics or drug users.

## Stages of Addiction

While developing dependence, several changes in characteristics of drug use occur.

In the earlier or mild phase of addiction, such as contact, experimentation, and occasional use, we see more freedom from the drug and less risks and damage to the individual drug user, although overdose and death can occur. The potential still exists for drug abuse. A person makes a choice at this stage to use the drug. In other words, the drug is used only when available and is used only in the presence of other people. Use is spontaneous rather than planned. The major reasons for continued use are primarily social—to "fit in." Most people in the earlier phases do not go on to become regular users. A 1990 study published in *American Psychology* suggests that experimentation can be a normal part of human development. For a healthy person, drug taking is not very important when compared to other experiences and activities in life.

The middle stages of addiction are those in which family, friends, and self are neglected at the expense of getting high. Because of drug use, at least one major life area—work, school, health, family, relationships, legal status, or financial status—is affected. Secretive and private use of alcohol and drugs is more frequent. Getting high alone is common. Guilt about use and irritation surrounding any discussion about drugs or alcohol set in. Physical addiction begins as the user falls closer to the late stages of addiction, described by some as "hitting bottom"—a zero state.

The late stages of addiction also have been called the terminal stages, because it is at this point that physical addiction and/or the deterioration of several major life areas develop. Nutrition is secondary to the high. Often, the drugs mask pain that is symptomatic of a serious illness such as hepatitis or endocarditis (infections of the liver and heart).

In the later phases, a lack of individual freedom from the drug develops. More physical damage is done to the individual; abuse is present, represented by a state of illness. The person is engaged in a self-defeating behavior that will cause loss of family and loved ones, money, health, and self-respect. Ultimately, the addict might die if not treated.

In other words, the individual probably devotes a lot of time, thought, and energy to getting the drug, taking the drug, discussing the effects of the drug, and associating almost exclusively with others who use the drug. He or she is considered psychologically dependent on the drug or, as is increasingly the case, dependent on several drugs (termed *polydrug abuse*) rather than on one specific drug. Addiction is present.

| Mild | Moderate | Severe |
|------|----------|--------|
| Use socially | Neglect family | Neglect health |
| Accept drugs | Use secretively | Use compulsively |
| Party mentality | Pressured financially | Neglect work |

## Factors that Cause Drug Abuse

### The effects of the drug (the high)

We roughly can locate the various drugs on a scale. On one side are the drugs with a strong addictive action (such as cocaine, heroin, and morphine); on the other are those to which an addictive power scarcely can be ascribed (such as aspirin, chlorpromazine, laxatives, or even petrol or vinegar). The addictive property of a drug depends on the bodily and psychic influences it exercises. The way in which these influences are connected with the chemical structure largely is unknown. All of the psychoactive drugs influence feeling and experience in the user.

In all cases the drug is taken for its desired action. What is desired depends on the person involved.

### The personal factors of the user

Personal factors, too, can make a difference. On one extreme are people who have a strong disposition toward excessive use and addiction, while at the other extreme are those who can seemingly "take it or leave it."

The risk of using any drug—even prescribed or over-the-counter drugs—is increased in an individual who is the "addictive personality" type. These people commonly display specific features: (1) high sensitivity to feelings of discomfort, tension, anxiety, and displeasure; (2) experiencing physical pain or very sensitive to pain; attempting to self-medicate; and (3) seek excitement and stimulation—very easily feel bored.

The risk factors can be stronger at certain times in a person's life than at others. Age, for example, is an important modifying factor. During puberty and adolescence, the risk for drug abuse appears to be increased. Our desire for change and excitement is higher during this age period, and peer pressure is more influential. Strong religious, philosophical, or political beliefs also can change a person.

Physical and psychiatric illnesses also can influence a person to use drugs. Many of these people probably should be under the care of a physician, but use alcohol and/or street drugs to self-medicate.

### The social meaning and value of a drug and of drug-taking

Drug use sometimes represents a way to join a group and be accepted into a culture or the company of peers. The social meaning of abuse includes ritualizing the use of a drug; seeking, buying, and using drugs becomes a social event with rules and procedures. A slang language and subculture often develops around drug use. Going to "cop" and going to cocaine parties might become part of the ritual.

Drugs can take on a positive meaning for this subgroup. For example, smoking marijuana openly was used as a political symbol during the 1960s. Cocaine use can be viewed as elegant, cool, fast. Users might be viewed as ambitious, energetic, and enlightened. Status might be derived from drug use, even among different drug subgroups. Alcoholics tend to perceive alcohol as a drug, and cocaine users sometimes see themselves at the top of the drug abuse pecking order. Heroin users sometimes are seen as detached or passive, while PCP users sometimes often are considered more impulsive types of people. Users believe that those who drink alcohol on a social basis aren't any better than they are. Comparing the use of illegal drugs with the legal and social use of alcohol might be an attempt by drug abusers to justify their habit. Rationalizations are a common sign of addiction and dependency whether the user is taking legal or illegal drugs.

## EFFECTS ON FAMILY MEMBERS

Addiction has an enormous impact on family members. The family is neglected more and more as addiction progresses. However, family members often become part of the problem. Spouses often cover for each others' addiction by making excuses to friends, family, and employers. This "enabling" protects the user and allows abuse to continue for a longer time period.

"Enabling" is action by others that saves the abuser from the consequences of his or her abuse. A family member is rescued from problems with work supervisors when the enabler calls in sick for him or her. The enabler saves the abuser from prison when they pay that fine, get the abuser to leave a situation when he or she behaves inappropriately, buy the best attorney, and even become a court witness backing the abuser.

The family usually is hurt the most when a person is addicted to drugs. The time and money that the addict ordinarily would have spent on his or her family and children instead are spent in obtaining and using drugs. Child neglect often produces long-lasting effects—damaging health and leaving emotional scars. Children feel hurt when their father or mother prefers drugs to them. A child who feels unloved and abandoned will seek attention in extreme ways. Also, a child who grows up seeing constant drug use will learn this as a way of life. Therefore, his or her chance of experiencing problems with drugs in the future increases.

The family often is very important—even to a person who is addicted and has been neglecting loved ones. The desire to improve the emotional and financial health of their families has motivated many men and women to change their destructive lifestyles. Those addicted must choose which is more important: their drug or their family.

## REFERENCE

Yochelson, S., and S. Samenow. 1977. *The criminal personality*. New York: Jason Aronson.

# IV.
# A GENERAL OVERVIEW OF DRUGS AND DRUG ABUSE TERMINOLOGY

This section will specify the general category of drugs described earlier as psychoactive. These drugs are substances that alter feelings, behavior, and perceptions. Generally speaking, seven categories or classes of psychoactive drugs are identified:

1. Sedative-hypnotics or general depressants

2. Narcotic analgesics

3. Stimulants

4. Hallucinogens (including marijuana)

5. Anesthetics

6. Clinical antidepressants

7. Major tranquilizers or psychotropics

Only the first four categories will be covered in depth, as most illegally used drugs fall into these categories.

## EXTENT OF USE

The most used or abused drugs in our country, excluding tobacco, fall under the sedative-hypnotic group. These drugs include alcohol, minor tranquilizers such as Valium and Librium, barbiturates, and other sedatives. Alcohol is the most frequently abused drug in this category, with 103 million current drinkers, approximately two-thirds of the population. The minor tranquilizers, some of them prescribed, follow second. Alcohol alone accounts for more than 100,000 deaths a year. In contrast, illegal drugs account for less than 4,000 deaths a year. Some of these deaths resulted from sniffing glue (toluene), gasoline, or other volatile solvents. These properties act as sedative-hypnotics but are more toxic than alcohol.

According to the National Institute of Drug Abuse, more than 37 percent (seventy-four million) of the American population has tried some type of illegal drug. Marijuana can be classified as a hallucinogen or in a class by itself and is one of the more frequently used or abused substances. More than 10 percent of the American population"between twenty and forty million"are users. An estimated sixty-seven million people have tried marijuana, including a majority of young adults. About 50 percent of high school seniors have tried it. Far fewer people use PCP or LSD, the next most popular hallucinogens.

The third most frequently abused drugs are classed as stimulants. Cocaine and crack cocaine have become a national epidemic, as this drug is extremely addictive when smoked. An estimated twenty-two million Americans have tried it, perhaps six million use it recreationally, and nearly one-half million can be labeled addicts. Amphetamines produce a similar feeling for the user, but are longer lasting. Dextroamphetamine and methamphetamine are probably as powerful as cocaine, although free-basing cocaine probably is more potent than injecting amphetamine, because it takes less time for the effects of a smoked drug to reach the brain. Ritalin and Preludin are stimulants of midlevel strength. Mild stimulants like coffee and cigarettes also can generate compulsive use patterns. Cigarettes especially have been found to be strongly addictive and related to serious health problems. If we add these milder stimulants into the category of drugs of abuse, then stimulants would be the most dangerous. Cigarettes alone account for more than 390,000 deaths a year among the 27 percent of the population that smokes.

A much smaller group of users prefer the narcotic analgesics. The word "analgesic" means painkiller. These are opiates like heroin and morphine and a variety of synthetic narcotics. Approximately one-half million Americans are heroin addicts.

An even smaller group—usually comprising young people—uses volatile solvents or inhalants. Solvents or inhalants are substances such as glue that contain toluene, lacquer thinner, amyl and butyl nitrate, or canned sprays. Overdose deaths are common because users put their heads in bags full of these substances and breathe the toxic fumes. Fortunately, as this is a true intoxication and a poisoning, drug abusers usually seek this method of getting high as a last resort. Brain damage from excessive inhalation of fumes easily can result.

Most of the other drugs compose only a small portion of the illicit drugs. Anesthetics like ether and nitrous oxide are psychoactive because they alter consciousness and relieve pain. Their abuse potential is low because they do not produce euphoria.

For the same reason, the lack of a high is why clinical antidepressants—drugs like Sinequan and Elavil—are not widely abused. These drugs elevate mood to a normal state but usually do not produce a high. According to some illicit users, however, "street Elavil" is available.

Major tranquilizers, drugs like Thorazine, Mellaril, and Haldol, also have a low abuse potential. They are used to control psychosis in mentally ill people. These drugs do produce sedation, but again, no feeling of euphoria generally is associated with use. In fact, they decrease the ability to feel pleasure.

## IMPORTANT TERMS

### Placebo Effect

When a person takes a drug that he or she expects will work, it will work. This phenomenon is known as the "placebo effect." In years past, placebos such as sugar pills have had amazing effects on some patients, producing favorable results. The sugar pill effect might be a form of self-hypnosis in which someone believes something so strongly that he or she imagines an effect.

## Potentiation

Drugs in the same category or class (except alcohol and sedatives) usually have an additive effect. The combined sedative effects of a Valium and a Librium produce a higher level of sedation. The effects of two hallucinogens or two stimulants usually combine to increase the effect. This additive effect is known as potentiation. Most similar drugs potentiate one another.

## Synergism

Combining some drugs produces a dangerously strong reaction, because they multiply in strength or produce new effects when mixed. It is dangerous to combine sedatives like Valium with alcohol, because one drug "boosts" the effect of the other, but by a different process. The effect is greater than additive: It has a "multiplier effect." For example, MAO inhibitors (drugs that prevent the breakdown of excitatory neurotransmitters, sometimes used as antidepressants) can make stimulating drugs quite dangerous. Synergism is a stronger interaction effect than potentiation. When combined, alcohol and barbiturates multiply the effect one drug has on the other. Most heroin addicts, for example, die only when alcohol or other sedatives also are taken.

## Antagonism

Some drugs cancel or lessen the effects of other drugs. A good example is a narcotic antagonist that has been developed to help narcotic-overdose victims. Naltrexone and Naloxone are drugs that almost completely neutralize the effect of narcotics. They are available in most hospital emergency rooms and have saved many lives. Another example of antagonism is using a major tranquilizer such as Thorazine to calm a bad reaction to a hallucinogen or to stimulants. Many people believe that giving coffee to someone who is drunk will help them recover from the effects of alcohol. Caffeine might be a partial antagonist to alcohol by helping to stimulate the alcohol-sedated brain. However, the effects of alcohol such as poor coordination and impulsiveness remain.

## Tolerance

Tolerance is defined as the effective dosage level in a given individual. Some people are born with a higher tolerance level than others. Most people develop a higher tolerance level to a drug as they continue to use the drug.

## Cross-tolerance

An alcoholic might require more medication for sedation and more painkillers to eliminate pain. This phenomenon is due to a corresponding rise in an abuser's tolerance to nonabused drugs in relation to the tolerance developed to a similarly acting drug. Cross-tolerance usually develops to drugs within the same class, such as sedatives. Heroin users also can better tolerate Demerol and Dilaudid and will need more than the average dose to reduce pain if they are injured.

### Cross-dependence

Cross-dependence means one drug can be substituted for another, even though that drug has never before been used by the addict. For example, Valium, Librium, or Xanax often are used to detoxify alcoholics, even though the individuals might never have had these drugs; however, as alcohol abusers, these people are cross-dependent on these drugs. These minor tranquilizers serve the same purpose as alcohol—they satisfy the craving and ease withdrawal.

### Use and Abuse

To some degree these terms are judgmental, and different people have different ideas about what they mean. Many people consider the word "abuse" to categorize the use of any illegal drug. Good reasons are behind this belief, because indulging in an illegal drug places a person at risk for arrest and also means that he or she is associating with criminals. However, even drugs legally obtained can be abused. For the purposes of this manual, "abuse" will be defined as *use that is detrimental to the health or well-being of an individual, his or her associates, family, or work.* Drugs can be abused by taking excessive doses, by a pattern of taking doses too often, or by provoking damaging behavior. In general, a person can distinguish whether a drug either has helped or has been a neutral factor in his or her life (use) or whether drugs have hurt his or her life (abuse).

## A SIMPLIFIED MODEL OF HOW DRUGS AFFECT THE BRAIN

The workings of our brain can be described using an automobile as a simplified model. This is a very rough model, but it might help some to visualize or understand how drugs affect the brain. An automobile has a number of systems necessary to work together so it can function correctly.

1. The engine needs gasoline for the motivation or "go power."

2. The car needs brakes to slow it down.

3. The car needs a clean windshield so information can enter—such as how the road curves or whether a light is green or red.

4. The car needs to steer to go in the correct direction and to avoid problems.

5. The car needs shock absorbers to reduce reactions to bumps in the road.

In a similar manner, the brain needs equivalent systems in order to function correctly. Normally, the brain is homeostatic (self-regulating), so all systems mesh together. Drugs can upset this balance.

Equivalent to gasoline, motivation within the brain depends on arousal chemicals. The body is motivated for action by adrenaline. The brain is motivated for action by this and a related chemical called noradrenaline. Cocaine and amphetamines, and caffeine to a lesser degree, flood the brain with this "gasoline," making the "engine" race. Normally the brain will respond to a stressful situation by becoming aroused. After the stressor is removed or handled, the brain can "take the foot off the gas" and slow the engine.

In contrast, with stimulant drugs in the system, the "gas pedal is held to the floor,"—in other words, the person cannot relax. Sometimes this "speeding" is enjoyable, but it does wear out the engine. In an attempt to maintain homeostasis, the brain will use its "brakes" (the serotonin system described below), and the "brake pads" will wear out. This "wearing out of brake pads" can become a permanent condition if stimulants are abused.

Depressant drugs such as alcohol, barbiturates, and to a lesser degree tranquilizers and marijuana, tend to choke off the "gasoline" supply, reducing mental power and alertness. Used in small amounts, it simply slows down the "engine" and reduces anxiety, but in high enough doses the "engine" will die. Alcohol and other sedatives will cause death if an overdose occurs.

Equivalent to brakes, the brain system, by using the inhibitory neurotransmitter serotonin, tends to slow down thoughts and reduce awareness. Serotonin is necessary for sleep and for relaxation. Damage to this system can be compared to brake pads wearing out or malfunctioning. LSD, mescaline, psilocybin, and to a lesser degree marijuana, tend to temporarily disable our "brakes" as if oil were put on the brake pads. When that occurs, our normal "slowing down" of awareness of thoughts and perception is reduced. This results in an increase in conscious awareness and a feeling that things are novel and interesting. Some find this pleasurable, but others become fearful when they find it difficult to control a flood of perception. Fortunately, these hallucinogenic drugs have only a temporary effect. However, sometimes stimulant drugs "wear out the brake pads," so the ability to relax and sleep is impaired for longer periods. Without our "brakes," paranoid thoughts often run wild.

Equivalent to receiving information about road conditions through a clean windshield, our brain needs to take in accurate information. This is a very complicated system, but information moving in the brain generally can be said to use a brain chemical called acetylcholine. This information chemical is disrupted by many drugs, especially general anesthetics such as ether, nitrous oxide, alcohol, and PCP. PCP and other anesthetics produce a "numbness" and diminished awareness. Through a "dirty windshield," the brain tries to guess at the correct information, and so one's imagination is used to compensate for the missing or scrambled information. PCP use can result not only in diminished awareness but actual hallucinations. If a driver accurately cannot know what the road is like, the car will go wild and crash.

Equivalent to steering, the brain's emotional system is able to choose what is good (pleasurable) or bad (disliked). The person "steers" toward what is likeable and avoids what is unlikable. The brain's reward chemical is called dopamine. Normally, a person maintains a perspective and makes accurate judgments. Drugs such as cocaine and amphetamines tend to overwhelm the pleasure system and to focus awareness in a compulsive manner on only part of the entire picture. For example, people who are on amphetamines or cocaine might repeat one action for hours. This inability to choose among the whole range of possibilities can be related to "the steering wheel getting locked in one direction." That direction is toward compulsiveness and irritability over a short period of time, and toward paranoia at higher doses or if stimulant drugs are abused over a longer time.

Equivalent to shock absorbers helping a car to ignore bumps in the road, the brain has a system to ignore pain. New pain should be focused on, but after awhile, it is better to ignore pain if nothing can be done to avoid it. Our body's natural chemicals called endorphins help us to ignore distracting pain. Narcotics, such as morphine and heroin, act like endorphins and "smooth out the bumps," enabling a person to drift along without worrying or feeling any pain. This is pleasurable, but as with any imbalance, one must pay sooner or later. The body quickly becomes adapted to the higher level of pain-killing chemicals and stops producing natural endorphins, and the person becomes physically addicted. That means if the heroin supply is cut off, the body is aware of many of the aches and pains ordinarily ignored or controlled. The body has gotten used to the "extra shock absorber" and has relied on it instead of the natural system. It takes several days before the natural level of endorphins is restored. During this withdrawal period, the body is overly sensitive to the normal bumps in the road of life. This time period without endorphins accounts for the withdrawal period following habitual heroin use.

This explanation illustrates that like a car, our brain has a number of necessary systems that normally remain balanced; it ordinarily enjoys a state of homeostasis. Small changes to any one system will be corrected by other systems. However, large changes can go beyond the limit of correction, and a car or a person will get into major trouble. At that time, an "overhaul" might be necessary, and outside help such as a mechanic or a drug program is needed to restore the normal balance.

The effects of all of these neurotransmitters occur when they are sent from one brain cell to another. Some neurotransmitters excite the receiving cell, some inhibit excitation. The area in which one brain cell sends neurotransmitter chemicals to another brain cell is called the synapse. Figures 1 and 2 illustrate how the synapse works normally and how it functions under the influence of cocaine.

## The Division of the Brain into Old and New Systems

The brain can be divided into several cooperating systems. The spinal cord sends information to and from the body. The "old brain" is shared by all higher animals, even fish and reptiles. One area of the old brain maintains basic functions such as breathing and arousal level. If this section is overly sedated, breathing stops. Another part of the old brain controls emotions, which can be considered motivations to approach or avoid elements in the environment. For example, the old brain will stimulate the drive to seek food when hungry. It can be said, therefore, that our basic impulses come from our old brain.

Humans have a "new brain" called the cortex, which normally controls the more primitive parts of the brain. The new brain is able to think in words as well as with feelings and images and is what makes humans different from other animals.

People need to wait for appropriate times to satisfy desires. The job of the logical part of the brain—the neocortex—is to say "no" to the impulses and desires of our old brain. For example, someone might see a candy bar in a store. The old brain might feel hungry and want to grab and eat the candy bar, but the logical new brain tells the old brain to wait and buy the candy bar before eating it. The new brain knows negative consequences would result from impulsively eating the candy. One of the problems arising from using alcohol and other sedatives is that the new brain becomes less efficient than usual; people often act emotionally and impulsively without thinking first about the consequences. For this reason, many fights and crimes involve alcohol use.

This division into old and new brains is, of course, oversimplified, but it is a useful concept in education. Demonstrate by using your hands. Ball one hand into a fist, which represents the old brain and its impulses. The new brain is represented by covering your fist with your other hand. Push your hands back and forth to show the concept of primitive impulses from the old brain and rational control by the new brain. Removing the covering hand demonstrates the disinhibiting effects of alcohol and other sedatives.

### The Synapse

The synapse is the connection at which information is transmitted from one brain cell to another. The body of the nerve cell has small "factories" where neurotransmitters are made. A neurotransmitter is sent out in vesicles or "bubbles," which pop out when the sending cell fires. In order to prevent overstimulation and to save the cell's supply of neurotransmitters, a pump system retrieves excess neurotransmitters, and an enzyme destroys what isn't retrieved. The receptor sites on the opposite side fire when the neurotransmitter lodges in the receptor site, passing on the message from one brain cell to another.

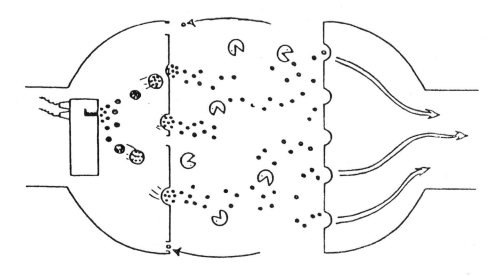

**Figure 1—A Simplified Diagram of the Synapse**

Cocaine and amphetamines prevent the sending brain cell from pumping back and storing used neurotransmitters. This creates a high degree of stimulation within the receiving cell. Although the factory works at full capacity, the supply of neurotransmitters becomes exhausted as the enzymes destroy these unprotected neurotransmitters.

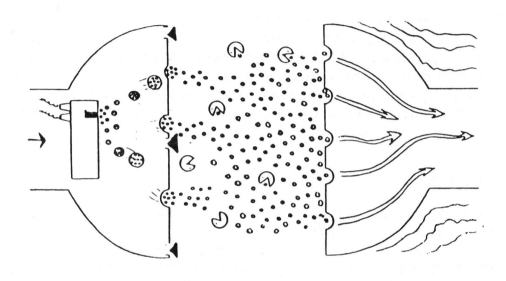

**Figure 2—A Simplified Diagram of an Overstimulated Synapse**

## NEUROTRANSMITTER SYSTEMS

The material in this section is probably too technical for most people. However, it might help interested people to conceptualize the mechanics of drug action. It admittedly is oversimplified in part because of the current state of knowledge in the field.

### Arousal

The ascending reticular activating system (the core of the old brain) controls overall arousal level. It is essential for alertness, concentration, and motivation. Major neurotransmitter for the arousal system: noradrenaline.

Noradrenaline is made by our bodies from the amino acid tyrosine, which is found in high concentrations in meat and dairy products. Amphetamines and cocaine stimulate this system by preventing the re-uptake of noradrenaline back into the sending neuron. This "loose" noradrenaline continues to stimulate the receiving neurons, producing excitement. However, the loose noradrenaline is destroyed by enzymes and is then not available.

Barbiturates, alcohol, other sedatives, and narcotics will decrease effectiveness of the arousal system. Marijuana appears to mildly decrease the release of noradrenaline, which might account for the "amotivational syndrome" and attention problems while "stoned."

### Sensory Inhibition System

Awareness of sensation, perception, and thoughts is controlled or filtered by this system, which usually works in conjunction with the arousal system to focus attention. Sleep is not possible without activity in the inhibitory system. The major neurotransmitter is serotonin (5-hydroxy-tryptamine).

Serotonin is made by our bodies from the amino acid tryptophan, which sometimes is used as a vitamin supplement. It is found in many foods, especially bananas and milk. LSD and other serotonergic hallucinogens (psilocybin, mescaline, and DMT) decrease the functioning of this filtering system, thus preventing sleep and expanding awareness of ordinarily inhibited perceptions. Evidently, these chemicals either fit into the "receptor sites" for serotonin but don't stimulate the receiving neuron, or they decrease the creation of this inhibitory neurotransmitter.

Marijuana also decreases the effectiveness of the serotonin system, increasing awareness of bodily sensation. It probably does so by reducing the amount of serotonin released from the "synaptic vesicles" when the brain cell fires. Marijuana appears to first affect the serotonin system, producing the "hallucinogenic" increase in sensory awareness. The noradrenaline system then is affected, causing relaxation and even laziness.

### Emotional System

This is the midbrain emotion-control center and helps produce emotions of happiness, sadness, fear, and anger. The major neurotransmitters are dopamine, norepinephrine and gamma-amino-butyric-acid (GABA). Dopamine appears to be the reward or pleasure neurotransmitter and motivates the initiation or repetition of thoughts or behaviors. A lack of dopamine results in apathy, depression, and Parkinson's disease, which is characterized by tremors and inability to initiate movement. Too much activity in the dopamine system is associated with schizophrenia—especially the paranoid type. Noradrenaline appears to be the main chemical involved in arousal, fear, anxiety, and avoidance behavior. GABA appears to calm neurons.

Minor tranquilizers such as Valium and Librium appear to make nerves more sensitive to the calming effect of GABA. However, after a few months the nerves become dependent on this artificial calming, so withdrawal can lead to seizures. Major tranquilizers such as Thorazine and Haldol decrease the strength of the dopamine system, preventing thoughts that are "wild" or self-reinforcing.

Cocaine is the drug that appears to directly stimulate the dopamine (reward or pleasure) system the most, producing pleasure directly. Cocaine and amphetamines both stimulate the noradrenaline system. These stimulating effects result from preventing the normal re-uptake of these neurotransmitters back into the sending cell, continuing the stimulation but also allowing the body's enzymes to destroy the natural supply of these neurotransmitters. A "run" on cocaine or amphetamines drains the body of these chemicals, leading to exhaustion and even clinical depression.

Amphetamines are like cocaine but are longer lasting. They mostly affect the noradrenaline system, producing more nervous arousal than euphoria. Lengthy periods of stress will cause exhaustion and can damage the body's ability to relax.

### Acetylcholine

The major system for transferring information involves the neurotransmitter acetylcholine. Our bodies make this from the amine "choline." The nerves that control our muscles use this chemical, and most of the brain information transmitted appears to use acetylcholine.

Anesthetics decrease the effectiveness of acetylcholine, and depressant/sedatives such as alcohol have the same effect. PCP (phencyclidine) is called a "cholinergic hallucinogen" because it disrupts awareness and information processing. At low doses it can "disinhibit" and produce excitement in a similar manner as alcohol. At medium doses it can produce hallucinations as perceptual ability is reduced and the mind tries to make sense of a disjointed awareness. At high doses, it can cause convulsions and coma. Pain is absent, and extremely violent behavior sometimes occurs. Because the sense of pain is dulled, users might strain themselves and tear muscles without realizing it. At high doses, PCP can produce convulsions and unconsciousness. The confusion evident in someone under the influence of PCP has been an element of many violent crimes, and PCP users are unpredictable.

### Endorphins

Endorphins are our body's natural opiates. They reduce awareness of pain, allowing one to concentrate on adaptive behaviors or on relaxing. Narcotics mimic the endorphins, putting people in a state in which they are dissociated from pain and worries. However, because the body stops producing its natural endorphins, it requires more narcotics as the body adjusts and tries to regain its homeostasis or balance. When narcotic use is discontinued, physical addiction is seen because the withdrawal symptoms occur until the body again begins to produce its own endorphins.

### Possible Actions of Specific Drugs on Neurotransmitters

Other than the effect of stimulants on neurotransmitters—fairly well-known information—much of the following is conjecture based on limited data. Further research might change psychology's conceptualization of how specific drugs affect our brains.

1. Heroin and other narcotics are drugs that stimulate our opiate receptors. They also shut off our "factories" that normally produce endorphins, so that an addict becomes dependent on an artificial supply. Narcotic antagonists occupy opiate receptor sites without causing action.

2. Cocaine and amphetamines deactivate the retrieval pump for the neurotransmitters dopamine and noradrenaline. These stimulating neurotransmitters remain in the synapse, continuing to stimulate the receiving cell to an unusual degree. However, the "trapped" neurotransmitters are destroyed by enzymes, and the brain runs out of its supply.

3. LSD probably turns off the production of serotonin, a neurotransmitter that inhibits awareness of unnecessary perceptions and thoughts as during sleep. The other serotonergic hallucinogens, which require much higher doses, probably block the receptor sites for serotonin.

4. THC (marijuana) probably increases the surface tension of the fatty neurotransmitter vesicles for serotonin and noradrenaline, allowing less to be released when the cell fires.

5. Alcohol and other sedatives make the cell walls less responsive, so that they cannot fire easily. Most sedatives also reduce hormone production.

## THE EFFECTS OF DRUGS ON DRIVING SKILL

Safe driving requires good vision, alertness to traffic and road conditions, quick reactions to unexpected problems, and the ability to make good judgments. Any physical condition or any drug that impairs these abilities can result in serious injury or death. A driver legally will be responsible for his or her actions. Being under the influence of any drug is not only an unacceptable excuse, it also is grounds for increased punishment, as everyone is expected to know that driving under the influence of any drug, including alcohol, is dangerous.

### Alcohol

Alcohol is the prime cause behind highway deaths. About half of all traffic deaths are alcohol-related. Nationwide, about 450 lives are lost each week to drunk drivers.

There are several important factors to know about alcohol and driving. In most states, a person with a blood alcohol content of one-tenth of 1 percent is considered legally drunk. At this level, people obviously are uncoordinated and usually will fail field sobriety tests consisting of walking a straight line, standing on one leg, and touching the nose with eyes closed. A person who is legally drunk might fall asleep at the wheel and have double or blurred vision. A 160-pound man is legally drunk after consuming five drinks in a two-hour period.

Someone who has consumed half the amount of alcohol of the legally drunk limit still suffers impaired driving ability. Studies have shown that even at this blood alcohol level, reaction time is slowed, a higher variability in lane position is evident, and loss of concentration related to decreased alertness results. Alcohol is a depressant, so it lessens the acuity of all nerve functions, especially in the parts of the brain in which rational judgments are made. A person under the influence of alcohol is prone to get angry quicker and to make foolish decisions.

### Barbiturates

Phenobarbital, methaqualone (quaalude), and similar barbiturates can be thought of as "alcohol in pill form." At both low and high medical doses, barbiturates affect driving skills more than does alcohol. The combination of alcohol and barbiturates especially is deadly.

### Valium, Librium and Other Minor Tranquilizers

Diazepam, the chemical name for Valium, has been shown to decrease driving ability at both low and high doses. The minor tranquilizers, chemically known as benzodiazepines, have less of an overall sedating effect than alcohol or barbiturates, and most of the sedation is related to antianxiety effects. Although a person feels fairly alert, the decrease in reaction time can be deceptive because it is not felt by the user who is tranquilized. The combination of benzodiazepines and alcohol is quite dangerous because they sedate in different ways. Therefore, the effects of the combination can be stronger than anticipated. Warnings about operating vehicles or heavy equipment while under the influence are on the bottles of all sedating medicines and should be taken seriously.

### Narcotics

Although little research has been conducted regarding the effects of heroin, morphine, or other narcotics on driving ability, the warnings about driving certainly make sense, as all narcotics have some sedative effects. If a person is "nodding out" or even feels slightly sleepy, driving logically would be more dangerous than if the person is alert.

### Marijuana

Marijuana has been shown to reduce driving ability, especially at higher doses. Someone who smokes two joints of medium-grade marijuana exhibits about half of the driving problems that a person who is legally drunk will show. One joint of marijuana also shows repercussions in driving skill in negotiating lane position when following curves and in making correct turnoffs. Three major problems appear to be aggravated by marijuana: Drivers show a decreased ability in tracking moving objects, trouble adjusting to the glare of oncoming headlights, and memory problems that could lead to forgetting where to go or making sudden moves on the road. The effects of marijuana can last several hours after the high is gone. It should be noted that in these studies, the marijuana used was only medium quality; a smaller amount of high-quality marijuana could produce the same effects on driving ability.

## LEGAL CONSEQUENCES OF DRUG POSSESSION OR DISTRIBUTION

From 1965 through 1986, more than eleven million Americans were arrested for possession or distribution of drugs. Nearly seven million of these arrests were for marijuana offenses. State and federal laws treat drug distribution as a serious offense, and the punishments can be severe. This also reflects the general attitude of the non-drug using population that is concerned that drugs are a danger to society and our youth.

The Anti-Drug Abuse Act of 1986 became law when it was signed by President Reagan on Oct. 27, 1986. Public Law 99-570 became effective and now is more commonly known in prison as the "new law." People with prior drug-related felony convictions can receive prison sentences ranging in length from ten years to life for drug convictions. If death or serious bodily injury to others results from the drug use, then a life sentence must be imposed (*Handbook on the Anti-Drug Abuse Act of 1986*. Department of Justice: 6).

First-time offenders sentenced for growing 100 or more marijuana plants, possessing one kilogram of hashish oil, or not less than fifty kilograms of marijuana can be sentenced to up to twenty years; people with prior records can receive up to thirty years. Life imprisonment can be the sentence if death or serious bodily injury resulted from the drug use in question.

The following page of information is reprinted from a Drug Enforcement Agency publication. It illustrates the criteria by which drugs are classified legally and the federal penalties for trafficking.

## REFERENCES

Blum, K. 1984. *Handbook of abusable drugs*. New York: Gardner.

Brecher, E. M., and *Consumer Reports* editors. 1972. *Licit and illicit drugs*. Boston: Little, Brown.

Gold, Mark S. 1986. *The facts about drugs and alcohol*. New York: Bantam Books.

Hoover, R. D. 1985. *Drugs of abuse*. Washington, D.C.: U. S. Department of Justice, Drug Enforcement Administration.

Julien, R. M. 1988. *A primer of drug action*. 5th ed. San Francisco: W. H. Freeman.

Lemberger, L., and A. Rubin. *Physiologic disposition of drugs of abuse*. New York: Spectrum Publications.

Ray, O., and C. Ksir. *Drugs, society, and behavior*. 4th ed. St. Louis: Times Mirror/Mosby.

Siegel, R. K. 1978. Substance actions. In *Drugs in perspective*, edited by W. P. Link, L. P. Miller, and B. Fisher. Rockville, Md.: National Institute on Drug Abuse, Division of Training.

White, W. L. 1978. An annotated history of the use, promotion, and prohibition of mood-altering drugs. In *Drugs in perspective*, edited by W. P. Link, L. P. Miller, and B. Fisher. Rockville, Md.: National Institute on Drug Abuse, Division of Training.

## FEDERAL TRAFFICKING PENALTIES

Narcotics Penalties & Enforcement Act of 1986

| CSA | PENALTY | | Quantity | DRUG | Quantity | PENALTY | |
|---|---|---|---|---|---|---|---|
| | 2nd Offense | 1st Offense | | | | 1st Offense | 2nd Offense |
| I and II | Not less than 10 years. Not more than life. | Not less than 5 years. Not more than 40 years. | 100-999 gm mixture | **HEROIN** | 1 kg or more mixture | Not less than 10 years. Not more than life. | Not less than 20 years. Not more than life. |
| | | | 500-4,999 gm mixture | **COCAINE** | 5 kg or more mixture | | |
| | If death or serious injury, not less than life. | If death or serious injury, not less than 20 years. Not more than life. | 5-49 gm mixture | **COCAINE BASE** | 50 gm or more mixture | If death or serious injury, not less than 20 years. Not more than life. | If death or serious injury, not less than life. |
| | | | 10-99 gm or 100-999 gm mixture | **PCP** | 100 gm or more or 1 kg or more mixture | | |
| | Fine of not more than $4 million individual, $10 million other than individual | Fine of not more than $2 million individual, $5 million other than individual. | 1-10 gm mixture | **LSD** | 10 gm or more mixture | Fine of not more than $4 million individual, $10 million other than individual. | Fine of not more than $8 million individual, $220 million other than individual. |
| | | | 40-399 gm mixture | **FENTANYL** | 400 gm or more mixture | | |
| | | | 10-99 gm mixture | **FENTANYL ANALOGUE** | 100 gm or more mixture | | |

| | Drug | Quantity | First Offense | Second Offense |
|---|---|---|---|---|
| | Others* | Any | Not more than 20 years. If death or serious injury, not less than 20 years, not more than life. Fine $1 million individual, $5 million not individual. | Not more than 30 years. If death or serious injury, life. Fine $2 million individual, $10 million not individual. |
| III | All | Any | Not more than 5 years. Fine not more than $250,000 individual, $1 million not individual. | Not more than 10 years. Fine not more than $500,000 individual, $2 million not individual. |
| IV | All | Any | Not more than 3 years. Fine not more than $250,000 individual, $1 million not individual. | Not more than 6 years. Fine not more than $500,000 individual, $2 million not individual. |
| V | All | Any | Not more than 1 year. Fine not more than $100,000 individual, $250,000 not individual. | Not more than 2 years. Fine not more than $200,000 individual, $500,000 not individual. |

*Does not include marijuana, hashish, or hashish oil. (See separate chart.)

## FEDERAL TRAFFICKING PENALTIES—MARIJUANA

Narcotics Penalties & Enforcement Act of 1986

| Quantity | Description | First Offense | Second Offense |
|---|---|---|---|
| 1,000 kg or more | **Marijuana** Mixture containing detectable quantity* | Not less than 10 years, not more than life. If death or serious injury, not less than 20 years, not more than life. Fine not more than $4 million individual, $10 million other than individual. | Not less than 20 years, not more than life. If death or serious injury, not less than life. Fine not more than $8 million individual, $20 million other than individual. |
| 100 kg to 1,000 kg | **Marijuana** Mixture containing detectable quantity* | Not less than 5 years, not more than 40 years. If death or serious injury, not less than 20 years, not more than life. Fine not more than $2 million individual, $5 million other than individual. | Not less than 10 years, not more than life. If death or serious injury, not less than life. Fine not more than $4 million individual, $10 million other than individual. |
| 50 to 100 kg | **Marijuana** | Not more than 20 years. If death or serious injury, not less than 20 years, not more than life. Fine $1 million individual, $5 million other than individual. | Not more than 30 years. If death or serious injury, life. Fine $2 million individual, $10 million other than individual. |
| 10 to 100 kg | **Hashish** | | |
| 1 to 100 kg | **Hashish Oil** | | |
| 100 or more plants | **Marijuana** | | |
| Less than 50 kg | **Marijuana** | Not more than 5 years. Fine not more than $250,000, $1 million other than individual. | Not more than 10 years. Fine $500,000 individual, $2 million other than individual. |
| Less than 10 kg | **Hashish** | | |
| Less than 1 kg | **Hashish Oil** | | |

*Includes hashish and hash oil. 

(Marijuana is a Schedule I controlled substance.)

Source: *Drugs of Abuse*, 1988 ed. published by the Drug Enforcement Administration.

# V.
# ALCOHOL AND OTHER SEDATIVES

## HISTORY AND ORIGIN

Alcohol has been known to man for at least 5,000 years and probably much longer. An ancient Egyptian papyrus describes the operation of a brewery in which wine probably was made in 3500 B.C. Fermentation or rotting is a natural process. Partially rotted berries could have been eaten by animals who were observed intoxicated by man, or man could have eaten these partially rotted berries or grapes, directly experiencing the effects of alcohol. More than 4,000 years ago, wine was taxed as a source of income for the government on the Greek island of Crete. Plato, an ancient philosopher, warned about the effects of alcohol and suggested that youths not be allowed to drink.

The Chinese philosopher Confucius also warned around 500 A.D. about the effect of alcohol. Several laws had been passed and repealed in China, first decreeing the use of alcohol legal, then illegal. In most of the world other than Moslem countries, alcohol has become an accepted and legal intoxicant. Europeans brought alcohol to the Americas.

Several laws were passed in early Virginia settlements making the first offense for public drunkenness punishable by a private "tongue lashing" by a minister. The second offense resulted in a public admonishment, and the third offense resulted in a fine and having to "lie in halter" for twelve hours. No treatment for alcoholism existed. Later, alcoholics were placed in sanitariums along with mental patients.

The prohibitionist movements have a fairly long history in this country. In 1853, Margaret Freelander of Syracuse, N.Y., began a famous prohibitionist tactic by entering a saloon and breaking up the bottles of alcohol with a wooden staff. In 1862, a federal tax was levied on alcohol, making it an important source of government income in view of the tremendous financial need of the country due to the Civil War.

By 1880, eight states had prohibited the use of alcohol. Alcohol again became legal in most of these states by 1904. In the latter part of the 1900s, opium and morphine were considered legitimate treatments for alcoholism. In 1914, the Harrison Act prohibited physicians from treating addictions by using narcotics. In 1919, the 18th Amendment to the Constitution took effect, making the sale of alcohol illegal. In New York and other cities, smoking marijuana became popular, since drinking was illegal. By 1930, there were about 500 "tea pads" where people could smoke all the marijuana they wanted for about a quarter.

Prohibition was said to be, in part, an attempt by the religiously oriented country people to control the wayward ways of city people. Alcohol use did decrease during prohibition. However, it remained fairly available, because a sizable minority of the population was willing to break the law. Some people made alcohol at home, while most did their drinking at fashionable private clubs called "speakeasies." In many areas of the country, the laws were little enforced or the demand was strong, and organized crime flourished. Battles were common between criminal organizations and between these organizations and the police.

Eventually, a political alliance developed between the people who wanted to drink and the people who believed prohibition was causing more problems than drinking itself. These factions elected representatives who had pledged to abolish prohibition, and a majority consensus formed. On December 5, 1933, prohibition officially ended, and the power to restrict alcohol consumption returned to each state.

Two years later in 1935, the first Alcoholics Anonymous (AA) group met in Akron, Ohio, organized by two "hopeless drunks," a physician and a businessman. AA essentially was the only treatment program for alcoholism for many years. The professional community viewed alcoholism as a weakness of character, while AA advocated that this addiction was an incurable disease. The AA philosophy of twelve steps slowly has gained respectability and has become the basis of many private treatment programs today. The acceptance of one's powerlessness over alcohol, confession, a spiritual awakening, and self-disclosure in a nonthreatening setting are the bases for this treatment. See Appendix E for a list of the twelve steps.

## BASIC FACTS AND COMPOSITION

Alcohol actually is a poison or toxin produced during fermentation. It usually is made from yeast digesting starch or sugar—yeast cells eat the starch and sugar and produce alcohol as a toxic waste product. When the alcohol content of a fermenting liquid reaches 14 percent, the yeast die in the toxic environment of their own waste. Alcohol cannot be found in greater concentrations than 14 percent in nature. In order to make stronger concentrations of alcohol, man creatively invented distillation. Alcohol evaporates at a lower temperature than water, so it can be separated from the liquid through a heating and condensing process. It is a solvent in which any oily substance can dissolve. As a solvent, it is used for cleaning, for extracting essential oils from plants, for thinning shellac used in woodworking, and as a gasoline additive. It increases the octane rating for gasoline, and as it mixes with water as well as oil, it helps prevent gas lines from clogging with ice.

### Blood-alcohol Content

Drinking a can of beer, a cup of wine, or a shot of hard liquor surprisingly will result in the same amount of alcohol in your blood (blood-alcohol content).

| 12 oz. can of beer | 4 oz. cup of wine | 1 oz. shot of liquor |
|---|---|---|
| 4% alcohol | 12% alcohol | 48% alcohol (96 proof) |
| .48 oz. alcohol | .48 oz. alcohol | .48 oz. alcohol |

A can of beer, a cup of wine, or a shot of hard liquor all contain about one-half of a fluid ounce of pure alcohol. It takes your liver an hour to change one drink into acetaldehyde, then acetic acid, then finally into carbon dioxide and water. Your liver gets rid of 95 percent of the alcohol through this breakdown. Sweating, breathing, and urinating get rid of only 5 percent. You cannot get rid of most alcohol unless it first passes through your liver, as most drugs do. The reason you urinate so much after heavy drinking is the "diuretic" effect of alcohol. The alcohol stimulates the brain to stimulate the kidneys to eliminate fluids through the urine.

If more than one drink is consumed per hour, that drink has to stay in a holding pattern until the liver is free again. The added alcohol is called your blood-alcohol content (BAC).

The following are examples of drinks and blood-alcohol content level in a 160-pound male for the first hour of drinking:

1 drink  = .02% BAC
2 drinks = .04
3 drinks = .06
4 drinks = .08
5 drinks = .10        This person is now legally drunk in most states. (Some states use .08% as the legal limit.) Someone who has consumed ten drinks is legally drunk for six hours.

Legal intoxication also can be reached by steady drinking. For example, since the liver only is able to metabolize between one and two drinks per hour, drinking two or more alcoholic beverages per hour will allow alcohol to accumulate, eventually resulting in legal intoxication.

Women generally will have a higher BAC, all things being equal, because women have proportionately more fat but less water than men of the same weight. Alcohol will mix with the body's water, and since women have less water the concentration of alcohol in their blood will be higher. Women also will have an even higher BAC level during menstruation as possibly even less water is available with which the alcohol can mix.

Many people smoke while they drink. Nicotine is a stimulant. Like other stimulants, nicotine acts as a vasoconstrictor or an agent that narrows your blood vessels so less blood can get through. One reason why so many drinkers might like to smoke while drinking is that smoking evens out the "high" by delaying the transfer of alcohol from stomach and intestines to blood because of this vessel narrowing. Another possibility is that the mild stimulation of nicotine keeps drinkers more awake. Whatever the reason, many drinkers report that they enjoy alcohol more when they smoke.

Individual differences also play a role. Why one person can drink so much and another can't might be due to family history or to one's physical makeup. Critical enzymes that help break down alcohol might be available less in some people than in others. Whether learned, cultural, or genetic, these differences in alcohol tolerance are real.

## Basic Statistics

About two-thirds of our adult population drinks alcohol. It is estimated that one of seven drinkers is a problem drinker. About eighteen million people abuse alcohol. This group of problem drinkers (7 percent of the population) consumes half of all the alcohol sold. Half of all men and about a third of all women are moderate to heavy drinkers. Alcohol abuse does have a significant impact on our society. Alcohol is linked to more than 100,000 deaths a year as compared to approximately 4,000 deaths a year due to illegal drugs. According to the National Institute of Health and State of Virginia Health Department:

76  percent of all murderers had been drinking
60  percent of all murder victims had been drinking
72  percent of assaults were by alcohol offenders
79  percent of assault victims consumed alcohol
72  percent of all robberies involved alcohol
52  percent of all spouse abusers have a history of alcoholism
38  percent of child abusers have problems with alcohol
65  percent of all child abuse is alcohol-related
64  percent of all suicide attempts involve alcohol
80  percent of all suicides involve alcohol
50  percent of all fatal car accidents involve alcohol
33  percent of all pedestrians killed in 1989 were drunk
45  percent of all fatal motorcycle accidents involve alcohol
40  percent of all fatal industrial accidents involve alcohol
52  percent of all fires involve alcohol
83  percent of all deaths due to fire involve alcohol
62  percent of all burns involve alcohol
69  percent of all drownings involve alcohol
50  percent of all spinal cord injuries involve alcohol
70  percent of all deaths due to falls involve alcohol
63  percent of all injuries due to falls involve alcohol
30  percent of divorces involve the heavy use of alcohol
40  percent (or 18,000 deaths) due to industrial accidents involve alcohol
47  percent of all industrial accidents (or ten million accidents) involve alcohol
20  percent of all hospital admissions costing $65.5 million per day involve alcohol

These statistics show about 170 deaths per day, excluding those deaths related to disease associated with alcoholism. In all, about 100,000 people die each year because of alcohol. About 35,000 die directly from the effects of alcohol, while another 60,000 die of indirect causes such as accidents. Thus, alcohol misuse is the third leading cause of death in the United States.

Additionally, alcohol is the number-one killer of youth because of car accidents caused while people are under the influence of alcohol. Most police officers who are killed are assaulted during a family argument or spouse abuse incident in which one or both of the family members are intoxicated.

Does alcohol pay for this damage? In terms of human life, never.

In terms of dollars, a 1975 study indicated:

### Costs of Alcohol in Billions of Dollars

| | |
|---|---|
| Lost Production | 19.64 |
| Health and Medical Costs | 12.74 |
| Motor Vehicle Accidents | 5.15 |
| Violent Crime | 2.86 |
| Social Responses (Treatment) | 1.94 |
| Fire Losses | 0.43 |
| | 42.75 billion |
| Profit from alcohol tax revenue | 10.00 billion |
| | |
| Society's loss because of alcohol: | 32.75 billion |

(J. Kinney and G. Leaton, eds. 1983. *Loosening the Grip: A Handbook of Alcohol Education*. St. Louis: C.V. Mosby Company)

This 1975 study shows that alcohol abuse, in addition to the loss of human life, accounts for a net loss to society of $32.75 billion. In 1981, the Research Triangle Institute published a study on the economic costs of alcohol to society. Their report indicates that this figure was over $100 billion a year, surpassing the 1975 estimate mentioned previously.

A 1986 study places the dollar value of lost production alone at $30.8 billion. This same study indicates that as much as 40 percent of industrial accidents are alcohol-related and that problem drinkers have 3.8 times as many sick days as nonalcoholics. In the fall 1989 issue of *Hollins Place Quarterly*, the financial cost of alcoholism is estimated at $120 billion per year. This same report states that the alcoholic beverage industry spends $1 billion on advertising alcohol, while less than $1 billion is spent on education and treatment. The National Institute on Alcohol Abuse and Alcoholism reported in 1991 that the 1988 cost of alcohol abuse is estimated to be $86 billion. Statistics vary, but it is clear that alcohol abuse is a major cost to society.

According to 1988 statistics from Mothers Against Drunk Driving (MADD), alcohol abuse also is responsible for more than 28,400 highway deaths each year. This number equals half of our highway death toll. Drivers who drink tend to have:

- Twice as many car accidents involving other operators or property

- Twelve times the likelihood of having a fatal car accident

- Five times the number of accidents in which someone is injured
- Twice the number of traffic tickets
- Three times the number of license suspensions

Drinking and driving is one of the principal reasons that life expectancy of fifteen-to twenty-four-year-olds has not changed while for other age groups, life expectancy has increased.

## PHYSICAL EFFECTS

The lethal blood alcohol level is approximately .4 percent for those who have not developed tolerance and about .6 percent for those who have. Assuming that the legal definition of .1 percent is used as the effective dose level, this makes the effective dose to lethal dose level approximately one to four, about the same as for heroin. Based on coroners' reports, approximately 400 deaths due to poisoning by alcohol occur per year. However, this figure probably is greatly underreported. A recent example involves a teenage girl who consumed a fifth of vodka; she went into a coma and died. Chronic alcoholics tend to maintain a .2 percent blood-alcohol level. Judging from this, you could say that alcoholics prefer to remain one-third of the way toward death.

### Effects on the Digestive System

Alcohol is an irritant and a solvent for many organic chemicals. Most people don't realize that pure ethyl alcohol (200 proof) is a fuel additive that helps boost the octane of gasoline. Pure alcohol is used to run race cars and can be used instead of gasoline as a fuel. No wonder alcohol irritates the digestive system. It is a solvent and can irritate any tissue with which it comes into contact. The tissues of the esophagus (the tube to the stomach), stomach, and small intestine can be reddened or even opened so that bleeding occurs. This painful internal reddening and bleeding of the esophagus is called esophagitis; if it occurs it the stomach, this condition is known as gastritis. Since alcohol stimulates the production of hydrochloric acid (a digestive juice) in the stomach, ulcers can occur. Ulcers are holes that appear when the stomach digests itself.

The pain from these ulcers can be masked by the alcohol, which has some anesthetic properties (Remember the old cowboy movies where they used a stiff drink to deaden pain?) Fairly large veins and arteries are located around the stomach area to help absorb nutrients from food into the bloodstream. When pain from these ulcers is not experienced and drinking continues, the alcohol and the hydrochloric acid burn deeper holes, often cutting open veins or arteries. The effect is similar to being stabbed in the stomach. The patient eventually dies, often suddenly, from internal bleeding.

Another digestive tract disease that occurs more frequently in drinkers is cancer of the digestive tract. These cancers, which are grayish-white in appearance, often go undetected. One type of cancer causes a blockage in the esophagus; the symptoms are painful swallowing and heartburn. At this late stage, the cancer might not be

## Approximate Blood Alcohol Percentage

| Number of drinks | Body Weight in Pounds | | | | | | | |
|---|---|---|---|---|---|---|---|---|
| | **100** | **120** | **140** | **160** | **180** | **200** | **220** | **240** |
| 1 | .04 | .03 | .03 | .02 | .02 | .02 | .02 | .02 |
| 2 | .08 | .06 | .05 | .05 | .04 | .04 | .03 | .03 |
| 3 | .11 | .09 | .08 | .07 | .06 | .06 | .05 | .05 |
| 4 | .15 | .12 | .11 | .09 | .08 | .08 | .07 | .06 |
| 5 | .19 | .16 | .13 | .12 | .11 | .09 | .09 | .08 |
| 6 | .23 | .19 | .16 | .14 | .13 | .11 | .10 | .09 |
| 7 | .26 | .22 | .19 | .16 | .15 | .13 | .12 | .11 |
| 8 | .30 | .25 | .21 | .19 | .17 | .15 | .14 | .13 |
| 9 | .34 | .28 | .24 | .21 | .19 | .17 | .15 | .14 |
| 10 | .38 | .31 | .27 | .23 | .21 | .19 | .17 | .16 |

Subtract .01 percent for each 40 minutes. For example, a 200-pound man has 7 drinks in two hours. His blood alcohol level is .13 percent minus .03 percent (three 40-minute periods), which equals .10 percent. This is legally intoxicated.

If much of your weight is fat, it will take less to get you intoxicated, as alcohol does not dissolve in fat as well as water. Because women tend to have a higher percentage of body fat than men, the above values may underestimate a woman's blood alcohol content.

In most states, a blood alcohol content of .10 percent is legally intoxicated and can result in drunk driving charges. In some states, this has been lowered to .08 percent. Easily measurable impairment begins at the .05 percent level. Most people die when their blood alcohol content reaches .40 percent, but alcoholics can tolerate as high as .60 percent (until their liver quits).

Know your legal limit of alcohol before driving. Avoid jail or an accident. If in doubt, be more conservative.

Exercise:     How many drinks will make *you* legally intoxicated?
How many will impair you at the .05 percent level?

operable and hence fatal. Cancer of the mouth and stomach also are more common in alcohol abusers. These cancers can be just as serious if not detected early enough.

Other digestive organs also are vulnerable. Acute pancreatitis, an often fatal disease, occurs when the pancreas, an organ that secretes digestive juices into the stomach, becomes inflamed due to alcohol consumption. This is a very painful condition and has a 40 percent mortality rate. Alcoholic hepatitis—in which the liver becomes inflamed—also can be fatal.

More frequently, alcoholic hepatitis precedes alcoholic cirrhosis, a condition in which liver cells die and are replaced by scar tissue. Cirrhosis is not reversible. A fatty liver—caused by excessive amounts of stored fat in the liver cells—often precedes cirrhosis. Cirrhosis usually is fatal even if drinking stops. A person can suspect cirrhosis if he or she finds that it takes fewer drinks to become drunk or to feel ill. Eventually, the brain is poisoned by waste in the blood that the liver cannot remove. Cancer of the liver also eventually can develop because of cirrhosis. Cirrhosis can develop in someone who consumes as few as three drinks per day over a long period of time.

Each drink of an alcoholic beverage contains roughly 150 empty calories. These calories add weight to the body, which causes additional risk factors. A "beer belly" can be caused by the extra fat or by a swollen liver.

### Effects on the Cardiovascular System

Diseases of the heart and circulatory system are less common but potentially as serious as the digestive diseases. Alcohol cardiomyopathy—in which the heart enlarges and weakens—can result from long-term alcohol ingestion. Beri-beri heart disease and cardiac arrhythmias caused by alcohol can result in heart failure and death. Elevation in blood-fat levels and blood pressure also are associated with heavy drinking.

Alcoholics are less immune to disease because of alcohol's toxic effects on the body's white or disease-fighting cells. Alcohol abusers bruise easily and heal at a slower rate because of alcohol's effect in reducing the blood platelet level.

### Effects on the Reproductive System

Like many drugs, alcohol is viewed by some as a sexual stimulant. This is true only if it serves to relax or disinhibit the user, since anxiety is a principal cause of sexual dysfunction. Like most drugs, however, the sex drive eventually diminishes as alcohol causes an imbalance in sex hormones.

Alcohol affects the levels of sex hormones present in men and women. Men can become more effeminate as the male sex hormone testosterone drops. Testicles might shrink, hair might thin, and sex drive diminishes. In women, the menstrual cycle is disturbed, often resulting in skipped periods and infertility.

### Fetal Alcohol Syndrome

Even unborn babies are affected as evidenced from malformations that are present at birth. As little as two drinks a day can result in Fetal Alcohol Syndrome (FAS). This syndrome is one of the leading causes of mental retardation and actually results in a deformed appearance in infants. FAS infants usually have small heads, narrow eye slits, underdeveloped facial features, low-set ears, and in some cases, hair on the face at birth. The hands sometimes have unusual creases in the palms, fingers might be joined together, or the fingers might bend unusually. Heart valve defects can occur. Damage to the infant's brain also can occur, resulting in an average IQ of 64 in the FAS baby as compared to an IQ of 100 in normal infants.

The risk of having an FAS child increases as the level of alcohol consumption increases. There is about a 10 percent risk (one out of ten) of having an FAS baby when the mother has two or more drinks a day during pregnancy. This increases to a 50 percent chance (five out of ten) of having an FAS baby at ten drinks a day. More recent evidence points to tragic emotional and behavioral problems in adults with FAS: Many adopted children with stable family relationships become disruptive in the home and at school. Impulse-control problems and antisocial activity tentatively have been linked to FAS. Studies suggest that many FAS adults end up in prison and in institutions as a result of emotional and behavioral problems due to subtle brain damage. More research is needed, however, to provide a definitive link.

### Physical Dependence

Alcohol is physically addictive just as are other sedative/hypnotic drugs (Valium, Librium, and the barbiturates) and the opiates (heroin, morphine, Dilaudid, and Demerol). Physical addiction means a person experiences actual physical discomfort, and symptoms appear after the substance is withdrawn following repeated use. Addiction can occur in as short a period as two weeks. Tolerance, or the ability to withstand higher doses without effect, develops to alcohol and the sedative/hypnotics.

The medical community generally agrees that withdrawing from alcohol is far more dangerous than withdrawing from heroin. Alcohol withdrawal can lead to death, but it is rare for a heroin addict to die during withdrawal. Consequently, minor tranquilizers are used to help withdrawing alcoholics avoid life-threatening convulsions. Drugs like Librium, Valium, and Xanax are administered to cushion the body's transition to restore the natural balance that alcohol has disrupted. The journey back to sanity can be a difficult one. In some cases, nausea, convulsions, seizures, hallucinations, and death can occur.

Brain damage, called Wernicke-Korsakoff's Syndrome, can result from poor nutrition associated with alcoholism. In some cases, this leaves the victim needing long-term institutional care.

This brain damage is characterized by the inability to maintain new memories. Long-term alcoholics afflicted with this disease often have memories dating back to their teen years but are not able to learn the name of a new acquaintance.

## PSYCHOLOGICAL EFFECTS

Alcohol is a central nervous system (CNS) depressant, as are the sedatives, barbiturates, and hypnotics (sleeping pills). These drugs act to relax the body and mind by slowing the workings of all nerve cells. Senses are dulled, coordination is impaired, and reaction time is longer. Also, the normal rational controls and restraints are impaired—in some cases almost completely. This is called "disinhibition."

A mildly intoxicated person might seem more lively and active because these normal restraints or controls have been dulled, and his or her impulses are disinhibited. It previously was mentioned that alcohol is involved in more than half of all murders committed. The reasons for this higher level of aggression relate to alcohol's disinhibiting effect. Alcohol suppresses or weakens our controls over emotions that normally are suppressed. These "primitive" feelings arise unchecked once a certain level of alcohol is ingested.

### The Old and New Brain

The brain can be divided into two distinct sections. One section, located in the center of the brain, can be called the "old brain." The old brain is the center of our feelings and drives. The centers responsible for maintaining automatic functions of the body like respiration, heartbeat, and digestion also are housed in that area. Some of the areas of the old brain store emotions such as hunger, thirst, sex, and anger. The old brain also is described as the "limbic system, the libido, or the reflex center." Emotions seem to be triggered by stimuli outside and inside the body. The smell of our favorite foods, an attractive sexual partner, or a threat to our safety normally might cause primitive emotions to be aroused. As we move further from the center to the surface and near-surface areas of the brain (the cortex), we find a higher level of rational functioning.

Humans are more sophisticated because of the "new brain." The new brain houses the areas of thought, control, compassion, morality, and judgment that normally help us restrain and control our emotions. Emotional maturity is our ability to delay gratifying these inner-level feelings. Therefore, we normally don't act before we think. For example, we normally don't assault someone who annoys us, even though we emotionally might feel like doing so. Our new brain basically tells us that these behaviors would not be appropriate or acceptable.

Alcohol is a sedative and a mild anesthetic. It numbs up or reduces the effectiveness of all brain cells—and thus, psychological function. All of the brain is affected, although each individual level seems to be affected in sequence. The first level to be disrupted seriously by alcohol intoxification is the complex new brain. Our sense of judgment, morality, control, restraint, and compassion is impaired to some degree depending on individual differences. Balance and coordination also are affected.

Once the new brain is impaired, the centers of the old brain take over. Our emotions and more primitive feelings might begin to control our personalities. An intoxicated person might start crying, laughing, or display other emotions for little or no apparent reason. He or she might act childishly, take risks, and behave rashly. Thousands of youths have been killed while speeding in a vehicle after their senses of judgment have been impaired by alcohol. Spouse abuse, murder, and numerous other acts of violence occur during this period of reduced inhibitions.

Since it normally takes the liver an hour to detoxify the alcohol in one drink, the old brain takes control for long periods of time. Like a child playing with a loaded gun, the old brain only has to make one error to result in serious consequences like jail or death. When someone becomes further intoxicated, only the automatic centers of the old brain (the brain stem) remain functioning to keep the person alive. When these deepest brain centers are too sedated to function, death occurs because of the inability to breath. Sometimes people suffocate on their own vomit.

The concept of the new brain controlling the old brain visually can be demonstrated by covering the palm of one hand with the fist of the other hand. The fist represents strong emotions, and the palm represents the controlling influence of rationality. The palm can be removed to demonstrate releasing inhibitions by alcohol consumption.

### The Process of Psychological Addiction

Long before physical addiction occurs, chances are good that the drinker has developed a psychological addiction. The psychological addiction to alcohol or drugs is more difficult than the physical addiction to break. Physical addiction can be broken by hospitalizing the user. Psychological addiction ultimately only can be broken by the users themselves. With alcohol, the psychological addiction normally happens slowly. It starts with experimentation and leads to social and recreational drinking, then regular and compulsive use. Finally, the grip of combined psychological and physical addiction takes its lethal hold. Because the process is so gradual, often the drinker fails to realize it is happening.

A system of mental defenses develops to protect the drinker's self-image. Rationalizations about drinking ("Everyone does it, and besides, it's legal"), denial ("I can stop any time I choose to"), projection ("It's your fault that I drink so much"), and generally one large "lie" all are created to justify the drinking. Soon, a secret irritation develops when drinking is discussed or when there is no alcohol around. Later, alcohol might be hidden, and drinking becomes more of a private activity in the isolation of one's own home.

Stress seems to trigger thirst. Sometimes before drinkers realize what has happened, they find themselves drunk—perhaps because they felt upset, angry, depressed, or even plagued with "normal" problems. Irritability and negative feelings such as guilt only escalate when a person gets sober, so he or she then is tempted to drink more and more. Although everyone is different, one statement can be made: The drinker, along with the entire family, is affected by the addiction.

## THE FAMILY DISEASE CONCEPT OF ALCOHOLISM

The tragic aspects of addiction involve its contagious character. The entire family is disrupted when one member is addicted. Often, the family develops a "siege" or "crisis" mentality so that everyone lives under fear and tension. Less order exists within this type of family, less time is taken for family leisure activities, and the spouse often takes on the role of co-alcoholic. The co-alcoholic lives in fear of the alcoholic's behavior. Generally, the spouse feeds into manipulations by the drinker—manipulations that place part of the blame on the spouse. It's not unusual for the alcoholic to say, "If it weren't for your nagging, I wouldn't drink so much." This mastery at blaming others is a symptom of the addiction.

### Effects on Spouses

The spouses of alcoholics often are called "co-addicts," because he or she also suffers from the emotional turmoil of alcoholism. The spouse might become an "enabler," helping the addict to avoid the consequences of irrational and abusive behavior. The spouse might suffer from physical and emotional abuse caused by the alcoholic. The spouse might become socially isolated, feeling shamed by the alcoholic's behavior. The spouse even constantly might feel guilty if he or she believes that he or she is the cause of the alcoholic's drinking. These thoughts and behaviors are irrational, of course, which is the reason that this person is sometimes called a co-alcoholic or co-addict.

### Effects on Children

Children also are affected by the drinker's behavior. While every family and child is different, in many families a pattern develops in response to the problem drinker's behavior. These patterns are not common to all families, and roles might vary, but they are typical in families in which alcohol or other drugs are the major focus of life.

Often the firstborn child takes on the leadership role. It is believed that these eldest fill the parenting void left by the addicted parent. What happens, however, is that these children prematurely are thrust into adulthood and must sacrifice their own childhood, an event they probably grow up to resent. These children sometimes grow up wanting to be alcohol abuse counselors, possibly to "save" their fallen parent.

Second-oldest children sometimes rebel against the family's disorganization. These children get attention through their rebellious acts. Sometimes these second-born children are in constant conflict with authority as their lack of respect for their own parents has transferred to their regard for the rules of society.

Third-born children often more openly display their fear of the alcoholic parent. Sometimes these children develop an active fantasy life to escape their fear. This withdrawal from reality can pose problems during childhood. In adulthood, these children sometimes marry problem drinkers; ironically, they might feel more comfortable with this type of person because they know what to expect.

Although the role addiction plays with family members is real, the patterns can vary. Some children seem to have been immune to the whole experience—they have gone on to marry and live normal lives. A much higher percentage, however, seems to be affected—they go on to live the same types of lives as their parents, falling prey to the same chemical that ruined their own childhood.

The trauma to children born to an alcoholic family is all too real. Reports of violence, child abuse, and verbal abuse are more common in the addicted family. Due to repeated experience, violence might come to be seen as an acceptable way to interact with others, and emotional instability becomes the normal way to live. Therefore, family cohesion is weak, and these values can be passed from generation to generation.

### Legal Responses

Public concern has risen due to the alarming statistics associated with alcohol abuse. We have entered a newer "prohibitionist" type of era, in which traffic laws for drunk driving have become very strict, incarceration is ordered for repeat offenders, and minimum legal drinking ages have been increased.

Alcohol does not excuse family or community violence, and offenders are sentenced just as with other violators. Many crimes continue to be committed under the influence of alcohol. Discussion has occurred regarding what type of role alcohol plays in crime. Some people who are criminally oriented use alcohol to bolster their courage for a crime they have planned; they then are able to commit more crime with less fear. Others, with their "new brain" anesthetized, commit impulsive acts that ordinarily would be inhibited.

Current legal trends indicate that crimes committed under the influence of alcohol will continue to be prosecuted. The fact that a person was intoxicated while committing is not a legal excuse because the person willingly consumed the alcohol. In fact, a person who becomes "mean and nasty" when drunk is seen as a greater threat to the safety of other people, so some citizens will advocate confining him or her longer to prevent further crimes. Similarly, traffic offenses and accidents resulting in injury or loss of life probably will result in stiffer penalties and possible prison sentences. The law reflects the public's determination to stop drunk driving and the needless loss of life.

## SUMMARY

Alcohol is responsible for the loss of thousands of lives and billions of dollars yearly. This central nervous system depressant acts to loosen normal levels of control, bringing forth impulsive and emotional acts that sometimes result in prison sentences. Deaths related to alcohol overdose and fatal accidents and other deaths directly related to alcohol use far outnumber those deaths resulting from the use of all illegal drugs combined.

Alcohol can cause a serious type of physical addiction that eventually damages every organ in the body except the ear. Psychological addiction usually precedes physical addiction and is accompanied by numerous excuses and lies about excessive drinking.

People who surround the alcoholic also are affected. The spouse and children especially might display guilt and anger similar to the guilt and anger displayed by the drinker. As with disorders like diabetes and heart disease, a familial link exists between alcoholics and their parents. Alcoholism is progressive. Unless treated, it will result in death.

Legal responses to drinking recently have become more aggressive. Stiffer penalties are exacted to those convicted of traffic offenses while intoxicated. A new prohibition does not seem politically possible, so the problem of alcohol abuse must be solved at an individual and small-group level. People must be taught to recognize the difference between responsible use and damaging abuse.

## OTHER SEDATIVES/HYPNOTICS

Although alcohol is by far the most abused sedative/hypnotic, other drugs that widely are abused can be grouped in this category as well. This sedative/hypnotic group of drugs also includes the minor tranquilizers, barbiturates, and general depressants. Drugs in the sedative/hypnotic group are known for their anxiety-relieving qualities. They work to temporarily reduce tension and nervousness and have been prescribed widely through the years for phobias and anxiety disorders.

### Barbiturates

Barbiturates are sedative/hypnotic drugs that are derived from barbituric acid. These drugs further can be classified by their duration of activity. Some work for only a short time period and others have longer lasting duration. In some drug combinations, the short- and long-acting varieties yield a drug that sedates in the short and long term. The barbiturates typically end with the letters "al." These drugs have names like Amytal, amobarbital, phenobarbital, and Seconal. The primary medical use of these drugs is as antiseizure medication, since they seem to sedate and relax centers of the brain that control seizure activity. Low doses of some of these barbiturates seem to help control seizures; the potential for addiction is low, since the doses are small.

Barbiturates were much more widely used as sleeping pills and sedatives during the 1950s until their reputation was marred by the large number of suicides and accidental overdoses by people under the influence of these drugs. For example, Marilyn Monroe died of barbiturate overdose; alcohol also served as a factor. Barbiturates, like other sedative/hypnotics, are synergistic (have a multiplier effect) with alcohol. Many people who suffer from anxiety and insomnia use alcohol. Because tolerance develops both to alcohol and to sedative/hypnotic drugs, people usually take more and more of these drugs to reach the desired effect. Unfortunately, the lethal dose, or the amount it would take to kill you, does not shift upward as much as the effective dose. What happens with barbiturates is that at some point, the amount needed to relieve the anxiety or insomnia is dangerously close to the lethal dose. When alcohol is added to the picture, the lethal dose is crossed since alcohol serves to multiply the strength of other sedatives. Consequently, the drug user dies of respiratory arrest.

### Benzodiazepines (Minor Tranquilizers)

These drugs basically were viewed medically as safer replacements for the barbiturates and at one point were believed to be nonaddictive. They are safer, because if taken alone, it is difficult to overdose to the point of respiratory arrest. Valium, Librium, Ativan, Dalmane, and Xanax are among the frequently used minor tranquilizers. Many alcohol detoxification centers use tranquilizers to aid alcohol withdrawal. Cross-dependence exists among all sedatives, so these drugs can be used to satisfy craving for other drugs or to cushion the effects of withdrawal. Minor tranquilizers should not be confused with the major tranquilizers, which are antipsychotic drugs like Thorazine, Haldol, and Stelazine.

In general, the benzodiazepines have a wide margin of effective dose to lethal dose. However, if alcohol also is ingested, lethal doses are much more likely to occur. Minor tranquilizers are addictive physically and are supposed to be prescribed only for short periods of time—perhaps to help a person recover from a traumatic experience. If a person uses Valium or other benzodiazepine for more than a three-month period, the brain changes and the person becomes dependent on the tranquilizer. Unfortunately, some physicians have kept their patients taking tranquilizers for long periods of time. In these cases, a lengthy withdrawal characterized by anxiety, irritability, and cravings occurs.

### Other Prescription Sedatives

Methaqualone (Quaalude) is a strong and highly addictive sedative. Its action can come on suddenly; consequently, this particular drug has been blamed for numerous traffic accidents and fatalities. Users also have been known to combine alcohol with this drug, which increases the likelihood of a lethal dose or severe intoxication. Because of these problems, this drug was pronounced illegal in the early 1980s and now legally cannot be prescribed.

Meprobamate, glutethimide, and chloral hydrate are other general sedatives. They are prescription items. Meprobamate contains muscle-relaxant properties and is less dangerous than glutethimide, which has properties similar to many of the barbiturates. Used as a sedative for tension and anxiety, glutethimide (Doriden) is a long-lasting drug whose potency may be a disadvantage because of the potential for overdose and abuse. Chloral hydrate was the first such hypnotic and sedative, predating the barbiturates but used for insomnia. It almost is identical to ethyl alcohol. Chloral hydrate has not been a widely abused drug in recent times.

### Inhalants

Volatile solvents such as airplane glue (toluene), butane, amyl and butyl nitrate, ethyl ether, paint thinner, and gasoline also are classified as sedatives and produce much the same effects as alcohol. However, they are more dangerous than alcohol because our livers cannot detoxify these chemicals as quickly and in some cases cannot detoxify them at all. Brain damage has occurred as the solvents dissolve cell membranes; they make the user feel intoxicated as well. Death can occur even quicker if a person places a bag over his or her head when breathing these fumes, because he or she can pass out and therefore will be unable to breathe fresh air. When compared to other drugs, a greater risk of immediate death exists with solvent inhalants.

Nitrous oxide is an anesthetic gas that sometimes is used to reduce the sense of pain experienced during minor operations such as dental fillings. When used medically, nitrous oxide is mixed with oxygen. It produces a "buzz" and reduces conscious awareness. Nitrous oxide is not poisonous. However, because the gas does not include oxygen, breathing it in its pure form can be dangerous if the loss of control automatically will lead to not breathing fresh air. Since it does not produce pleasure, nitrous oxide is not a major drug of abuse, but still some people do play with it. The more informed users breathe it from balloons, but the ill-informed can hurt themselves by breathing the gas directly from a high-pressure tank, which can freeze lungs.

### Drug Interactions

Sometimes drug abusers use sedatives to relax after they've used amphetamines or other stimulants. The sedation helps to slow down a system that has been keyed up by the stimulants. This can lead to physical and psychological addictions to sedatives as well as to the stimulant drug. Another danger is that heroin or other narcotic addicts sometimes use barbiturates or alcohol to reduce discomfort when the narcotic is not available. When the narcotic is used again, the combination of a sedative and a narcotic can be lethal.

### Psychological and Physical Dependence

Like alcohol, abusing any sedative can result in psychological as well as physical dependence. Psychological dependence involves intensely craving and actively seeking the drug, while the physically addictive properties actually result in physical symptoms. As with alcohol withdrawal, stomach cramps, convulsions, and seizure-like reactions can occur. Withdrawal from the sedative/hypnotic group can be dangerous, as with alcohol, and close monitoring might be necessary.

### Abuse Potential

Quaaludes, thought by many street users to be a sexual stimulant, at one time were frequently abused. Because of the widespread abuse of this drug, it was made in 1983 a Schedule 1 drug, which means that now its only legal use is in research. Therefore, not even a licenced physician can prescribe this drug now. Underground laboratories continue to manufacture quaaludes, however, so an illegal supply still is available.

Most sedative drugs legally can be prescribed. Abuse results when these drugs are misused and doses higher than those prescribed are taken. For the many people diagnosed with legitimate nervous disorders, these drugs have been a blessing.

Other people have become addicted physically to these drugs as their tolerance slowly builds. Because some patients potentially can abuse these drugs, records are kept, and physicians are responsible for monitoring the dosage levels of their patients. However, it is not unusual to find entire medicine cabinets filled with these types of drugs because they are effective—at least in the short term—against anxiety disorders and insomnia. In the long term and at higher doses, these medications actually create more problems for the user since use becomes a necessity to avoid nervousness. Tension increases as sleep becomes increasingly more difficult to achieve. Sedatives actually block dream sleep, which is the most essential and relaxing stage of rest. Using drugs beyond their prescribed limits is a dangerous practice.

Sedatives are powerful drugs that can lead to physical addiction. When properly used at prescribed levels, they are effective in treating seizure disorders, anxiety, and insomnia. Long-term use of higher dosages of sedatives not only causes psychological addiction but also physical addiction. In several instances, users actually have died because of the multiplier effect of other sedatives on alcohol. Although the amount needed to get high increases, the lethal dosage level does not increase appreciably. A user might need almost as much of a sedative drug to get high, eventually, as it takes to kill him or her.

## REFERENCES

AA World Services. 1976. *Alcoholics Anonymous.* 3d ed. New York: AA World Services.

Alcohol Safety Action Program. 1986. *Virginia's favorite drug is her most popular killer.*

Jellinek, E. M. 1960. *The disease concept of alcoholism.* New Haven, Conn.: Hillhouse Press.

Johnson, V. 1980. *I'll quit tomorrow.* New York: Harper & Row.

Kinney, J., and G. Leaton, eds. 1983. *Loosening the grip: A handbook of alcohol information.* 2d ed. St. Louis: C. V. Mosby.

# VI.
# NARCOTIC ANALGESICS: THE OPIATES

Analgesics are drugs that alleviate pain. Aspirin, Tylenol, ibuprofen, and other nonnarcotic analgesics relieve pain, but do not share the emotionally sedating qualities of narcotics. The nonnarcotic analgesics normally are not drugs of abuse; however, they sometimes are used for suicide attempts or by people who don't understand that the drugs can be dangerous at larger doses. However, narcotics can be both physically and psychologically addicting.

Opium is the raw sap extract of the Papaver Somniferum seed pod. This flower, more commonly known as the poppy, produces several naturally occurring opiates. The psychoactive opiates found in opium are morphine, codeine, and thebaine. Morphine composes most of the opium sap extract and is the most powerful, while codeine is found in smaller proportions. Only traces of thebaine can be found in opium.

The semisynthetic derivatives of opium are heroin, hydromorphone (Dilaudid), and oxycodone (Percodan, Tylox). These drugs start with a base of morphine, codeine, or thebaine and are changed through a chemical procedure. For example, heroin is morphine treated with acetic acid.

The synthetic narcotics are made exclusively using laboratory procedures. Two such drugs are Meperidine (Demerol) and Dolophine (Methadone). "Designer drugs" include Fentanyl, a relatively new synthetic that is short-acting and is effective at even less a dose than heroin.

## HISTORY

Opium is one of the oldest drugs known to humanity. Its properties as a medicine probably were known to the ancient Sumerians in the Near East where opium is alleged to have been first cultivated. Opiates have proved effective in reducing pain without impairing other senses, in eliminating stomach cramps, as a cough suppressant, and in the treatment of diarrhea.

Around 1200 A.D., Arab traders took opium into the Far East. Alcohol was illegal in China, but opium was not. In 1729, Emperor Yung Cheng decreed smoking opium illegal, and China was the first nation of the world to pass laws regarding this drug. Those who were discovered selling the drug in opium shops were sentenced to death by strangulation.

In the 1700s and 1800s, China was dominated by the British Empire. The British grew opium in India and smuggled it into China, where it was illegal. Many Chinese were victims of addiction, but dishonest customs officials were bribed so imports continued. The smuggling trade increased greatly from around 1720 until 1838, when the Chinese government arrested many British merchants and burned some

2.4 million pounds of opium. This started the first of two wars between Britain and China, which the British won due to superior naval power. The opium trade increased until around 1880, when as many as half of all Chinese men were opium addicts. Moral outrage in Britain at the turn of the century finally curbed this smuggling. An international agreement, called the Hague Convention of 1912, was designed to solve the opium importation problems in China and the Far East.

In 1762, an over-the-counter opium preparation called Dover's Powder was used widely in England. Laudanum, an alcohol and opium syrup, legally was available in America as a sedative and pain reliever during the late 1800s. Historians have remarked that while the men were getting drunk in the saloons, the women of that period were becoming opium addicts at home. Even some of the members of the prohibitionist movement apparently used these opiates, which were ingredients of many patent medicines. However, their concern was the violence associated with drunkenness. Some men and women habitually ate opium balls in America and were addicted, but this practice was considered a personal disgrace rather than a danger to society.

As America grew, so did the country's railroad system. Many of the workers on U.S. railroad lines were Chinese men who smoked opium. Opium use increased during this period and spread across all the country's ethnic groups. Opium had been used widely for medicinal purposes in America for many years, but smoking opium for recreation became popular near the end of the century—a practice many citizens considered immoral. The use of opium, morphine, heroin, or any other drugs was not controlled until this century. However, the estimated number of opium addicts still was less than 1 percent of the total population. Narcotics users were pitied rather than treated as criminals.

### Early Laws

Two laws passed during in the early 1900s attempted to control opium and cocaine use. The Pure Food and Drug Act of 1906 required all medicines containing opiates or cocaine to be labeled as such. The government wanted people to know what they were buying. Opiates and cocaine still could be purchased legally in most parts of the country, both from physicians and over the counter. In 1914, the federal government took a stronger stand against these drugs and indicated that opiates and cocaine could be used only in the course of professional practice. This law, called the Harrison Act, originally was designed to control narcotics by making them available only through physician prescription.

In 1920, the Supreme Court decided that the realm of professional practice did not include allowing physicians to offer opiates to addicts so the addicts could maintain their habits. Several thousand doctors were imprisoned because they refused to stop prescribing narcotics to addicts. Many doctors began to legally prescribe stimulants as substitutes—possibly as a way to circumvent the law and to continue treating addicts. This law was revoked in 1925, but by then most physicians were unwilling to risk their reputations to maintain addicts.

Interestingly enough, opium was considered a cure for alcoholism, morphine allegedly was a cure for opium addiction, and heroin was a possible treatment for morphine addiction. Now methadone, a synthetic opiate, is considered a treatment for heroin addiction. Heroin actually received its name because of the belief that the drug was a "heroine" over addiction. Little was known at that time about the disease process of addiction—many people thought addiction only could occur in the stomach.

### Growth of the Illicit Market

Opiate smuggling and distribution became a factor in American life after narcotics largely were prohibited. However, organized crime emerged as a force in America during—and possibly even as a result of—alcohol prohibition, which lasted from 1919 to 1933. The end of prohibition signaled the end of a very lucrative source of illegal income from the coffers of these crime families. However, the sale of narcotics remained profitable. The new crime money was found in the illegal importation and sale of heroin. This continues today, as nearly one-half million heroin addicts live in this country. If cocaine becomes more expensive, heroin could become more popular. History indicates that as cocaine becomes inaccessible, heroin becomes a substitute drug.

### Current Medical Use

The opiates long have been used to alleviate pain. They also have several side effects; the most distinctive side effect is the slowing of the digestive system. Although narcotics contain some sedating qualities, the main effect is to reduce the sense of pain while allowing the user to remain conscious.

Opiates and other narcotics widely are prescribed. Physicians are careful to supply only the amount necessary to control pain, because overuse can lead to addiction. An often misunderstood fact is that the effect of one narcotic is basically the same as the effects of the rest. The differences lie in the length of action, the amount needed to obtain a desired effect, and the drug's ability to enter the brain. Heroin is not much different from morphine or other narcotics—it simply gets to the brain more easily.

In America, heroin is classified as a Schedule 1 narcotic, which means that the drug only can be used legally for research in this country. In countries such as England, physicians still are allowed to prescribe heroin and indicate that it is a more effective drug than morphine for treating pain and as a maintenance drug for addicts. It also is prescribed for minor pains, including sore throats, because a smaller dose of heroin in needed to obtain the desired effects in the brain and has a less constipating effect on the digestive system. Although heroin is a stronger drug than morphine, no special quality makes these drugs significantly different. Generally, all opiates and other narcotic analgesics act similarly, although potency and length of action varies. The information contained in this chapter concerning heroin generally can be considered applicable to all other narcotics; all are addictive physically and all easily can be addictive psychologically as well.

### Future trends

"Designer"/synthetic drugs that can be more easily obtained through the manufacturing process might eventually replace all of the natural/semisynthetic opiates found on the illicit market. Methadone was developed in Germany to synthetically replace morphine during World War II and was named in honor of Adolph Hitler (Dolophine). Demerol and Dilaudid were developed later. A "designer" drug called Fentanyl is many times more powerful than heroin and is manufactured illegally as well as legally. Fentanyl is a short-acting narcotic, quite useful in surgery. However, it is also being sold on the street in some areas. The effective dose is smaller than a grain of salt. Unfortunately, many people will die because of the high level of potency of these drugs, and many will be left disabled by disorders like those mimicking Parkinson's Disease caused by improper manufacturing procedures by "street cooks."

## PHYSICAL EFFECTS

Narcotics commonly are injected intravenously (called "shooting up") or subcutaneously (called "skin popping"). Medically, many are taken orally, but because the effect is slower, people using narcotics to get high tend to inject. Inhalation is possible but less popular. In Vietnam, the drugs reportedly were so pure, one could absorb enough to get high simply by rubbing the substance on the skin.

All the narcotics have similar effects. However, they differ widely in the duration of the effect and the amount needed to stimulate the effect. Heroin (diacetylmorphine) passes into the brain ten times more easily than morphine, which explains its increased potency. The liver must metabolize heroin into monoacetylmorphine and then into morphine. It then is excreted primarily in the urine.

### Potency

Street heroin traditionally is 2 to 5 percent pure. When this purity exceeds 5 percent, the following two related events usually occur: Several users, usually "chippers" or occasional users, die because of overdose, and numerous people who were not using begin to use. When a user overdoses on heroin, sometimes co-users are eager to find where the victim got these "good" drugs.

Recently, heroin of 50 to 75 percent purity has been reported, even at the street level. This could lead to many problems if users are not informed of the purity level.

### Effective Dose to Lethal Dose Ratio

A fairly small ratio–approximately one to three–exists between the dose of heroin or other narcotics required to stimulate the desired effect and a lethal dose. The actual amount varies from individual to individual as well as within an individual as his or her tolerance develops. This slim margin of safety, combined with the uncertainty of the "cut" percentage in street heroin (usually only 2 to 5 percent heroin), makes this very dangerous to use. The National Center for Health Statistics reports that death certificates placed the blame on opiates for the death of 595 people in 1987.

Most overdose deaths for confirmed addicts were not attributable to the heroin itself, but to the addition of alcohol or barbiturates to the heroin. One study found that half of the heroin users died within a five-year period of use—many of them "weekend chippers" who had not developed a tolerance. The most common cause of death was overdose; other causes cited were related incidents such as fighting during robberies. A Bureau of Prisons study for which nearly 250 heroin addicts were interviewed found that all but two had friends or acquaintances who had died of narcotic overdose. In recent years, the purity of street heroin has increased, leading to greater chance of accidental overdose.

If too much of a narcotic is absorbed too quickly—especially if alcohol or barbiturates are present—breathing stops and the lungs fill with fluid from the blood. The breathing sounds like that of an asthma sufferer; then it finally stops. When the oxygen supply is insufficient to nourish the heart muscle, the heartbeat then fades away. To provide first aid to an overdose victim, keep the person awake and moving, provide artificial respiration if breathing stops, and take him or her to a hospital emergency room as soon as possible so that a narcotic antagonist can be administered.

## Central Nervous System Effects

Narcotics primarily act on the central nervous system. The major medical action is "analgesia," the dulling or elimination of pain. With narcotics use, this occurs with relatively little effect on the other senses of touch, pressure, vision, and hearing. Drowsiness is common, and some alertness and mental acuity diminishes; the primary concern is that the brain's respiratory center is sedated. Therefore, it's dangerous to operate motor vehicles while under the influence. The opiates also suppress the brain stem's "cough center." The electrical brain waves change to a state similar to sleep. However, narcotics reduce the amount of dream sleep, which can result in a negative psychological effect.

Although central nervous system sedation is the primary effect of narcotics, users also might experience excitation of the "vomiting center." It is quite common for new users to feel nauseous and to vomit repeatedly.

## Effects on the Eyes

Pupils constrict with opiate use (an effect called "pinpoint pupils"), and users never develop a tolerance for this reaction.

## Cardiovascular Effects

Normal medicinal doses do not affect heart rate or blood pressure. Blood pressure might decrease at higher doses.

### Effects on the Gastrointestinal Tract

With opiate use, the digestive process suffers a general decrease in productivity, which can result in severe constipation. Water absorption is enhanced, although the level of digestive secretion is reduced. The feces dehydrate and harden; therefore, opiate use is effective in relieving diarrhea, but if used in excess, a dangerous blockage can be created. A number of complications can result from this lack of proper digestion; common ailments include aspiration pneumonitis, ulcers, cholecystitis, pancreatitis, biliary colic, and biliary rupture. Users do not develop a tolerance to the constipating effects of opiates.

### Effects on the Genital-urinary Tract

Several complications also can result from the loss of sensation and increased tone in areas of the urethra, bladder, and sphincter. Urinary retention, stones, bladder rupture, and uremia become more likely in the heroin user.

### Effects on the Lungs

The opiates can cause the bronchial musculature to constrict and air tubes in the lungs to close. At moderate to high doses, breathing can become more difficult. Pneumonia and carbon dioxide narcosis become increasingly likely.

### Complications from the Use of Needles

Numerous complications can result from unsanitary practices in using these drugs. Drug abusers constitute the second largest group of Acquired Immune Deficiency Syndrome (AIDS) victims. It is estimated that as many as one third of all long-term intravenous drug users are infected with the inactive AIDS virus; many more infections are suspected in areas in which users commonly share needles. Most AIDS victims in the prison system acquired the disease from intravenous drug abuse.

Hepatitis is the second largest threat. Viral hepatitis is a dangerous infection of the liver. Jaundice can develop as the infection advances, leaving the victim very weak. Pain in the liver area often is mistaken for withdrawal pain or is masked by the strong analgesic effect of the narcotic. If untreated, hepatitis can lead to cirrhosis, resulting in death.

Bacterial or fungal endocarditis also is prevalent. This infection of the lining around the heart or of the heart itself can be fatal and is difficult in advanced stages to treat. Those who are properly diagnosed sometimes are hospitalized for months. Again, pain is masked by the drug.

Sclerotic occlusions in the veins can develop. Veins actually deteriorate from repeated puncturing and the effects of chemicals and bacteria, leaving "track marks." Internal scabbing and infection destroy these veins. Therefore, the addict must become more creative—shooting deeper or perhaps shooting under the tongue or in the groin, for example—to find a useable vein and satisfy his or her craving.

Skin abscesses also can occur. Abscesses can result from a bacterial infection in the skin and are sped along by an immune system weakened from improper diet and health care practices. These abscesses actually leave pus-filled holes in the body.

### Antagonists

Barbiturates and alcohol sedate the respiratory centers, thus the risk of death greatly is increased. Narcan is a true antagonist of opiates and can eliminate the effects of narcotics within minutes after administration. If an overdose victim can be taken to a hospital in time, Narcan might save his or her life.

### Tolerance

The body develops tolerance to the drug's euphoric, respiratory depressant, analgesic, and sedative effects. Users do not develop tolerance to the constipating effects nor to the pupil-constricting effects.

### Factors Leading to Death

The most common cause of death by drug abuse is respiratory arrest, in which the breathing stops and fluid fills the lungs. Also, serious medical conditions such as endocarditis and hepatitis can be masked by the pain-killing effect of narcotics. Death also can result from the sometimes poisonous impurities or "cut" in the drug. A "hot shot" can result when a dealer cuts his or her drugs with substances such as cleaning powders rather than with the more common quinine, milk, or sugar powders.

### Withdrawal

Physical withdrawal, sometimes called "the jones," usually begins four to eight hours after the last dose. Physical withdrawal manifests in flu-like symptoms of weakness, intestinal pain and cramps, cold sweating, "goose bump" flesh (hence the term "cold turkey"), diarrhea, intense yawning, insomnia, and dilated pupils. The withdrawal period, even for a totally dependent heroin addict, usually lasts only five days. However, withdrawal takes longer for the longer-lasting narcotics. Methadone seems to be the worst; addicts report aching bones, sleep problems, and unease lasting months after methadone use has ended. People who have been on methadone maintenance for years report withdrawal lasting up to one year.

Although it can be severely uncomfortable, withdrawal from narcotics is not life-threatening except in rare cases in which the addict suffers from such a severe heart condition that any stress could prove dangerous.

## PSYCHOLOGICAL EFFECTS

Heroin produces a sleepy, dreamy, and pleasant state described as "the nod." The pleasure might feel like it comes from the stomach area and has been described as "orgasmic." This relaxed pleasure apparently lasts longer than the nervous pleasure derived from cocaine and might help the cocaine user to "come down" more easily. It is not unusual for cocaine abusers to mix the two drugs.

## Addictive Potential

For several reasons, heroin and the opiates represent a highly addictive class of drugs. Not only is physical pain eliminated with use, but psychological pain is eliminated as well. The drug provides a quick release from feelings of anxiety and tension. People who use opiates quickly learn to bury their feelings in the drug as the addiction gains a stronger grip.

## User Profile

It has been speculated that the more neurotic types of emotions are controlled by heroin. Hence, individuals prone to anxiety and a low self-image will be attracted to this drug. Illicit heroin is found more commonly in poorer sections of cities in which crime might be more prevalent. A subculture might evolve around the drug, or the user simply could be criminally oriented. Many heroin addicts report that they feel comfortable with the lifestyle—not just the drug—and they enjoy the "copping" routine. Many users feel hopeless about their future because of poverty or other problems and escape into narcotics for brief moments of happiness.

Professionals such as physicians who are addicted tend to use prescription drugs like Demerol, morphine, Fentanyl, and Dilaudid. These drugs can be obtained by circumventing the rules governing their control. For example, a nurse could pocket half a dose or a dose that has been refused by a patient. Drug users might obtain their drugs from professionals by complaining of pain from legitimate or illegitimate injuries. Veterans can get painkillers like Tylox, Percodan, and Talwin.

## Psychological Addiction

Psychological addiction is represented by the craving and irritability that sometimes persists following physical withdrawal. This craving stems from identifying the drug with its effects. Craving can be triggered by places, people, or times. It is difficult to resist psychological craving when drugs are visible and no constraints are in place. Almost everyone has experienced some type of craving. Craving can be illustrated by imagining a very hungry person who sees his or her favorite dish of food. Craving heroin is similar, although more extreme, to craving certain types of food. When food is around, for example, the craving is most difficult to resist. Thinking about food also will make the craving worse. When television advertisements or other stimuli serve as reminders of food, the thought of eating begins to exert control.

Generally speaking, it is the psychological addiction that is the most difficult to break. Physical addiction generally lasts only a few days. Psychological addiction can last a lifetime. It is not unusual for an inmate to serve a several-year prison sentence drug-free and return to using heroin almost immediately on release because of the "triggers" present in the community. Sometimes inmates set themselves up for failure by seeking old drug-abusing "buddies" or frequenting areas in which drugs are sold. Sometimes this behavior is intentional and consciously directed at returning to the drug subculture; other times, it is not so obvious to the user. Unfortunately, many people feel more comfortable in this subculture and repeat the cycle of addiction and detoxification several times. It eventually becomes a way of life.

### Progression of Addiction

Initially, the addict uses heroin to get high, to feel good, and to alleviate anxiety. As tolerance develops, the drug abuser no longer can feel the same level of high and must use larger doses. Because the habit is expensive, criminal behavior can escalate as tolerance climbs even higher. Eventually, the user takes heroin not to get high, but to stave off the inevitable effects of withdrawal. Addictive narcotic use becomes a matter of avoiding pain, not a matter of finding pleasure.

## REFERENCES

Gold, Mark S. 1984. *800-Cocaine*. New York: Bantam Books.

Goode, Erich. 1989. *Drugs in American society*. 3rd ed. New York: Knopf.

Judson, H. F. 1975. *Heroin addiction*. New York: Random House.

Julien, R.M. 1988. *A primer of drug action*. 5th ed. San Francisco: W.H. Freeman.

Link, W.P., L.P. Miller, and B. Fisher. 1978. *Drugs in perspective*. Washington, D.C.: NIDA.

National Institute on Drug Abuse. 1986. *Cocaine use in America*. Prevention Networks (ADM 86-1433).

# VII.
# AMPHETAMINES AND OTHER STIMULANTS

Stimulants, also known as "uppers," refer to several groups of drugs that tend to increase alertness and physical activity. Some people use stimulants to counteract the drowsiness or "down" feeling caused by sleeping pills or alcohol. This up and down cycle can be extremely dangerous to the body. Amphetamines, cocaine, Preludin, Ritalin, nicotine, and caffeine are all stimulants. For the sake of simplicity, stimulants can be divided into three strengths or levels of high, medium, and low potency. Of course, dose, mental state of the user, and individual differences make a difference in the potency of all drugs.

## LOW-POTENCY STIMULANTS

### Tobacco

Tobacco is such an addictive drug and is such a great health problem in the United States (with 390,000 deaths attributed each year to its use) that it will be covered in a separate chapter. At this point, it should be noted that tobacco is considered a low-potency stimulant as far as the central nervous system is concerned. Its effects on the heart and circulatory system are detrimental, and it is a leading cause of heart attacks, strokes, and arteriosclerosis (hardening of the arteries). It also damages the lungs and is the major cause of lung cancer and emphysema.

### Caffeine and Related Xanthines

Caffeine is a stimulant found in several plants, including coffee beans, tea leaves, cola beans, and (to a lesser extent) the cacao bean from which chocolate derives. It chemically is similar to theophylline, an asthma medicine, and to theobromine, the main stimulant in chocolate.

The history of coffee dates back many centuries. The earliest reference to coffee is found in an Arabian medical book written around 900 A.D. Coffee first was cultivated for its stimulant effect—to help people stay awake for religious services, for example. In 1600, owning or visiting a coffee house in the Moslem eastern Mediterranean was punishable by death. Conservative Moslems viewed coffee as intoxicating and therefore forbidden by the sacred book of Moslems, the Koran. This sentence also was enacted to disperse political malcontents who frequently held their meetings in coffee houses. This prohibition eventually was lifted. The use of coffee spread to other parts of Europe in the early 1600s. There were sporadic attempts to prohibit it—again, in part because coffee houses were seen as places where news and antigovernment agitation occurred.

Tea also contains caffeine, but in lower doses. Tea was mentioned in a Chinese manuscript dated around 350 A.D., but it did not become a worldwide drink until the early 1600s. Tea played a role in the American independence rebellion; an import tax on the product was one of the complaints against the British in the mid-1700s. Although much of America's tea was smuggled then into the colonies, coffee was considered a more patriotic drink. Today, more coffee than tea is drunk in America, while the reverse is true in England. Iced tea was introduced for the first time at the St. Louis World's Fair in 1904.

The main source of caffeine for soft drinks is the cola nut. Although the original Coca-Cola also contained cocaine, the ingredient was deleted in the early part of the century. Many soft drinks contain caffeine, often a dose equal to half a cup of coffee.

Chocolate's main source is the bean of the cocoa tree. The average cup of cocoa contains some caffeine (10 milligrams) and a larger amount (200 milligrams) of a related drug called theobromine. Theobromine is much less potent than caffeine to the central nervous system but produces more heart stimulation and smooth-muscle relaxation.

### Over-the-counter Drugs

Many of the drugs sold in stores contain large amounts of caffeine. The largest doses are found in Vivarin or No-Doz, which are sold as stimulants. However, many other medications such as headache pills, water-loss pills, and cold remedies contain large amounts of caffeine. Consumers should read the ingredients of any medications they buy.

### Doses in Various Products

An average cup of tea contains 40 to 70 milligrams of caffeine. An average cup of coffee contains 65 to 115 milligrams. A chocolate bar contains about 20 milligrams and a cup of cocoa about 4 milligrams. The caffeine level in American caffeine-containing soft drinks ranges between 36 and 59 milligrams. An over-the-counter stimulant, Vivarin, contains 200 milligrams. The danger of using caffeine in pill form is that people accidentally can overdose.

### Physical Effects of Caffeine

The effects of a dose of caffeine begin within half an hour and peak in about two hours. Half of the caffeine is metabolized by the body in three hours. Tolerance can be developed—steady users need two to four times their initial dose for equivalent effects. The lethal dose is about 10 grams.

Caffeine blocks the brain's receptors to adenosine, a chemical that inhibits arousal by preventing the brain from releasing stimulant chemicals. Thus, when caffeine is taken, more of the brain's stimulant chemical (adrenaline) is sent to other brain cells. Caffeine causes increased brain wave arousal, and more adrenaline is released in the body. Sleep is disturbed, and at higher doses breathing rate and perspiration increases. The rate at which the body burns food increases slightly, and fatigue is reduced.

Caffeine benefits people suffering from some forms of headache that relate to expanded blood arteries leading to the brain. Caffeine constricts these blood vessels. If a person takes caffeine regularly and then stops (on weekends, for example), headaches commonly occur. This is considered a physical withdrawal symptom.

Caffeine has other detrimental effects. High doses result in many of the same effects as other stimulants such as amphetamines and cocaine and can lead to a paranoid psychosis. This might occur if someone consumes about 1 gram in one dose or if the person habitually uses fairly high doses. However, even moderate doses can lead to nervousness, irritability, insomnia, and ulcers. People with psychiatric problems can lose control when using any stimulant, including caffeine. People who are troubled with panic or anxiety attacks can stimulate this problem by using too much caffeine.

Caffeine reportedly produces birth defects and skeletal-development problems when high doses are fed to pregnant rats. However, this phenomenon has not been shown at lower doses in humans. It is wise, however, for pregnant women to avoid using much caffeine or any other drug. It also is worth noting that rats fed large doses of caffeine become highly aggressive, launch unprovoked attacks on other rats, and even becoming self-mutilating.

In summary, caffeine, although legal, is a low-potency stimulant that must be used in moderation.

## MID-POTENCY STIMULANTS

### Strychnine

Strychnine is used as a rat poison, and it causes death by convulsions. In the past, small doses were used as a stimulating tonic. However, because of the danger of a fatal overdose, this drug is not used for humans. Unfortunately, some unscrupulous drug dealers sometimes add strychnine to batches of stimulants or hallucinogens to increase the effect. This is very dangerous and demonstrates the danger of the illegal drug market.

### Ritalin and Cylert

During the 1950s and 1960s, long-term amphetamine use with hyperactive children and children with attention deficits was discouraged. Two nonamphetamine stimulants, methylphenidate (Ritalin) and pemoline (Cylert) therefore were introduced as amphetamine substitutes. These drugs only differ slightly from amphetamines in their chemical structure and probably work the same way. They generally have been considered less potent forms of stimulants, although dosage level is a relevant factor as with any drug.

### Preludin

The stimulants of mid-level strength also include phenmetrazine (Preludin). Preludin, nicknamed "bam," is a diet pill that was popular in Washington, D.C., in the 1970s and early 1980s. Heroin addicts mixed their opiates with bam to make a form of speedball. Preludin also was dissolved with heat and water and injected alone for the stimulant properties. Preludin has been prescribed mostly as an appetite suppressant.

## HIGH-POTENCY STIMULANTS

### Cocaine

Cocaine is probably the most addicting stimulant, both because it is more euphoric and because it wears off quickly so that people who use it tend to do so often. Because it is abused so widely, it is discussed in a separate chapter.

### Amphetamines

The most potent stimulants are the amphetamines. These high-potency stimulants generally include three closely related drugs: amphetamine, dextroamphetamine, and methamphetamine. Their street names include "ice," "speed," "crank," "meth," "monster," "white crosses," "uppers," "dexies," "bennies," and "crystal." In pure form, they are yellowish crystals that are manufactured in tablet or capsule form. Abusers also sniff the crystals (although this is painful) or make a solution and inject it.

No difference is discernible to the user between amphetamine, methamphetamine, and dextroamphetamine. However, they do differ in potency—methamphetamine is the strongest—and dextroamphetamine has fewer side effects.

Amphetamines increase heart and breathing rates and blood pressure, dilate pupils, and decrease appetite. In addition, the user can experience a dry mouth, sweating, headache, blurred vision, dizziness, sleeplessness, and anxiety. Extremely high doses can cause people to flush or become pale; they can cause a rapid or irregular heartbeat, tremors, loss of coordination, and even physical collapse. An amphetamine injection creates a sudden increase in blood pressure that can cause death from stroke, very high fever, or heart failure.

In addition to the physical effects, users report feeling restless, anxious, and moody. Higher doses intensify the effects, and the user can become excited, overconfident, and in some cases paranoid or psychotic.

Amphetamines were synthesized first in 1887. Amphetamines are chemically similar to the natural hormone adrenalin, which is produced in the body to give a burst of energy during the "fight or flight" reaction. Adrenalin (also known as epinephrine) is a natural stimulant first described in 1899. A Japanese chemist first isolated methamphetamine in 1919, although no legitimate medical use for this drug existed until 1927. The Harrison Act prevented physicians from prescribing morphine to heroin addicts; consequently, amphetamines sometimes were used to help detoxify or treat heroin addiction.

The stimulating properties of amphetamines were put to use first beginning in the 1930s. The German army dispensed amphetamines to soldiers for blitzkrieg warfare, in which they overwhelmed the opposition with fighting sustained over days.

Amphetamines helped the German soldiers stay awake, although of course they later had to recuperate. Amphetamines were used by all sides during World War II, and after the war Japan had to deal with a large part of its population that was abusing the drugs. It commonly has been reported that soldiers were issued amphetamines to overcome combat fatigue during the Vietnam era.

Medically, amphetamines were used in inhalers as decongestants and for asthma, although better drugs have been found since. Amphetamines once were used widely for weight control, but it was determined that the weight loss was only temporary, so the drugs aren't approved for weight control unless other methods have been tried with no success. Additionally, amphetamines are used to treat narcolepsy, a disorder characterized by excessive sleepiness and ironically, for hyperactivity in children, in which the stimulants act as sedatives. Both of these uses still are considered legitimate by the medical community. Amphetamines also have been used to treat low blood pressure and to decrease fatigue, although the latter use is controversial medically.

In America, the habit of injecting amphetamines and of mixing heroin and amphetamines ("speedballing") became popular during the Korean War in the 1950s. Later, injectable amphetamines were removed from pharmacies in an attempt to curb an increase in illicit use that had begun in the early 1960s; however, they still are used in inhalers. As prescribed drugs, amphetamines once commonly were used to reduce sleepiness and still are used illicitly by long-haul truck drivers to stay awake. The problem with this is the driver becomes so exhausted that he or she only stares at the road without remaining truly observant.

Amphetamine use became popular in San Francisco during the 1960s, and experimental and recreational use spread throughout the country. The drug subculture then was dominated by marijuana and LSD users who accepted drugs as a legitimate form of recreation. The use of amphetamines by this isolated group slowly declined because of peer pressure against the drug. Members of the drug subculture coined the phrase "speed kills" to describe the negative emotional effects of long-term amphetamine use.

Over the next two decades, methamphetamine usually was snorted, injected alone, or mixed with heroin. The drug, which was made in illicit laboratories or extracted chemically from legally purchased inhalers, was called "crank" or "monster" and was popular in certain regions of the United States, especially around Philadelphia. Amphetamines replaced cocaine in speedballs because of the relatively low cost and length of the high. Amphetamines commonly were associated with motorcycle gangs or clubs.

### "Ice"

During the 1980s, amphetamine use was largely replaced by cocaine or "crack" abuse. More recently, a smokeable form of methamphetamine called "ice," "glass," or "batu" has surfaced in Hawaii. Because of cost and length of intoxication, ice could replace cocaine as the drug of choice for many. In Hawaii, two "meth" cases match every cocaine case. The problem with amphetamines seems to be getting worse—1988 to 1989 showed a 75 percent increase in reported cases of abuse. Methamphetamine reportedly is being shipped into Hawaii from the Far East, possibly Korea, Hong Kong, or the Philippines. The drug reportedly was first popularized in Hawaii by Filipino youth gangs and is popular among a wide section of the population there.

Crystal methamphetamine also is produced legitimately by Abbot Laboratories under the brand name of Desoxyn and is a Schedule 2 drug available by prescription with vault-type security and registration with DEA. This drug is available as a small white tablet with the letters "ME" stamped on one side and what appears to be a reversed "a" on the other side.

The illicit market manufactures meth in clandestine laboratories. "Crystal meth" normally is found in a white powdery or crystalline form. Although this drug has been snorted, injected, or swallowed for a number of years, the drug now reportedly is smoked in the Far East and in Hawaii. Reports from Hawaii indicate that 1 gram of ice can produce ten to fifteen "hits" or doses, and that one-tenth of a gram or an effective dose sells for as little as fifty dollars. The effects can last up to fourteen hours depending on the amount taken and the purity of the substance.

Reports from Hawaii mention two types of street meth: a water- and an oil-based version. The water-based type looks like rock candy and is formed in the same manner. It burns more quickly than the oil-based type and leaves a white residue in glass pipes where it is heated into fumes to inhale. The base version is a yellowish oil skimmed from the top of a heated mixture of meth and baking soda and then cooled in freezers. This type of meth burns more slowly than the water-based version and leaves a charred residue in the pipes.

The type of pipes preferred reportedly have been six-inch glass, with rounded and enlarged ends to help cool the gaseous state of the drug. The meth is dropped through a hole one-half inch in diameter, and it is covered by the finger once the meth has been heated into gas. A wet towel is sometimes used to cool the pipe for storage or further use. The user's fingertip sometimes is burned by the hot glass when the hole through which the meth was dropped is covered to prevent losing the gaseous vapor.

### Origin and Composition

Amphetamines are similar chemically to arousal hormones in our bodies called adrenalin (epinephrin) and noradrenalin (norepinephrine). Consequently, these drugs are suspected of mimicking or boosting the body's own natural stimulants. Amphetamine is less potent than dextroamphetamine, which is likewise less potent—gram for gram—than methamphetamine.

Most of the illegal amphetamines in this country come from illicit laboratories. A minority of these drugs are diverted from prescription sources. Look-alike drugs that resemble stimulants but contain legal substances such as caffeine are sold in "head" shops.

In order to increase profits, illicit amphetamines often are cut or mixed with other drugs such as a local anesthetic called Procaine or even with other powdered substances such as strychnine. Strychnine is a muscle stimulant that causes paralysis at higher doses.

### Dosage and Pathway

Four methods have been used to put stimulants into the body. In order of increasing potency, these methods are:

- Orally, by pill or capsule
- Snorting or absorbing through the nasal membranes/sinus cavities
- Injecting into a vein
- Freebasing or inhaling fumes of methamphetamine base or rock

It takes about three minutes for the user to achieve a high by snorting, one half minute by injection, and a few seconds by smoking. The intensity of the high is affected by the amount and purity of the stimulant, the route of administration or speed that it enters the brain, and the user's acquired tolerance. Generally, a dose of 10 to 30 milligrams of dextroamphetamine and even less methamphetamine will last six to eight hours and produce alertness, hypervigilance, and excitability. The standard dose of ice is .10 grams or 100 milligrams, indicating that it usually is impure.

### Physical Effects

Although stimulants can be effective in treating asthma, narcolepsy, hyperactivity, obesity, and a form of epilepsy, their use is not without physical consequences. Amphetamines narrow blood vessels and thus raise blood pressure, increase the respiration rate and body temperature, and increase general activity level.

Amphetamines appear to have two effects on the synapses of nerve cells. Not only do they increase the release of norepinephrine, one of the body's own arousal hormones, but they also prevent the breakdown of this norepinephrine so that it stays active for a longer period of time. In this way, the person using amphetamines experiences initial excitement, but then depletes his or her own natural supply of neurotransmitters, consequently becoming exhausted and depressed. Eventually the body's storehouse of norepinephrine is depleted and, much like with cocaine, depression can follow in the withdrawal stage.

Chronic food and sleep deprivation, in addition to the depleted neurotransmitters, produce a schizophrenic-like behavior pattern characterized by paranoia. Amphetamine psychosis is difficult to differentiate from a schizophrenic psychosis.

Most heavy or long-term amphetamine users report a constant irritability, nervousness, difficulty sleeping, and suspiciousness. Many also report headaches, trouble concentrating, and sleep difficulties even after they have stopped using these drugs for many months. It is not clear whether stimulants have aggravated existing psychiatric conditions or whether long-term internal chemical changes result from long-term amphetamine use. These people sometimes improve after they are administered low doses of phenothiazines such as Thorazine. Antidepressants also have shown some promise in treating the depression following amphetamine withdrawal.

Unlike cocaine, amphetamines do not have an anesthetic effect. Amphetamines do constrict blood vessels, but do not produce a numbness like cocaine. Constricted blood vessels will slow the absorption of amphetamine from the nasal tissues and also will reduce circulation in nasal tissues. Amphetamines tend to make skeletal muscles more tense. Strangely enough, amphetamines dilate or open the bronchial tubes (air passages). This is why asthma sufferers are treated with low doses of amphetamines placed into inhalers.

Amphetamine overdose is uncommon. Most first-time users can tolerate high doses, although the likelihood of heart failure, aneurism, and instant death do increase because of the increase in heart rate and blood pressure associated with this drug. The predominant danger of using amphetamines is the gradual physical deterioration that occurs in long-term users. The addiction and long-term effects of this drug seem to cause weight loss, increased susceptibility to infections, deteriorated health, and abnormal heart rate.

### Effective Dose to Lethal Dose Ratio

The lethal dose of amphetamines probably exceeds 1,000 milligrams. The effective dose, as mentioned, could be 10 to 100 milligrams. Since tolerance does build, more drug is needed to attain the desired effect. The lethal dose does climb as tolerance builds, so a high-tolerance user probably would need more to overdose than a novice. Overdose deaths commonly are not reported, although the death rate due to increased aggression and criminal involvement probably is higher for users than for nonusers. Because the advent of smoking amphetamines is relatively recent, insufficient data exists about overdose deaths from smoking ice. If amphetamines parallel cocaine in overdose rate, many thousands of emergency-room visits and hundreds of deaths per year will be seen in the 1990s.

### Withdrawal

Withdrawal occurs when a compulsive user of amphetamines or stimulants stops using the drug. The intensity of the withdrawal depends on several factors, including the manner in which amphetamine is administered, the frequency of use, and the dosage. Most stimulant withdrawal follows a definable course that varies according to the potency of the stimulants used. These withdrawal symptoms usually involve exhaustion, depression, irritability, sleeplessness, loss of energy, and sometimes an intense craving for stimulants. The usual pattern, though, is for the amphetamine user to sleep for several days during the withdrawal period. Since depression occurs during the early stages of withdrawal, suicide might be more likely during this time, especially if the person has personality, legal, or financial problems.

Amphetamines do not produce a addiction in the sense that bodily organs convulse or are otherwise physically disturbed during withdrawal. Amphetamines do produce withdrawal symptoms that are at least in part physical (exhaustion and depression caused by depletion of neurotransmitters), especially among those who inject or smoke methamphetamine. However, the physical symptom basically is exhaustion. Although physical dependence is unlikely, a strong psychological dependence can develop. People can begin to believe that they need stimulants in order to function, and people can develop a craving for the effects. This craving for the high can lead to severe neglect of health, including malnutrition, because these drugs suppress hunger and thirst.

The most common adverse effect on the family is financial and emotional. The user who becomes dependent on this drug allows it to be the focus of his or her life—even more important than friends and family. Amphetamine addicts will lie, take money from their family, ignore responsibilities, and prefer to be high rather than spend time with loved ones. Amphetamines become their primary love in life and their major source of pleasure.

Hepatitis, skin infections, tetanus, and possibly AIDS are chronic medical complications associated with intravenously using amphetamines. Seizures sometimes are experienced by heavy amphetamine users regardless of the route taken in administering the drug. Heavy users of these drugs experience "shakes," depression, and fatigue when they crash after staying high for days at a time. Chronic users suffer from dental problems, malnutrition, and sexual dysfunction; sometimes death from overdose occurs.

Death from amphetamine overdose can occur, although it is rare. The sudden increase in blood pressure can rupture arteries in the brain. Heart attack is the most common cause of overdose death. The heart speeds up, but the blood supply to this muscle is choked because of constricted blood vessels. This results in a heart attack, and the victim sometimes dies. Smoking methamphetamine is the most dangerous way to use the drug, because large doses enter the bloodstream through the lung tissue. It is common for a person to physically waste away until he or she reaches a life-threatening state. If the use of meth increases, the number of deaths also is expected to increase.

Long-term heavy use of amphetamines can lead to malnutrition and various diseases that result from vitamin deficiencies. Lack of sleep, weight loss, and depression also result from regular use. Frequent use of large amounts of amphetamines can produce brain damage that results in speech and thought disturbances and difficulty sleeping long after use. In addition, users who inject amphetamines can get serious and life-threatening infections from unsterile equipment or self-prepared solutions that are contaminated. Lung or heart disease and other diseases of the blood vessels also can be contracted; these can be fatal. Kidney damage, stroke, or other tissue damage also can occur.

### Psychological Effects

Users report that a psychological dependence can develop to amphetamines. This dependency is typified by a feeling that the drug is essential to normal functioning. These users frequently continue to use amphetamines to avoid the depression they feel once the drug's effects wear off. In addition, people who use amphetamines regularly might develop tolerance.

Users associate increased irritability, nervousness, intense craving, and aggressiveness with stimulant dependence. The higher potency stimulants can produce more serious psychological conditions, including intense depression after withdrawal and severe paranoid or delusional psychosis. People who use large amounts of amphetamines over a long period of time also can develop an amphetamine psychosis: They might see, hear, and feel things that do not exist (in other words, suffer hallucinations), have irrational thoughts or beliefs (delusions), and feel as though people are out to get them (paranoia). Chronic users reportedly have hidden in closets, under beds, or in dark rooms while pointing guns at imagined enemies. During the chronic paranoid state, the user believes law enforcement agents are closing in and that a potential crisis is imminent.

People in this extremely suspicious state frequently exhibit bizarre and sometimes violent behavior. These symptoms usually disappear when people stop using the drug. However, sometimes the psychosis does not clear so quickly and the user needs psychiatric hospitalization.

When people abruptly stop using amphetamines, they might experience fatigue, long periods of sleep, irritability, hunger, and depression. The length and severity of the depression seems to be related to how much and how often the amphetamines were used. All stimulants place the body in a condition termed "stress," a state necessary in emergency situations but wearing out the body's resources. Therefore, the need to sleep following withdrawal from amphetamines is a rebound effect in which the body attempts to replenish depleted chemical reserves.

## LOOK-ALIKE STIMULANTS

Look-alike stimulants are drugs manufactured to look like and mimic the effects of real amphetamines. The drugs usually contain varying amounts of caffeine, ephedrine, and phenylpropanolamine. These three legal substances are weak stimulants and often are found in over-the-counter preparations such as diet pills and decongestants. More recently, new drugs called "act-alikes" have been manufactured to avoid new state laws that prohibit look-alikes. The act-alikes contain the same ingredients as the look-alikes but do not physically resemble any prescription or over-the-counter drugs. These drugs are sold on the street as "speed" and "uppers" and are expensive, even though they are not as strong as amphetamines. They often are sold to young people who are told they are legal, safe, and harmless. This is one reason they increasingly are being abused.

### Effects of Look-alike Stimulants

Some negative effects of look-alikes, especially when taken in large quantities, are similar to the effects of amphetamines. These effects include anxiety, restlessness, weakness, throbbing headache, difficulty breathing, and a rapid heartbeat. In several cases users with high blood pressure have suffered cerebral hemorrhaging and death. Often, in an emergency, look-alike drug-overdose cases are misidentified by physicians and poison control centers, which can cause problems in determining the proper treatment.

One of the greatest dangers is that these drugs easily are available and are being used by young people and others who do not normally abuse drugs. Once people start using these drugs, they can be at high risk for using other drugs.

Because look-alikes are not as strong as real amphetamines, they are extremely dangerous for people who deliberately or accidentally use the same dose of real amphetamines as they would take of the look-alikes. For example, people who buy look-alikes on the street might unknowingly buy real amphetamines and take enough to cause an overdose. On the other hand, people who have abused amphetamines might underestimate the potency of the look-alike drugs and take excessive amounts that can result in a toxic reaction.

Although caffeine is an ingredient in several look-alike drugs and is legal, caffeine is a drug. Overdoses are not common, but they can take the form of nervousness and insomnia when taken in liquid form. More severe overdoses easily can occur when the caffeine is taken in pill form, such as with No-Doz or Vivarin. An overdose can result in confusion, convulsions, and paranoia. Like all drugs, caffeine can be used and it can be abused.

## SUMMARY

Stimulants include the high-level, mid-level and low-potency types. High-potency stimulants have been on the increase in certain parts of the country. Amphetamines are the most potent stimulants, and the effects last for many hours. A newer, more potent smokeable variety called ice is popular in Hawaii and is expected to spread to the mainland.

Stimulants like cocaine can produce in the user paranoia, psychosis, delusions, and aggressiveness followed by depression during the withdrawal phase. Users also can die from cardiac fibrillation, stroke, aneurism, and respiratory collapse. Stimulant users also typically suffer from malnutrition because these drugs have an appetite suppressant quality.

Using stimulants intravenously carries the same bacterial and viral risks as injecting heroin. Hepatitis, HIV, venereal disease, and a myriad of other diseases can be spread through dirty needles. Sexual promiscuity also can be more likely in the earlier stages of stimulant abuse, which can increase the risk of the spread of AIDS. For the aforementioned reasons, the high-potency stimulants can be considered dangerous drugs.

# VIII.
# COCAINE

## HISTORY

Cocaine is an alkaloid extracted from the leaves of the coca, a plant that has been cultivated in the Andean highlands of South America since prehistoric times. Native Peruvians who live in high altitudes have used the coca leaf to provide energy, reduce hunger, and alleviate headaches. It is legal for them to use it in the form of raw leaves and in the form of tea. It also is legal to export a limited quantity of the active ingredient, cocaine, for medical uses. However, much of the coca production is diverted to crude factories where cocaine is extracted for illegal export.

When the Spanish conquistadors came to South America, they initially tried to suppress coca use largely because of its ties to the native religion they were attempting to eliminate. However, they found that coca was useful in getting the native mine and field workers to work harder in high altitudes with little food or rest. Eventually, the conquistadors began to pay workers in part with coca leaves. Using raw coca leaves, which contain only small amounts of cocaine as well as several vitamins and minerals, normally is not a problem and actually can be beneficial. It is noteworthy that when Native Peruvians select leaves to chew, they prefer the sweeter leaves that contain a mixture of alkaloids, not the more bitter leaves with high concentrations of cocaine. Legal in Peru, coca tea is a mild stimulant that helps people adapt to high altitudes. However, the use of the concentrated cocaine extract often causes severe problems.

Coca rarely was seen outside South America until the mid-1800s, when German scientists isolated the active ingredient, cocaine. It was experimented with as a medical drug and at first appeared promising as a treatment for alcohol and morphine addiction and for depression. However, it was not long before the dangers of abuse—which can include compulsive use, convulsions, paranoid psychosis, and even death—were published.

By the turn of the century in America, cocaine was an ingredient in many "patent medicines" for which the ingredients did not have to be revealed. These medicines often did make people feel better, but their dangers were not well-publicized. Cocaine was also a main ingredient of a popular turn-of-the-century soft drink, Coca-Cola. The original drink contained cocaine, but the company voluntarily discontinued this ingredient prior to the passage of the Pure Food and Drug Act in 1906. Even today "Classic Coke" uses flavoring from the coca plant, although all the cocaine has been removed. The Harrison Act of 1914 prohibited physicians from using cocaine or opiates in treating addiction.

### Legal Medical Use

Cocaine is classified as a Schedule 2 drug. It has approved medical uses, although a high potential for dependency is noted. It is used medically as a local anesthetic and to reduce bleeding from mucous membrane surgery. Mucous membranes include the inside of the nose, mouth, and anus—that is, any skin that normally is moist. The most common medical uses involve tooth extraction, gum surgery, and the removal of nasal polyps. When used medically, the amount administered is only the amount necessary to produce numbness and reduce bleeding. The patient usually doesn't feel any mental effects.

### Extent of Illegal Use

A 1985 survey found that some 3 percent (5.8 million) of the American population used cocaine within the past month. Approximately 5 percent of high school students and 25 percent of the young adult sample (ages eighteen to twenty-five) reported using it at least once in their lives, although fewer reported using the drug within the past year. One measure of the extent of use is the number of cocaine-related emergency-room admissions in the sixteen largest cities: The 1985 figure was just under 10,000, including nearly 500 deaths. The 1989 emergency-room figure was just under 50,000; the number of deaths is not available. Recent figures suggest that cocaine use reached its peak in 1988, but this is not certain.

The degree of use also is indicated by testing the urine of those arrested. In the District of Columbia, the percentage of arrestees who tested positive in 1989 for cocaine was 58 percent; however, the number since has declined.

Education appears to be affecting cocaine use. An annual survey of 1,200 high school seniors has determined a drop in the number of students who reported using cocaine the month before. This number was 6.2 percent in 1986 and decreased to 2.8 percent in 1989. This decrease in use counters the number of students who said they could get the drug if they wanted to; this number increased to nearly 60 percent in 1989.

An unfortunate trend among habitual users is to switch from snorting cocaine to smoking it, which is more dangerous. However, snorting evidently remains the preferred method of consumption.

## ORIGIN AND COMPOSITION

About 75 percent of the cocaine available in our country comes from Colombia, while another 25 percent reportedly comes from Bolivia, Peru, and several other countries. According to the National Institute on Drug Abuse, about 144,600 pounds of cocaine were consumed by Americans in 1986 as compared to 62,000 pounds of the drug consumed in 1983. In the Andes Mountains, cocaine is extracted in crude laboratories. Coca leaves are soaked in kerosene, gasoline, acetone or other solvents and soda to extract the cocaine and produce a coca paste. This paste, sometimes called "bazooka," can be smoked, and it has become a real problem in South America. It usually contains dangerous solvents—sometimes lead from leaded gasoline solvents. The coca paste then is combined with hydrochloric acid to produce cocaine hydrochloride, the white powder or crystals of cocaine. High-quality cocaine hydrochloride is usually 80 to 90 percent pure. Even using the best coca plants, other alkaloids are produced that cannot be removed easily.

In order to increase profits, cocaine dealers usually add other ingredients to the drug. The safest "cut" is mannitol, but other cuts include numbing agents such as procaine, various sugars, and sometimes amphetamine. Unconfirmed reports exist that white plastic shavings have been used as an adulterant to melt with the cocaine when it is heated. These other ingredients can cause additional physical problems. Also, someone who is accustomed to adulterated ("stepped on" or "cut") cocaine might overdose if the purity of the cocaine purchased unexpectedly is higher.

### Manufacturing for Street Use

Cocaine hydrochloride is water-soluble white powder. It usually is sniffed (snorted) and sometimes is injected. Some users now vaporize cocaine base—although it isn't water-soluble, it evaporates at a lower temperature.

Cocaine base can be made by using two different methods. The freebase method takes more work and uses flammable solvents, but it produces a purer result. To make freebase cocaine, the cocaine hydrochloride first is mixed with ammonia or other strong base to change the water-soluble cocaine hydrochloride into cocaine base. The cocaine base, which is not water-soluble, is extracted by an organic solvent such as ethyl ether. After the solvent is removed, the cocaine base then can be smoked.

Freebasing quickly has been replaced in popularity by the rock form of cocaine called "crack," which easily can be made with kitchen items. This method often is called "dirty basing" or "street base." The salt of cocaine—cocaine hydrochloride—is heated with baking soda and water, and lumps form. The resulting rocks of baking soda and cocaine are called crack. This method of production is preferred by many dealers because it is quick, but also because most of the "cut" remains in the rocks and the baking soda increases the weight as well. "Crack" or rock cocaine thus is an impure form of cocaine base. More information on crack is included at the end of this chapter.

### Dosage and Pathway

Cocaine hydrochloride consists of two types of substances: an alkaloid base (the cocaine part) and a salt (the hydrochloride part). Cocaine hydrochloride easily dissolves in water. Cocaine base does not dissolve in water, and its boiling point is much lower. Cocaine is ingested primarily by three methods:

- "Snorting" or absorbing cocaine hydrochloride through the nasal membranes or sinus cavities

- Injecting cocaine hydrochloride into a vein

- Freebasing or inhaling fumes of cocaine base/crack

It takes about three minutes for the user to feel the initial effects when snorting, one-half minute when it is injected, and perhaps ten seconds when it is smoked. The intensity of the high is affected by the amount and purity of the cocaine, the speed at which it enters the brain, the emotional and physical state of the user, and the user's acquired tolerance. Generally, a line of cocaine used for snorting contains about 25 to 30 milligrams, but less is used for injecting or smoking.

## PHYSICAL EFFECTS

Although cocaine is used by the medical profession to block pain and reduce bleeding, it generally is recognized as a stimulant and euphoriant. Cocaine interacts with substances in the central nervous system that carry messages to various parts of the brain. It narrows blood vessels and thus raises blood pressure, increases the respiration rate and body temperature, and increases general activity level.

Cocaine appears to alter the effectiveness of two neurotransmitters in the brain. Neurotransmitters are chemical messengers that transmit information from one brain cell to another. The neurotransmitter dopamine is involved with the brain's pleasure or reward system and helps a person learn to repeat an act that led to the release of dopamine. The second neurotransmitter affected by cocaine is noradrenaline, which involves alertness and nervousness. (To simplify, dopamine can be called the body's "joy juice," while noradrenaline can be called the body's "energy juice.").

Normally, these neurotransmitters are "shot out" of a brain cell when that cell communicates to another cell; after the other cell receives the message, the extra neurotransmitter is pumped back into the sending cell. Cocaine appears to prevent the unused neurotransmitter from being pumped back into the sending brain cells. The extra neurotransmitter stays near the receiving brain cells and continues to stimulate those cells, producing an unusual degree of excitement. This excitement comprises pleasure (dopamine) and nervous alertness (noradrenaline). However, the extra neurotransmitter is destroyed when it isn't protected within the brain cells, and the brain's supply becomes exhausted.

In this way, someone who uses cocaine experiences initial excitement, but then depletes his or her natural supply of these neurotransmitters and becomes exhausted and depressed. It takes time for the body to replenish its natural supply, but the typical response of a cocaine abuser is not to rest and recuperate, but to take even more cocaine in order to stay high. Although the body does not become dependent on cocaine to a point where spasms and physical pain develop, the loss of brain chemicals can produce psychological symptoms of irritability, exhaustion, and depression.

When cocaine is snorted frequently and in substantial doses, it is highly destructive to nose tissue. It irritates the delicate nasal membranes until they crack and bleed almost constantly. The constriction or narrowing of blood vessels slows the absorption of cocaine from the nasal tissues and also prevents blood from reaching these tissues, causing areas of cell death. Prolonged snorting causes holes to develop in the septum, the cartilage and skin between the two nasal passages. Plastic surgery sometimes is required to repair the damage. Perpetual cold-like symptoms—a constantly running nose, red skin around the nose, and a persistent dull headache—are common in chronic cocaine snorters.

Cocaine's physical effects on other parts of the body include constricting blood vessels and producing numbness in any area on which it is placed. The blood-vessel constriction elevates blood pressure. This effect, in combination with cocaine's heart acceleration, can lead to a heart attack. Cocaine produces a general increase in muscle tone in the short run, and users often experience a feeling of increased physical stamina. However, as abusers normally don't eat or drink properly, the body becomes weakened.

Chronic medical complications associated with intravenously using cocaine include hepatitis, skin infections, tetanus, and possibly AIDS. Seizures sometimes are experienced by heavy cocaine users regardless of the introduction route. People who suffer from epilepsy report that cocaine lowers their threshold to seizures. Heavy users of cocaine experience "shakes," depression, and fatigue when they "crash" after staying high for days at a time. Chronic users suffer from dental problems, malnutrition, and sexual dysfunction, and sometimes they die from overdoses.

In a recent study of 165 men and fifty-one women seeking treatment for cocaine-related problems, almost half (46 percent) of those treated used other drugs including alcohol (34 percent). The chief complaints by members of this group (72 percent of whom were considered heavy cocaine users) were chest pains (39.5 percent), anxiety (21.9 percent), shortness of breath (21.9 percent), palpitations (20.6 percent), dizziness (12.9 percent), and headache (12 percent). Besides these complaints, 9 percent of this group were considered psychotic and 5.2 percent had suicidal ideation. Out of this sample, two died from cardiac arrest after cocaine use and were pronounced dead in the emergency room (Brody et al. 1990).

### Cocaine and Sex

When used in small doses by a healthy person, cocaine can stimulate sexual excitement. It sometimes is applied near the head of the penis to produce numbness and to delay ejaculation. Cocaine never should be applied to the vagina or to either the male or female urinary openings. Tissue damage can occur. Larger doses of cocaine produce so much nervousness that males often are unable to maintain an erection. Prolonged abuse exhausts and weakens the body, decreasing sexual ability and interest. It commonly is reported by chronic abusers that the desire for cocaine becomes much stronger than the desire for sex.

A recent study was done with more than 1,300 males in their thirties who visited a fertility clinic because they were not able to impregnate their wives. Recent use of cocaine was related to low sperm count, deformed sperm, and sperm that were unable to swim properly. This study did not find that alcohol and marijuana cause sperm problems (*Fertility and Sterility*, Feb. 1990).

### Effective Dose to Lethal Dose Ratio

Because tolerance to cocaine develops quickly, a user is able to take a dose in the evening that might have been lethal if he or she had taken it earlier that morning. It is difficult to say what dose is lethal. A "kindling" effect develops in which some nerves appear to increasingly become sensitive to the convulsive and irritating effects of the drug, while other nerves are not affected in this way—or even become less sensitive, especially to the euphoric effects. Some people have died after exposure to as little as one-fifth of a gram, while others repeatedly take one gram at a time. Sometimes someone has a medical condition that isn't dangerous unless cocaine is taken. Some people lack the enzyme the body uses to metabolize cocaine, and so a small dose will stay in the body much longer than it might in other people, continuing to overstimulate the heart until a heart attack occurs. Other people (such as basketball player Len Bias) have arteries leading to the heart that will spasm or can experience cardiac fibrillation (a quivering heart) more easily than normal. In other words, a small dose can kill even an athletic man.

Cocaine was blamed for nearly 500 deaths in 1985, and the number of deaths since has increased. Based on coroners' reports, cocaine was blamed for 777 deaths in 1987, according to the National Center for Health Statistics. The increased use of cocaine—and especially the increased use of smoking the drug—encourages a rough estimate: Nearly 1,000 Americans die each year from cocaine overdose. The most common cause of death appears to be a rapid heart rate combined with constricting blood vessels leading to the heart muscles, producing a heart attack. Many users have experienced chest pain while using cocaine, and these chest pains indicate a near heart attack. Other reasons for death include bursting blood vessels in the brain due to sudden rises in blood pressure, heart overstimulation leading to fibrillation (quivering) rather than normal beating, and death from fever and convulsions.

## PSYCHOLOGICAL EFFECTS

Although cocaine does not produce physical withdrawal effects, it is considered one of the most psychologically addicting drugs existing. Numerous experiments on animals indicate that this drug replaces the body's natural craving for primary reinforcers such as food, water, sex, and shelter. That is, repeated use produces intense cravings—cravings so strong that a person can become a slave to this drug. Monkeys and rats will continue to use cocaine instead of drinking or eating—to the point of death. Psychological addiction can be much more compelling than physical addiction. Addiction means slavery.

Leading experts Dr. Mark Gold, author of *800-COCAINE*, Dr. Sidney Cohen, author of *The Substance Abuse Problems*, and Dr. Oakley Ray, author of *Drugs, Society and Human Behavior* all say cocaine definitely is addicting.

The following are criteria for addiction:

1. Increased tolerance is experienced.
2. Withdrawal is experienced.

3.  Acquiring and using the drug affects job and family.

4.  Using the drug contributes to illegal activities.

Cocaine abuse certainly can lead to addiction by these criteria.

### Tolerance and Dependence

In the past, addiction to cocaine was believed to be rare, because relatively small doses were snorted. Because tissue in the nose constricts from cocaine, less of this drug entered the bloodstream. Injecting and smoking cocaine introduces much larger amounts of this drug into the body. Very high doses of cocaine now are consumed when a user injects cocaine into his or her veins or inhales cocaine base. Tolerance for the drug quickly increases so that more and more of the drug is needed to obtain the desired high. The compulsion to keep using becomes so great that the desire for the drug soon outweighs all other drives such as hunger, thirst, and sex. The craving or psychological dependence induced by cocaine is extreme in some people, particularly those who smoke freebase/rock or inject cocaine. Eventually, the cocaine has a limited pleasant effect, and paranoid thoughts and actions develop. For example, users have reported hiding in their homes with loaded guns waiting for law enforcement officials to enter.

### Withdrawal

Withdrawal occurs when a compulsive cocaine user stops using the drug. The intensity of withdrawal depends on several factors, including the manner in which cocaine has been administered, the frequency of use, and the dosage. Cocaine withdrawal usually involves exhaustion, depression, irritability, sleeplessness, loss of energy, and intense craving for the drug. Suicide can be more likely during this time—especially if the person has used all of his or her resources in quests for the drug or if the person believes he or she has lost the respect of other people.

## EFFECTS ON THE FAMILY

Acquiring and using the drug affects job and family. The most common adverse effects on the family are financial and emotional. The user who becomes dependent on this drug allows it to become the focus of his or her life, and it becomes even more important than family and friends. Cocaine addicts will lie, take money from their family, ignore responsibilities, and prefer to be high rather than spend time with loved ones. Cocaine becomes their primary love in life and their major source of pleasure. Many people have lost houses, cars, jobs, and freedom because of their desire for cocaine.

Chronic cocaine use causes exhaustion and sometimes serious medical problems, which in turn affect family members, friends and fellow workers. The Centers for Disease Control in 1982 stated that 11,000 cocaine abusers (about 950 per month)—triple the number reported just three years earlier—were admitted to federally funded drug abuse programs in 1980. This does not include the 3,000 or more private centers that treat drug abusers. Treatment can be expensive and long-term.

Self-help groups continue to provide much support, although a period of hospital confinement can help someone to get through the withdrawal phase and to begin new behavior patterns.

Considering the psychological and physical effects of heavy cocaine use, it would be impossible for family relationships and job performance to remain unaffected. Relationships, values, and priorities change in respect to the chronic user's single-minded drive to obtain and use cocaine.

Cocaine is the ultimate reinforcer. In one experiment using animals, monkeys pressed on a bar repetitively (12,800 times) in order to obtain a single dose of cocaine. They worked for cocaine, preferring it over food, even though they were starving. They even ignored receptive females introduced into their cages, continuing to press the bar to receive the drug. The monkeys received electric shocks in order to obtain large doses of cocaine, even though they could have received lesser doses and avoided the shock. In an unlimited access situation, the monkeys self-administered cocaine by bar-pressing until they died of brain seizures. These monkeys reportedly had been normal animals until they were administered the drug, and they did not have any situational stresses. All the monkeys responded in this compulsive manner. If humans had unlimited access to cocaine, they probably would behave like the monkeys. The highly rewarding properties of cocaine can make obsessive users of mature and well-adjusted people.

## COCAINE CONTRIBUTES TO ILLEGAL ACTIVITIES

Acquiring cocaine is illegal. Cocaine users risk losing their health, important relationships with their wives, husbands, parents, siblings, and children, their jobs or careers, and their freedom. People who normally would not consider breaking the law will risk a prison term in order to obtain cocaine.

Cocaine use certainly can contribute to illegal acts for which one can be incarcerated. Many offenders deny that cocaine use contributed to their illegal activities, saying that money, peers, and the thrill of subverting the law were the main motives for their actions. For others, the compulsive drive to obtain and use cocaine was the prime cause that led them into associations and activities that contributed to their incarceration and legal problems. These people can benefit from a drug treatment program, if they are receptive to the notion that they need treatment.

Numerous clinical reports indicate that users often sell all their possessions believing they later will be able to replace everything. Eventually, some even sell the use of their bodies, becoming prostitutes. Later, as funds are depleted, other types of crime appear. Selling cocaine, robbery, and numerous other crimes are committed by previously law-abiding citizens. The criminally oriented escalate their activities, possibly up to ten-fold, during this desperate state of addiction.

## TREATMENT FOR COCAINE ADDICTION

Successful treatment typically goes through the following stages:

1. The abuser reaches a stage of unhappiness that cannot be denied or rationalized. The stage frequently is referred to as "bottoming out." Legal problems and incarceration sometimes create a shock strong enough to convince the cocaine abuser to examine his or her life and decide to change.

2. At this point, the abuser has to change associations such as friends and peers and his or her identity and way of thinking. Individual and group counseling can help in this process.

3. A superior alternative must be found. The patient must rediscover the value of friends, relatives, health, work, and self-esteem that a drug-free life can offer.

Dr. Mark Gold is the author of several books about cocaine and is a nationally recognized expert on the drug. According to Dr. Gold, a cocaine abuser must adopt several resolutions in order to avoid relapsing.

1. He or she must avoid drug users altogether.

2. He or she must not stay in a room or at a party at which someone is preparing to use or is using drugs.

3. He or she must not help friends find drugs or accompany a friend on such an expedition.

4. He or she must not touch or handle any drugs at any time.

5. He or she must not accept or fill any drug prescriptions without program approval.

6. He or she must avoid going to places where drugs will be available—to a rock concert, for example.

7. He or she must realize that one can think about and even crave cocaine, but not use it. He or she also must realize that he or she is required to honor the treatment commitment in the face of all temptations and pressures to quit.

If relapse occurs or if contact is made with the drug, people should be aware that this does not necessarily constitute a failure. Failure is met when a person relapses and doesn't seek help, but instead continues on a self-destructive course. Failure means lying about relapse to self and others. Failure means completely turning away from programs, wellness activities, and support systems. While contact with this drug is not advisable, relapse does not constitute a complete failure unless the user turns away from his or her program and support systems in the process.

### Referral Sources in the Community

800-COCAINE is the cocaine hotline available for providing information and referral. A self-evaluation questionnaire in Dr. Gold's book of the same name can be helpful.

Cocaine Anonymous (CA) is based on the twelve-step disease model and is available in most metropolitan areas. The guidelines for CA follow:

1. Do not associate with cocaine users. Leave a place if you find that cocaine is present.

2. Switching to other drugs or trying to cut down on cocaine is futile. The message is: "Stop using cocaine and other drugs."

3. Make amends with the people you hurt while you were a cocaine junkie. In that way, the shame and guilt will be reduced.

4. Examine yourself, identify the flaws in your character, and cultivate spiritual awareness. These activities will help you to prevent slipping back into the old ways.

5. Look around you in CA. Are these people happier and more content than your cocaine-using friends were?

6. Recovering addicts can help the addict who wants to recover.

7. Addiction is a progressive illness that cannot be cured, but it can be arrested for a lifetime through total abstinence.

For additional information regarding Cocaine Anonymous, contact CA Central Office, 712 Wilshire Boulevard, Suite 149, Santa Monica, CA 90401; 213/553-8306.

## CRACK OR ROCK COCAINE

Crack is crystallized freebase cocaine sold in ready-to-smoke "rocks." Quantities range from "dime rocks" to "eight balls" to "tracks" to "boulders." The most popular unit is the rock, which is sold in ten- to twenty-dollar amounts. The word "freebase" literally describes the pure cocaine alkaloid freed from its hydrochloride salt. The crystals are nicknamed crack because of the cracking sound they make as they are smoked.

### Making Base

Crack can be made by two different methods. In the "dirty base" or "street base" method, cocaine hydrochloride and any "cuts" are mixed with baking soda and water, heated, and then stirred until small rocks form. The resulting rocks, comprising cocaine base and baking soda, then are sold to the customer. The residual baking soda in the rocks not only "cheats" the customer by diluting the concentration the customer believes he or she is purchasing, but it also contributes to lung damage when the product is smoked.

In the "clean base" method, a solvent such as ether is mixed with water and cocaine hydrochloride. The cocaine base separates from the hydrochloride and cuts occurs because the base does not dissolve in the water, although the cuts and hydrochloride will dissolve in the water. The cocaine base and ether then is separated from the water mixture and dried, leaving the cocaine base. Although this method produces a cleaner or purer form of cocaine over the "dirty base" method, using ether is dangerous because it is highly flammable. Small amounts of ether can remain in the cocaine base, and an impatient user could explode the substance by trying to smoke it before it is fully dried. These solvents also can cause lung damage because they irritate lung tissue.

Most of the rock cocaine sold on the street is produced by the dirty basing method, because drug dealers trying to make a better profit prefer the quicker and easier baking soda and water method that does not remove all previous cuts and adds some additional weight. Crack especially is insidious and dangerous because of its accessibility. It often is sold in small ten- to twenty-dollar vials that are priced within most people's financial limits and that can create an almost unbreakable need for continued use. Crack actually is more expensive per dose than powdered cocaine because it is cut heavily and is sold in smaller amounts. This is a marketing ploy that helps dealers make more money.

### Route of Administration

Unlike cocaine hydrochloride powder, which is snorted, injected, or swallowed, crack is smoked. The blood vessels in the lungs are numerous and unlike those in the sinus cavity do not collapse enough to limit intake (cocaine is a vasoconstrictor).

Consequently, dangerously high doses that are extremely addictive are taken in, rendering the user eager to seek the high from crack. Crack is to cocaine as heroin is to opium, whiskey is to beer, and THC is to marijuana. Crack cocaine usually is heated into vapor using a small blowtorch, but users sometimes "chase the dragon" by putting it on aluminum foil, heating it from below, and sniffing the rising fumes.

### Levels of Intoxication

Smoking cocaine freebase or crack gives the user a far more intense and rapid euphoria than snorting cocaine powder. However, this euphoric high lasts only about five to fifteen minutes and is followed almost immediately by an equally unpleasant crash characterized by irritability, agitation, and intense cravings for more of the drug. Because the effects are so short when smoked, the paranoia often experienced tends to die rapidly, and violence is less likely to occur than with longer-lasting stimulants.

However, the short duration makes smoked cocaine very addictive as a person has to smoke again and again to stay high. This repeated use creates a strong learned association between the pipe and positive feelings, and this emotional connection can be hard to break. It is common for cocaine smokers to continue until their supply runs out, feeling unable to stop. However, they never feel as high as they did following the first hit of the day when they still had undepleted natural energy. With many drugs, levels of use are described as experimental, social/recreational, regular, heavy, and compulsive. Crack cocaine holds the dubious reputation of causing severe addiction quickly, bypassing the social/recreational levels and moving the user quickly to chronic compulsive use that is limited only by finances.

### Physical and Psychological Risks

Data collected on the 800-COCAINE hotline through May 1986 show that the majority of callers who smoked cocaine base had experienced severe and life-threatening medical and psychological side effects: chest congestion (65 percent), chronic cough (40 percent), brain seizures with a loss of consciousness (7 percent), severe depression (85 percent), loss of sexual desire (58 percent), memory lapses (40 percent), violent behavior (31 percent), and suicide attempts (18 percent).

Many cocaine users claim they had some control while using cocaine, but no control while using crack. Clinical reports indicate the addictive potential of this new form of the drug is probably the most addictive we ever have faced. Some users report the intensity of the high as stronger than injecting cocaine. Indeed, it takes crack less time to get to the brain than injected cocaine.

### Frequency of Reported Use

Data collected by the National Institute of Justice on ninety-seven crack users (*NIJ Reports*, November/December 1989:7) indicates that use is limited by finances, although 30.9 percent used one to five rocks per week, 34 percent used six to twenty rocks per week; 15.4 percent used twenty-one to forty rocks per week; 12.3 percent used forty-one to eighty rocks per week; 5.1 percent used eighty-one to one hundred rocks per week; and 2.1 percent used more than one hundred rocks per week. It also was reported that 66 percent of users purchased their crack in crack or dope houses; 13.4 percent smoked shared crack given to them by associates; 9.3 percent bought off the street; and another 9.3 percent bought from user-sellers.

An eight ball (one-eighth of an ounce) is equivalent to 2.5 to 3.5 grams of cocaine and yields about forty-five to fifty-five rocks. It is believed that rock cocaine sometimes is cut with B12, benzoyl, and other fillers like powdered plastics. These either don't separate from cocaine as easily during the cooking process or they cause a swelling in the rock. The common notion that amphetamines are used as cuts has not been supported by the NIJ study.

### Slang Terms

Research into the most common names for crack (NIJ Reports, November/December 1989:9) in order of frequency are: "rock," "rox," "boulder," "yeaho," "stone," "roxanne," "eight ball," "dime," "caine," and "bump."

Crushed crack that is spread on tobacco and smoked is called "Fifty-one" or "one-fifty-one" in some parts of the country. Crack sprinkled into marijuana is called "thirty-eight." Processing methods might account for the street names "ether based," "synthetic," and "chemical." Brand names listed in the NIJ publication include "eye-opener," "swell up," "speed," "pony," "eastside player," and "wrecking crew." Other brand names include "fish scales" and "devil's dandruff." The combination of cocaine base and PCP has been called "space-basing."

### Summary

Cocaine hydrochloride is to crack as beer is to grain alcohol. Crack is a highly addictive form of this drug and even has caused long-term cocaine users who have claimed to have some degree of control when sniffing to become hopelessly addicted when they turn to the pipe. Sadly, many of the users are young, and the social, emotional, and psychological changes incurred by crack use will be long-standing. The addictive probability is not matched by any other drug seen to date. Unlike most other drugs, crack can be addictive instantly for some people, producing sensations in the user that produce an overwhelming desire to use the drug repeatedly.

## REFERENCE

Gold, Mark S. 1984. *800-COCAINE.* New York: Bantam Books.

# IX.
# TOBACCO

## HISTORY

Tobacco is the one widely used drug unique to North America, although its use began to spread all around the world approximately 500 years ago. Columbus and other European explorers of his time were amazed to see Native Americans "drink smoke" from rolls of dried leaves set on fire. Other natives burned the same leaves in pipes in order to "drink" the smoke. Natives who agreed to travel to Europe brought their tobacco with them, and sailors on the ships tried this curious smoke and found that they liked it. Nicotine, the active ingredient in tobacco, could be used as a mild stimulant, but it also had the contradictory effect of acting as a tranquilizer. The sailors also learned another fact about tobacco: that after they had smoked for a while, they had to continue smoking several times a day or experience a miserable craving that only tobacco could satisfy.

What might surprise today's cigarette smokers is that tobacco use often had religious meaning to Native Americans. They used tobacco that contained much more nicotine than cigarette tobacco and would smoke to the point of intoxication. This was believed to be a way to communicate with the spirit world.

Tobacco did not have to be smoked to produce its stimulant or tranquilizing properties; it also could be chewed and could be snorted intranasally in the form of snuff. However, it was found to be addicting in every form. Because of the steady demand for tobacco, it was quite valuable in times of short supply. In England during the 1600s, tobacco could be exchanged for an equal weight of silver. Because of its addictive nature and its high prices, many a rich estate was drained to support this habit. At about the same time, tobacco was a major commodity to be exchanged for African slaves. The price was set at about 500 pounds of tobacco for a slave taken by other Africans during raids of enemy tribes.

Because of its addictive qualities, attempts have been made over the years to limit or prohibit its use. For example, the Sultan of Turkey in 1633 decreed the death penalty for those caught smoking tobacco. Even though many smokers were executed, the habit persisted. About the same time, the Russian czar ordered whipping or slitting of the nostrils as punishments for smoking; again, the demand for tobacco didn't end. The steady demand has remained true in every nation in which the tobacco habit was started. Tobacco farming was a major economic factor in the growth of early America, and even to this day America exports tobacco around the world.

In earlier days, most tobacco was smoked in cigars and pipes, inhaled as snuff, or chewed. The cigarette was not unknown but commonly wasn't used until this century. The explosive rise in cigarette consumption was due to three major factors.

One was the public condemnation of chewing tobacco and the related juice-spitting. Spitting was blamed for spreading tuberculosis. The development of milder tobacco that could be inhaled deeper without as much coughing and the invention of machines to mass-produce cigarettes were the other factors. American cigarettes became popular around the world partly due to widespread distribution during two world wars.

The tobacco industry is a major economic force. The production level of cigarettes in 1970 was 583 billion, which suggests a daily per-capita consumption of eleven cigarettes for each American adult. The percentage of Americans who smoke has dropped over the last thirty years, but it remains a significant portion of the population. In 1955, some 54 percent of men smoked, and about 24 percent of women smoked. By 1965, nearly 30 percent of women had taken up this habit, while the percentage of male smokers changed very little. About that time, the U.S. Surgeon General publicized the dangers of tobacco smoking, and the percentage of American smokers steadily has dropped. It appears that health education and the change in public acceptance have been the primary reasons for the decline in use for this legal drug. Today, approximately 30 percent of men and 24 percent of women smoke. Others use snuff or chew tobacco. Many of these individuals wish they could stop, but find it very difficult.

### Laws Regarding Tobacco

Tobacco has been a major agricultural product since the early years of America and as such has enjoyed favorable treatment under the law. Tobacco was a major crop during the early settlement of America, and its growth was encouraged in most of the original colonies. To this day, U.S. government programs ensure economic stability for tobacco growers. Tobacco products are taxed heavily, which is a source of revenue. Tobacco is also a major export to other countries. In these ways, the tobacco industry benefits our nation.

However, recent medical research indicates that the costs to society outweigh the benefits. The costs of individual addiction and health problems have motivated laws banning the sale of tobacco products. By 1921, the year after alcohol prohibition, fourteen states prohibited cigarettes. However, as people continued to smoke, this prohibition proved too difficult to enforce, and in 1927 the last statewide cigarette prohibition law was repealed.

Almost all the states now forbid tobacco sales to minors, but studies have shown that most smokers pick up the habit in their early teenage years. In fact, 60 percent of smokers had begun smoking by the age of fourteen. An antismoking organization traveled to retail stores across the country and found that some 70 percent of the stores sold cigarettes to youths under the age of fourteen. This lax enforcement is one reason behind teenage smoking. The reasons teenagers smoke are complex and include peer pressure, a desire to have adult status, and responding to cigarette company advertising.

Since 1966, each cigarette package has displayed a mandatory health warning. In 1970, tobacco companies were forbidden by law to advertise on television and radio.

This ban has had little effect on the percentage of smokers, however, although it might have countered the percentage of potential increase that might have occurred if the ban hadn't existed. It should be noted that tobacco products continue to be advertised on billboards and in magazines, newspapers, and sports-related materials. Most of this advertising is youth-oriented and uses attractive, athletic models with white teeth to sell the products. This picture is deceptive, of course, as tobacco use leads to shortness of breath, a smoky smell that often repels others, and stained teeth.

In a 1978 report issued by the office of the Surgeon General, cigarettes were blamed for 325,000 premature deaths per year. The same year, 54 million Americans smoked 615 billion cigarettes. In 1988, the Surgeon General stated that nicotine, like heroin and cocaine, is addicting. The most recent (1989) statistics released by the Surgeon General blame tobacco for 395,000 deaths each year. However, tobacco companies continue to enjoy an unusual freedom from product liability claims; some 200 lawsuits have been resolved in favor of tobacco companies who have claimed that no conclusive evidence exists that cancer is caused by cigarette smoking. However, anyone who started smoking after 1966 when the warning labels were added to cigarette packages has less of a legal standing, as he or she has accepted known risks.

The greatest change in legal status occurred in recent years with the advent of laws prohibiting smoking in areas in which other people might be subject to secondhand smoke. Many public and large private establishments have been divided into smoking and nonsmoking areas. Recent legislation prohibits smoking on shorter airplane flights. Nonsmokers have demanded the right to breath clean air, and this appears to be the trend. A new form of nicotine—in chewing gum—meets the needs of users and of those who don't want to be affected by smoke. However, this gum presently is available only by prescription and contains such high doses of nicotine that smokers get dizzy after chewing it for a short time. It is reasonable that a lower dose nicotine gum will become legally available without a prescription and used by those who desire nicotine but who don't wish to offend others. Legal nicotine gum also would reduce some of the medical problems associated with tobacco.

It could be claimed that a major contradiction in antidrug laws is that tobacco, which kills 100 times the number as illegal drugs, is tolerated.

## PHYSICAL EFFECTS

The active ingredient in tobacco is nicotine. It is poisonous in a high enough dose and can be used as an natural insecticide. Organic farmers often mix ground tobacco leaves in water, then spray the water (containing nicotine) on plants they wish to protect. In the wild, nicotine helps the tobacco plant ward off the attacks of many insects. In fact, it is believed that most of the psychoactive chemicals found in plants are natural protectors for the plants.

Nicotine is a stimulating alkaloid with addicting properties related in some ways to cocaine; like cocaine, nicotine is classified as a stimulant. Tobacco users tend over time to increase their dose of nicotine to an "optimal" level. If they switch to low-nicotine cigarettes, they will smoke more to obtain the same dose. For a novice smoker or for the experienced smoker who takes an unusually high dose, the effects include lightheadedness, dizziness, and some nausea. But the desired effect—mild euphoric stimulus—also is present.

The effect of tobacco in the mouth is an increase of saliva, especially if the tobacco is in the chewable form. Smoked tobacco paralyzes lung cilia, the tiny hairs that clean out the lungs. This prevents the cilia from removing tars and other pollutants from the lungs. Paralyzing the cilia is dangerous, as a one-pack-a-day smoker breathes in one quart of tar each year. During sleep when no smoking occurs, the cilia can be active and push tars and other material toward the throat. This is why smokers tend to cough in the morning—and don't cough as much later in the day unless they exercise.

The senses of smell and taste are dulled in smokers. When people stop smoking, they often find that they eat more. This partly can be attributed to nervous eating, but it also is because the food tastes better than it did when the person was a smoker.

Because the small blood vessels are constricted, nicotine affects the cardiovascular system by increasing the heart rate and blood pressure. Circulation to the extremities in smokers tends to be impaired, and skin temperature is lower due to less blood flow. Because of less blood flow to the skin, smokers seem to develop more wrinkles than nonsmokers.

One organ affected by blood pressure problems is the penis. Nine out of ten men who complain of failure to achieve or maintain an erection are smokers and often find they can perform better sexually after they have quit smoking. The constriction of blood vessels increases the risk of heart attack as the blood supply to the heart muscles also is constricted. The increase in blood pressure doubles or triples the risk of stroke—clogging the blood supply to parts of the brain—and the risk of brain hemorrhage, in which blood vessels burst within the brain.

Respiratory diseases such as pneumonia and chest colds—probably due to impaired cilia—are more common among smokers. Chronic bronchitis is a cough and shortness of breath due to irritated and swollen air passages. Emphysema involves scar tissue that takes the place of healthy lung cells in the air sacs called alveoli. This scar tissue cannot expand and contract like healthy lung cells, so breathing is difficult. Bronchitis is reversible but emphysema is not, and it can lead to disability and even death.

Cancers of the mouth, throat, and esophagus most often are caused by a constant irritant such as smoke. Cancers of the kidney, pancreas, and bladder also are related to smoking. Lung cancer is fatal in nearly all cases.

Pregnant women who smoke or chew tobacco endanger their fetuses. They suffer a higher rate of miscarriage, stillbirth, and premature birth. Their babies have lower birth weights. Because nicotine constricts blood vessels, the lessened blood flow could cause problems during fetal development. Fetal development also is affected by the carbon monoxide inhaled by the mother. Carbon monoxide is a poison that prevents red blood cells from normally carrying oxygen. In large doses, carbon monoxide can cause death; at lower doses, it can kill sensitive brain cells.

## SOCIAL CONSEQUENCES

In addition to medical health hazards, cigarette-caused fires are another major problem. In 1984, cigarette-caused fires killed 1,570 people and seriously injured another 7,000. Cigarettes cause about one-third of residential fires. It is noteworthy that alcohol also is involved in about half of these fires as falling asleep with a lit cigarette is the usual cause.

Many smokers began their habit in order to appear "cool" or socially acceptable or perhaps to appear grown-up and mature. However, in society today, smoking often is considered unattractive. The clothing and furniture of smokers tends to be scarred with burn holes and to smell of smoke. The smell of smoke often bothers others and causes arguments when smokers don't respect nonsmokers' rights to clean air. Worse, a person who might have been interested sexually can be turned off by yellow, stained teeth and the breath of a smoker. It has been said that kissing a smoker is like licking a dirty ashtray.

## ADDICTIVE POTENTIAL

Although nicotine produces a brief euphoric stimulation, this effect is fairly mild. The addiction potential is not attributed to the pleasure factor as much as to avoid withdrawal effects. Withdrawal effects include irritability, cravings to smoke, increased number of awakenings during sleep, increased eating, decreased heart rate, and increased confusion. Studies of mental abilities during withdrawal show that response speed consistently worsened within the first twenty-four hours of tobacco deprivation and improved slightly over the next nine days, but it did not return to normal speed during this time. After the subjects resumed smoking, response speed returned to normal levels. The cravings and mental disturbances during withdrawal can last for weeks, even for months. A number of men who have quit both heroin and tobacco have said that tobacco was more difficult an addiction to end as the withdrawal symptoms last much longer.

Another element of the addiction relates to the behavior of smoking. The habitual behaviors such as lighting up, taking a "drag," holding a cigarette, and blowing smoke all serve to combat boredom and to reduce tension. Ending these habits and substituting other activities is part of the problem that smokers must solve when quitting.

## QUITTING

Quitting the tobacco habit is not easy. Some people apparently just make up their minds to stop, do so, and they never have a problem. However, most smokers do have problems quitting, and even if they do stop smoking for long periods, experience cravings for months or even years. These cravings occur especially after eating, when the quitters are around others who smoke, or in times of boredom or stress. In general, the first two weeks are the hardest. If someone can abstain that long, then he or she can stay clean for good. The cravings then seem to decrease if the person turns his or her attention to other concerns.

As with quitting other drug habits, success in quitting smoking involves motivation, confidence, coping skills, and social support. A number of aids and programs have been found useful by many ex-smokers. Some ways to do it yourself include setting a target date and building up your confidence that you can quit at that time. When that date arrives, throw away all your cigarettes and matches to make it harder to restart. Quitting along with a friend often is helpful, as pride becomes a motivator. Take up an exercise such as jogging or lifting weights. This will make you feel better and will help your lungs clean out faster.

Don't expect too much at once. Estimate how much money you will save, and after a length of time use some of that money to buy yourself a treat for good behavior. Think of smoke as disgusting and something to avoid. Make a list of reasons to quit: health, increased energy, money, increased attractiveness, setting a good example, and feeling pride in proving your inner strength. If you start to slip, look at your list for support.

Quitting cold turkey has worked for many people. In fact, this is the method recommended by the American Cancer Society. Other smokers find that cutting down first before quitting helps. Cutting down can be done by smoking only half of a cigarette, changing brands, using a filter, inhaling less, setting a daily quota, or stretching the periods between cigarettes. Many have found that by cutting back to half a pack a day for at least two weeks, they see two positive results. One is that saying "no" to oneself becomes a habit. The second is that withdrawal symptoms from half a pack will be less severe than from higher doses.

Other hints include placing a rubber band around your pack as a reminder that you plan to quit or placing your pack in a place that is more difficult to reach. Some people find that smoking by using the other hand helps break the habit, as movements are more conscious and less habitual. Another way to make smoking more conscious is to keep a log of each time you light up and what you are doing at the time.

Because the tobacco habit is linked more strongly with habitual behaviors rather than a physical addiction to nicotine, people must substitute other activities for smoking. Suggestions include chewing on toothpicks or sugarless gum, drawing pictures, drinking water when a craving occurs, exercising regularly, starting new hobbies, and even drumming or twiddling with one's fingers.

Many of those who quit do slip and start smoking again. If this happens, don't feel like a failure. Nicotine is a powerful addiction. Learn from your slip and resolve to quit again. But be careful not to let the slip turn into full-time smoking. Believe that you can succeed.

# REFERENCES

*Drug abuse and drug abuse research.* 1986. The second triennial report to Congress from the Secretary. Washington, D.C.: United States Department of Health and Human Services.

*How to stop smoking.* South Deerfield, Mass.: Channing L. Bete, Inc.

National Institute on Drug Abuse Research. 1979. *The behavioral aspects of smoking.* Monograph no. 26. Washington, D.C.: United States Department of Health, Education and Welfare.

*Stop teenage addiction of tobacco.* Palo Alto, Calif.: Tobacco and Youth Reporter.

# X.
# HALLUCINOGENS

Hallucinogens are psychoactive substances that can produce perceptual distortions when taken at effective dosage levels. These drugs primarily cause changes in body awareness and visual distortions, such as changes in color and size perception. They also can cause visual hallucinations—users imagine they see things that aren't really there. Hallucinogens have been called psychedelic (mind-expanding), psychotomimetic (psychosis-imitating), illusionogenic (illusion-producing), and psychodysleptic (mind-disrupting).

A number of chemicals are in this drug class, including LSD ("acid"), psilocybin ("magic mushrooms"), mescaline ("peyote"), PCP ("angel dust"), and a variety of chemicals known by abbreviations, including MDA, MDMA, DOM, TMA, DPT, DET, and DMT. Hallucinogens can be further classified into three groups of drugs with similar effects: The first group includes LSD, psilocybin, bufotenine, DET, and DMT. These drugs all appear to disrupt the functioning of the serotonin brain system, which filters sensation and thought awareness. Without this filtering, sequential step-by-step thought processes are overwhelmed by normally unconscious sensations and images.

The second group are the hallucinogenic amphetamines and include drugs such as mescaline, MDMA, MDA, DOM, and TMA that add the stimulating effects of amphetamine to the hallucinogen effect. In the third category is PCP, an anesthetic that disrupts information processing and causes both numbness and confusion. Of the hallucinogens, it is the most dangerous, because users are more unpredictable and can become violent without feeling pain.

Cannabis preparations such as marijuana, hashish, and hash oil all contain THC, which acts as a tranquilizer as well as a hallucinogen. Cannabis products are classified as hallucinogenic but are discussed in a separate chapter.

## LSD

LSD is the abbreviation for the chemical term d-Lysergic Acid Diethylamide. LSD has numerous street names, including acid, microdot, orange sunshine, purple haze, and windowpane, and it has been sold as mescaline and peyote.

### History

During the Middle Ages, ergot, a fungus that grows on rye, sometimes was baked in bread. A chemical produced by this fungus called ergotamine resulted in agonizing burning sensations, confusion, convulsions, miscarriages, and blood circulation problems that resulted in hand and foot gangrene. Many victims sought refuge at the shrine of St. Anthony at which they recovered largely because of their ergotamine-free diet. Ergotism became known as "St. Anthony's Fire." Throughout history, accidental ingestion has caused this type of poisoning. In 1926, 11,000 Russians died after accidentally overdosing on ergotamine.

LSD is a chemical made from ergotamine. LSD itself has not been proved to cause any tissue damage, and no human death has been caused directly by overdose. However, because ergotamine is a chemical precursor of LSD, a possibility exists that poor chemical processing could introduce ergotamine as a contaminant. The Food and Drug Administration doesn't regulate the purity of illegal drugs.

LSD first was derived from ergotamine in 1938 in Switzerland by Sandoz Laboratories. However, the hallucinogenic property of the drug was not recognized until 1943, when a chemist named Albert Hoffman accidentally took an LSD "trip" after the substance accidentally was rubbed onto his skin. He reported that for about two hours he experienced a stream of fantastic images and a kaleidoscope-like display of colors. Three days later he took a larger dose that he still considered very small, but which we now know was unusually large. For some six hours, Hoffman experienced colored patterns, perceptual distortions of vision and time, feeling of being out of his body, and fears of going crazy.

Because this drug produced visual hallucinations, it was investigated as a possible way to mimic and learn about mental illness. A great deal of LSD research occurred from the 1950s until 1966. It did not prove beneficial to schizophrenics and had mixed results for others. In fact, the conditions of paranoid schizophrenics who were administered LSD worsened. A consistent finding in research was that the setting or situation is very important, because people under the influence of LSD are very suggestible. Some patients reported new insights and increased creativity and said they became aware of beauty they formally had ignored. Others called the experience frightening and said they would never again take the drug. LSD has been used with mixed clinical findings to treat chronic alcoholics and heroin addicts.

A 1960 study of LSD and mescaline in some 25,000 doctor-supervised sessions found an attempted suicide rate of one in 2,500. The incidence in which psychotic reactions lasted more than two days was one in 1,500. The rate among mental patients was somewhat higher: one in 830 attempted suicide and one in 550 experienced prolonged psychotic states. A 1969 study of some 50,000 professionally supervised LSD sessions found a suicide rate of one out of 2,150. In a less-controlled situation, a higher rate of these problems can be expected due to illegality. But general research suggests that LSD-produced psychotic or suicidal reactions occur less frequently than when they are produced by PCP. However, because suggestibility is such an important factor with hallucinogens, more suggestible people probably suffer greater-than-average risks of psychotic reactions or suicidal behavior.

Much of the early nonscientific experimentation with LSD was among movie stars and other prominent people in California. It came to national attention in 1957 when *Life* magazine praised the drug as part of its "great adventure" series. Other *Life* articles in the early sixties included a piece on LSD as a new antiaggression drug and an article on LSD-influenced art.

During the 1960s, Harvard professor Timothy Leary experimented with LSD and psilocybin and became excited about their potential for therapeutic change. He actively promoted the uncontrolled use of these drugs and advocated a "Tune in, turn on, and drop out" philosophy. He was a political radical, promoting LSD trips by the millions as a way to change American society. The drug generally was viewed by society as unpredictable, although many people took the drug to express defiance against authority, for "personal growth," or simply for experimentation. The U.S. Army and the CIA also experimented with the drug during this period for possible use as a confusing agent for interrogation and for war.

As LSD and related drugs became more popular, fears of uncontrolled use and unpredictability also grew. A state of near panic arose, and in 1966 most hallucinogens were classified illegal. Use declined during the seventies. LSD seems again to be returning to popularity in some parts of the country and might be sold as mescaline, peyote, or THC. Survey estimates of the number of American youths who have tried hallucinogenic drugs shows a decline from 5 percent in 1982 to 3 percent in 1985. The American experience with hallucinogens appears to have been largely by whites (13 percent), with fewer Hispanics (6 percent) and blacks (3 percent). The usual pattern of use is to experiment and then leave it alone.

### Origin, Composition, Production, and Forms

LSD is odorless, colorless, and tasteless. A related but far less powerful chemical, lysergic acid amide, is found in morning glory seeds. However, this related chemical has far less visual potency than LSD but still produces unpleasant nausea, and thus rarely is used. LSD can be derived from ergot, but most of it is synthesized from other laboratory chemicals.

LSD is so potent that an extremely small quantity can be placed on sugar cubes, blotter paper, or small tablets, which then can be swallowed. A minimal effective dose is 60 micrograms (60 millionths of a gram). Two common forms of LSD are "microdots"—dried drops of LSD on paper and "windowpanes"—small squares of gelatin.

Although it is very powerful drug, threats about contaminating a city water supply are unfounded as the chemical easily is destroyed by the chlorine used in the water as a disinfectant.

### Dosage and Pathway

LSD normally is taken orally. A normal dosage of LSD is 50 to 150 micrograms, equivalent to 100,000 to 300,000 doses to the ounce. This is a very small quantity and consequently, LSD is considered the most potent drug known. Only one out of each 10,000 molecules actually enters the brain, a fact that serves to further illustrate the potency of this drug. Most LSD is metabolized by the liver and finally is excreted in the feces within three days. The drug readily passes the placental barrier in pregnant women.

The effects of an oral dose peak within two to three hours but will continue for at least six hours. Usually, all effects are over after twelve hours, and a person then can sleep. Higher doses increase the intensity of the effects rather than the length of time affected.

Tolerance develops rapidly to LSD, although no physical dependence or withdrawal symptoms develop. It is rare for users to take daily doses, because tolerance to further doses lasts at least three days and up to one week. During this time, dosage must be increased greatly to produce equivalent effects. Even with very large doses, the effects might be no stronger than as if the user had taken marijuana. The majority of users take LSD monthly or weekly at the most.

## Effective Dose to Lethal Dose Ratio

Experiments using mice determined that half of the mice die when given a dose of LSD equivalent to fifty to sixty micrograms per kilogram of body weight. This is equivalent to a dose of 35,000 to 42,000 micrograms for a seventy-kilogram man. Another study estimates a human lethal dose at about 14,000 micrograms. These doses are hundreds of times greater than the usual dose. So far, no human death has been attributed to the direct effects of LSD poisoning, although irrational behavior has taken its toll.

## Factors That Can Influence Potency

As with any drug, the setting, purity, dose, expectations, mood, cultural factors, and personality factors such as intelligence, suggestibility, and imagination all play a role in the reaction to the drug. A person's behavior while under the influence of the drug can be somewhat unpredictable as anything that happens can affect his or her emotional reaction.

## Physical Effects

LSD disables the perceptual filtering system, which appears to be the major effect. This filtering system, which uses the neurotransmitter serotonin, reduces awareness of unimportant thoughts and perceptions. Serotonin is necessary for sleep, when almost all awareness is filtered out. Serotonin also is a necessary component while people are awake, because it shifts attention by ignoring less important perceptions and allows relaxation. This filtering system also is involved with habituation to new stimuli—that is, ignoring most of what we are accustomed to. Without the filtering system acting as a "brake," people are more aware of thoughts and feelings. It could be said that those under the influence of LSD, like those suffering from schizophrenia, are less in control of what they can ignore. By disabling the natural "braking system," LSD stimulates the central nervous system.

After ingesting LSD, the user's pupils will dilate, he or she is unable to sleep, and might salivate more. The eyes might water more, and the person can feel chilled although usually a slight rise in body temperature occurs. Increases in heart rate and blood pressure might occur, and the user usually experiences a loss of appetite. Several of these effects also commonly are experienced with stimulants.

Some bothersome effects of the drug might be mild nausea, chills, trembling, blurred vision, and ringing in the ears. Dizziness, distraction from pain, increased dreaming, and tingling sensations also might be felt. What frightens people the most is the feeling of being unable to control the experience.

Studies of electrical brain activity show a shift in activity from the left to the right hemispheres. The left side of the brain generally acts in a logical step-by-step manner and controls the activity of the right hemisphere, which thinks in images and generalities. Most people have developed one area of the left hemisphere that dominates and controls the rest of the brain, but LSD disrupts that normal control. The result is a great increase of conscious awareness but also less ability to stick to a task.

## Psychological Effects

The general psychological effects include increased awareness, distorted perception, increased emotional sensitivity, distorted judgment, and effects on behavior. Users have been known to hurt or even kill themselves because of faulty beliefs, and the occurrence of flashbacks (memories of drug perceptions) has been reported within several months after use. While LSD does not appear to directly create moods such as euphoria or sadness, people tend to exaggerate their emotional reactions while under the influence of this drug.

## Effects on Perception

Several distortions of time and sensation occur. Sometimes everything seems to be alive. Time often becomes irrelevant or seems to slow down. A person might believe that barriers have dissolved and that he or she is connected in some way to things outside. Sensations, including those surrounding one's own body, might intensify and seem strange or new. Ordinary elements might seem novel and beautiful as if the user is seeing them for the first time. Visual afterimages, more intense colors, and patterns all might appear. Actual hallucinations or "visions" also occur—especially if the eyes are closed—although the person remains aware that these visions are drug-induced. Synesthesia, in which different senses are mixed and the user sees colors in response to sounds, has been reported. Generally, conscious awareness greatly is increased, but the ability to logically deal with this rush of perception is decreased.

Surprisingly, LSD, which generally increases awareness, has been found to provide longer pain relief than morphine to victims of advanced cancer. Pain relief might last for weeks. This probably is explained in terms of expanded awareness: Cancer patients under the influence of LSD are still aware of their pain but also are aware of much more than the pain on which they previously focused and can learn to keep their focus on other elements.

### Effects on Emotion

General sensitivity to emotions becomes apparent. Emotional suggestibility is a drawback, for it is as if a person's emotional defenses are gone, leaving him or her open. Euphoria, detachment, mystical feelings, paranoia, and panic all increase. "Bad trips" reportedly occur at least once by one-quarter to one-half of all users. Users sometimes fear they are out of control or are going insane.

### Effects on Thinking

Large doses of hallucinogens result in significant impairment of attention, concentration, short-term memory, judgment, problem solving, and eye-hand coordination.

A user might feel separated from or a stranger to himself or herself. One's identity sometimes seems to blend with the surroundings. Users might believe they are being reborn or are remembering other significant past events. Religious experiences are reported by 25 to 95 percent of initial users, depending on the setting.

Bringing previously unconscious thoughts and emotions to conscious awareness potentially is helpful in psychotherapy. However, due to its illegal status, this drug no longer is used by psychiatrists.

### Effects on Behavior

The usual behavior of a person under the influence of LSD is to quietly indulge in sensations. Isolated incidents of violence such as murder or assault are rare. However, incidents of self-injury do occur and usually result from a faulty belief in personal superhuman power. In one instance, a student under the influence drilled a hole in his head; in another case, a woman set herself on fire. A number of people have jumped to their deaths from windows reportedly due to a delusion that they could fly. LSD is dangerous for people who are paranoid or at risk for psychosis, as it can trigger a psychotic episode. While LSD use is reasonably safe when professionally supervised, bizarre behavior is possible and can lead to physical harm if the drug is used unsupervised.

### Long-term Effects

The brain quickly develops a tolerance to LSD. More and more of the drug is needed to produce the same level of effect, and little happens when LSD is taken after a previous dose. Cross-tolerance also develops to other hallucinogens. Physical addiction or withdrawal symptoms have not been demonstrated, and tissue or genetic damage has not been found. However, psychological dependence might occur in people if they believe they need a drug to see beauty or to be happy.

Several negative long-term effects can occur. Increased suggestibility, paranoia, unusual beliefs, confusion, flashbacks, and risk of psychosis are potential dangers. Studies of psychological functioning among users have so far shown no signs of brain damage, but long-lasting emotional scars have been reported by former users.

Flashbacks are rare, usually mild and short-lasting, more frequent under stress and fatigue, and very rarely occur more than four months after LSD use. The exact mechanics of flashbacks are not understood. Some people believe flashbacks are due to drug storage in the brain, while others believe the drug brings out borderline mental illness. The most common explanation is that flashbacks simply are memories of drug experiences.

## PSILOCYBIN OR PSILOCIN

### History

The "magic mushroom" has been part of mystical religious ceremonies for thousands of years. When Spanish conquistadors came to Mexico and Central America, they found natives practicing an ancient religion that included using psilocybin mushrooms to obtain visions. A different mushroom was used for similar purposes by Siberian tribesmen in Asia and is praised in a Hindu religious book written nearly 4,000 years ago. Psilocin and psilocybin first were isolated by Sandoz Laboratories by the same chemist who first isolated LSD. Dr. Albert Hoffman isolated psilocybin from mushrooms in the late 1950s. It was studied along with LSD and mescaline as a psychiatric drug. It was promoted by Timothy Leary and others as a drug for the masses and, like LSD, was outlawed in 1966 due to fears about uncontrolled use.

### Origin and Composition

Psilocybin has been found in ninety different kinds of mushrooms. However, approximately 5,000 species of mushrooms exist, and it's dangerously possible to confuse psilocybin with poisonous species. Psilocybin and the chemically similar psilocin usually are found in the same variety of mushrooms. A chemical copy can be synthesized in the laboratory.

### Dosage and Pathway

The typical dosage is from one to four mushrooms or four to ten milligrams of the drug. The effects are felt after thirty minutes and peak about ninety minutes after ingestion, although the effects last for around six hours. The drug is powerful, but it generally is considered less potent than LSD. Most of the drug exits the body after eight hours, although traces can be detected after a week has passed.

### Effective Dose to Lethal Dose Ratio

Experiments conducted on mice have found that half of them are killed at a dose of 280 milligrams of psilocybin per kilogram body weight. This is equivalent to a dose of 19,600 milligrams for a seventy-kilogram man—a measure thousands of times greater than an effective dose. No human deaths have been attributed to psilocybin. However, many people have died from the poison found in other mushrooms; therefore, eating a mushroom without consulting an expert is foolish. Also, one variety of psilocybin mushroom that also contains a poison was responsible for the death of a six-year-old boy.

### Physical Effects

As with most drugs, the context of use is important. For hallucinogens and specifically for psilocybin, the context of use is even more significant because of the role the increase in suggestibility plays.

Generally speaking, the same physical effects noted earlier with LSD also are apparent with psilocybin. Since the drug is not as potent, these effects are less intense. Smaller increases in blood pressure, heart rate, and pupil dilation are noted than with LSD. Because the trip is shorter, the user suffers less from exhaustion. Psilocybin resembles the body's natural serotonin, the neurotransmitter that is used by our perceptual-filtering system. This attention system temporarily is disabled under the influence of psilocybin.

Like LSD, the same bothersome feelings of nausea, chilliness, limb numbness, and trembling can occur.

### Psychological Effects

Perceptual distortions and colored visual hallucinations are the primary effect. Synesthesia (seeing sounds), euphoria, disorientation, anxiety, and even panic can occur.

### Long-term Effects

As with all hallucinogens, tolerance and cross-tolerance is evident along with the danger of psychological dependency. Physical addiction or the presence of withdrawal effects has not been documented. Psychosis can occur in those susceptible. As with LSD, long-term use can lead to paranoia or unusual beliefs.

## MESCALINE

### History

The tops of the small peyote cactus were the principle source of mescaline for Native Americans, who have used this drug during religious ceremonies. The drug has been used as early as 300 B.C. in Mexico and also used by tribes celebrating religious ceremonies in the southwestern regions of the United States. Even today, the Native American Church legally is permitted to use peyote during their religious practices. Nearly half of the U.S. Native American population belongs to this church.

Mescaline first was isolated from the peyote cactus in 1856. The drug legally could be used by anyone in America until 1966; it then was outlawed along with the other hallucinogens because of fears about its increasingly widespread use. Until then, peyote could be purchased through mail-order houses.

### Origin and Composition

Mescaline can be found in a few species of cacti, especially peyote. These cacti generally have few spines, so this chemical might be their defense against insects. The peyote cactus is the principle source of the drug, which can be expensive to manufacture and rarely is found on the street. Most drugs sold on the street as mescaline are either PCP or LSD, which can be more profitably manufactured.

### Dosage and Pathway

The drug normally is taken orally—users either chew the peyote buttons or ingest it as a powder in gelatin capsules. The typical dose is 200 to 600 milligrams, which lasts for four to eight hours. Most mescaline is excreted in pure form from the body.

### Effective Dose to Lethal Dose Ratio

Experiments on mice have determined that half of the mice are killed when administered a dose of 500 to 600 milligrams per kilogram of body weight. This is equivalent to a dose of 35,000 to 42,000 milligrams for a seventy-kilogram man. This is hundreds of times the usual dose. No human death has been attributed directly to mescaline poisoning.

### Effects

As with the other hallucinogens mentioned, the effects depend on the context of use. A fearful, paranoid person who does not know that this drug has been given to him or her might experience extreme panic while others expecting pleasant effects remain calm while under the influence. Generally speaking, mescaline is weaker in potency than psilocybin, which in turn is weaker than LSD. It has some amphetamine-like stimulating action in addition to its hallucinogenic effect.

### Physical Effects

Generally, the drug produces a physical reaction that is similar to the reaction noted previously for LSD and psilocybin. Increases in heart rate, blood pressure, temperature, and pupil dilation are evident. Nausea also can occur and reportedly is stronger than that which occurs with LSD. This nausea is much stronger when mescaline is taken in its natural form of peyote because of the other chemicals in the plant. Structurally, mescaline is similar to amphetamines although it isn't considered toxic even at higher doses. Mescaline apparently has a wider range of safety than the synthetics. The effects of the related synthetics of mescaline including STP (DOM), MDA, MDMA ("ecstasy"), and MMDA considerably are more toxic—nausea, tremors, and convulsions—at higher doses. Also called hallucinogenic amphetamines, these synthetics act like amphetamines at low doses and like hallucinogens at higher doses.

### Psychological Effects

Distortion of senses is evident along with excitation and nausea. At high doses, kaleidoscopic movement of colors, hallucinations within the five senses, time distortion, and ego doubling (thoughts of being out of the body) have been reported. Many have reported religious experiences, and Native Americans use mescaline to communicate with the spirit world. At lower doses, users often experience a feeling of well-being and increased positive feelings toward others.

### Long-term Effects

As tolerance develops toward mescaline, cross-tolerance develops toward other hallucinogens. The drug can produce psychological dependency in some people, although this is not common. Physical addiction or withdrawal symptoms are not evident. Overdose leading to death has not been documented in humans. Increased use is correlated with heightened passivity and psychosis in predisposed individuals.

## PCP

This unpredictable drug was developed as a surgical anesthetic but was found to have hallucinogenic, depressant, anesthetic, and stimulant properties dependent on dose and individual differences. The drug generally is considered a hallucinogen, although it is not similar in action to the other hallucinogens.

### Names

The technical name of PCP is "Phencyclidine" or 1-(1-phenylcyclohexyl) piperidine hydrochloride. Slang terms include "angel dust," "wack," "THC," "dust," "lovely," "loveboat," "rocket fuel," "John Hinckley," "butt naked," and "keys to St. E's."

### History

PCP was made in 1926 as a surgical analgesic and anesthetic for humans. The frightening side effects of the drug led to its withdrawal in 1965 from use for humans. PCP continued to be used with animals until 1978. Today it only is made in illicit laboratories that purchase controlled chemicals normally used to manufacture plastics.

The early illegal use of PCP occurred in the late sixties when it often was sold as "THC." It was tried experimentally by users of other hallucinogens, but it was rarely the drug of choice. However, because of its easy manufacture and low cost, it was more available than many more preferred drugs, and its popularity spread.

### Origin and Composition

Nearly ten chemicals are needed to make PCP, including two main precursors—piperidine and cyclohexanone. The manufacturing process is dangerous since ether is used, and many labs have blown up when someone simply lit a cigarette or flicked a light switch.

PCP can be made into a liquid, powder, or crystal and also can be found in capsule or tablet form. Normally, PCP is smoked in mint, parsley, oregano, marijuana, or tobacco cigarettes that are dipped in the liquid or laced with powder. The drug smells like a mixture of chlorine, ammonia, and fish oil, and some dealers have used insecticides or formaldehyde to produce a strong chemical odor to fool users.

### Dosage and Pathway

The typical dose is ten to 100 milligrams in a period of twenty-four hours. The drug usually is smoked, although it can be ingested or snorted. PCP usually stays active in the body for four to six hours and is stored in fat deposits. PCP can be found in the urine of users for several days.

### General Effects

The effects derived from PCP vary from user to user and from time to time. In most cases, the user feels a "numb" state with no pain, a mild euphoria, and the ability to ignore problems. Some have used this drug continuously for years with no apparent brain damage. Others have become psychotic or brain damaged after just a few experiences with the drug. Because the drug is manufactured illegally, the purity and composition might not be known to the user. Much of what is experienced is dose-related.

### Low Doses (5 milligrams)

PCP can have stimulant as well as depressant properties at low doses. Agitation and excitement, incoordination, blank stares, rigid muscles, loss of feeling in body parts, uncontrolled eye movement, inability to speak, profuse sweating, and oversensitive hearing might all be present. Hallucinations like "melting faces" or extremely vivid imaginations have been reported. Users have reported using their minds to imagine anything they desire. Increased strength, assaultive and bizarre behavior, and poor judgement also are evident, even at low doses. Incoordination and dizziness frequently are reported effects of the drug. Increased heart rate, pupil constriction, and a warm tingling sensation also are noted.

### Moderate Doses (10+ milligrams)

The anesthetic properties of the drug are more potent at moderate levels. The user might feel paralyzed but aware or might be in a short coma. The eyes might be open and exhibit rapid, uncontrolled eye movement. Vomiting, excessive salivation, shivering, flushing, sweating, paranoia, decreased sensation, grossly impaired judgment with repetitive movements, and psychotic-like behavior also might occur at moderate dose levels.

PCP users are feared by police, as police officers have witnessed gruesome crimes perpetrated by people under the influence of the drug; they also are leery of the possibility of people high on PCP becoming violent and showing unusual strength. When high on PCP, people feel no pain and while in a frenzy often harm themselves and others. Users reportedly have broken bones or been shot and not realized it.

### High Doses

At high doses, the drug potentially is lethal. Death can result from respiratory depression, pulmonary edema, or brain seizure activity. Convulsions, fever, paranoia, high blood pressure, and prolonged coma usually precede death, which can occur more frequently than previously thought. A near-death overdose might be followed by a recovery phase marked by confusion and delusions that last several weeks. In some cases, overdose leads to a psychosis lasting a few months. Most deaths from PCP, however, are caused as a result of poor judgment or by accidents that occur at low or moderate dose levels.

### Physical Effects

At high doses, coma, stupor, large elevations in blood pressure, seizure activity, violent convulsions, and possibly death results. Seizure activity is common, and users have a high risk of needing emergency medical care due to psychosis and agitation.

### Effective Dose to Lethal Dose Ratio

Toxicity studies have found that half of the test animals were killed at a dose of 179 milligrams/kilograms when administered orally and at a dose of 15.9 milligrams/kilograms when injected with the drug. Smoking probably is similar to the injection route due to rapid increase in blood levels. This means that approximately 1-1/3 grams of pure PCP will kill half of the seventy-kilogram men injecting or smoking this dose, an effective-to-lethal-dose ratio of one to ten. Because it can remain in the body's fat, a lesser dose can cause death after prolonged use.

### Psychological Effects

A PCP high can be a numbness that some people find satisfying. Some people find it confusing and frightening. The user might feel confused, depersonalized, time and body distortion, depressed, hear voices, see "monsters," or feel a floating sensation, relaxed, and calm. Impaired judgment and aggressive behavior is more likely. Several people under the influence have committed murder and apparently suffer amnesia regarding their crime. In Washington, D.C., a woman under the influence of PCP reportedly placed her baby in a freezer; in another incident, an elderly woman was brutally raped and murdered by assailants who were under the influence. Arrestees have reported fighting with police while feeling no pain, and one man reportedly threw his baby out a window, believing it was a devil.

### Behavioral Effects

Bizarre behavior frequently is reported. Running naked (hence the name "butt naked"), pulling out one's teeth, increased strength and decreased awareness of pain that results in torn muscles, car crashes, drowning, and similar accidents are more likely. Some users report increased sexual interest and aphrodisiac-like properties, but more often a numb withdrawal is the result. Others report they've stared at the same object for hours on end. Eventually, many users prefer to use the drug continuously and feel uncomfortable if not intoxicated.

### Long-term Effects

Using PCP results in an increased level of tolerance as well as psychological dependence. Physical addiction or withdrawal has not been demonstrated. Long-term use can result in brain damage in which retention and memory are affected and emotion is flat. "Rubberheads" and "burnouts" are two terms used to describe people who have been brain-damaged from PCP use. Psychosis also can result from extended or even short-term use. A certain percentage of PCP users need psychiatric hospitalization (hence the name "keys to St. E's"), which could be short-term or could be permanent. Flashbacks also commonly are reported even years after last use. These flashbacks can be as intense as the actual use of the drug itself but more often are of a lower intensity. Temper outbursts, confusion, laziness, speech problems, slowed reflexes, weight loss, depression, anxiety, and a general disorientation all are reported results of long-term use.

## SUMMARY

Hallucinogens encompass many different types of drugs that generally alter perception as well as mood. These drugs can be stimulant-like (LSD or mescaline) or sedative/depressant-like (PCP). Generally, high doses of these drugs would be needed for a lethal overdose. LSD has been associated with disturbed behavior, psychotic thinking, and flashbacks. Drugs such as "ecstasy," DOM, DET, and STP have mild hallucinogenic properties and act mainly as euphoric-type stimulants. Numbness and irrational aggressiveness commonly are associated with PCP use, while a disturbance in thinking also can occur primarily in memory. Because of the disruption of perception and the psychologically addictive aspects of these drugs, the young and suggestible particularly have been vulnerable.

## REFERENCES

Axton, J. E. 1985. *LSD and the marketplace: A report on street acid*. Phoenix: Do It Now Foundation.

Cohen, S. Lysergic acid diethylamide: Side effects and complications. *Journal of Nervous and Mental Diseases* 130:30-40

Dye, C. 1985. *Acid: LSD today*. Phoenix: Do It Now Foundation.

Dye, C. 1985. *Dusted: Facts about PCP*. Phoenix: Do It Now Foundation.

Grinspoon, L., and J. B. Bakalar. 1979. *Psychedelic drugs reconsidered*. New York: Basic Books.

Holbrook, J. M. 1983. Hallucinogens. In *Substance abuse: Pharmacologic, developmental, and clinical perspectives*, edited by G. Bennett, C. Vourakis, and D. S. Woolf. New York: Wiley.

Kuznik, F. 1985. PCP: A nightmare drug. *The Washingtonian* (January): 121-25.

McGlothlin, W., and D. Arnold. LSD revisited—A ten-year follow-up of medical LSD use. *Archives of General Psychiatry*: 35-49.

Peterson, R. C., and R. C. Stillman. 1978. *Phencyclidine: A review*. Washington, D.C.: National Institute on Drug Abuse.

# XI.
# CANNABIS (MARIJUANA)

Cannabis is better known in America as hemp when the fibers in its stem are used for rope. When used as a drug, it is usually called marijuana, the Spanish word for intoxicant. Marijuana refers to the leaves of the plant. Three varieties of cannabis are known: Cannabis Sativa is the most common, as it is used both as rope and for the psychoactive ingredient known as tetrahydrocannabinol, called THC for short. Cannabis Indica is lower in fiber but higher in THC content. A third variety, Cannabis Ruderalis, is rare outside of Siberia and is not considered good quality. Cannabis or marijuana has several slang names, including "grass," "weed," "pot," "reefer," "herb," "hemp," "tea," and "Mary Jane." It is known as "ganja" in India and as "dagga" in Africa.

## HISTORY

Cannabis has been used for rope, clothing, and paper and for medical, recreational, and religious purposes for thousands of years. It probably is native to central Asia, for archaeologists studying early humans have found seeds dated as far back as 8,500 years ago. The first recorded use of cannabis in medicine occurred in China around 2737 B.C. As early as 1000 B.C., cannabis was used in India as part of the Hindu religion as an aid in meditation. Its cultivation spread around the world during ancient times, especially in interest of uses as fiber. It was used for rope, clothing, in medicine, and recreationally by ancient Romans and Arabs, who were active traders. It is the most durable natural fiber for ropes on ships.

Ancient Chinese physicians had limited medicines and recommended cannabis as treatment for a variety of illnesses from constipation to rheumatism to asthma to absent-mindedness. Over the years it apparently has been used to treat depression, to increase appetite, as an external antiseptic (germ-killer), to help women with premenstrual syndrome, and as a mild analgesic (painkiller).

In colonial America, hemp was the second largest export and in 1762, farmers were fined for failing to grow it. Several of our first presidents even grew it, but probably for its fiber use. As early as 1630, almost all the early rope and half of all American clothes were made from hemp fiber. The wagons that pioneers used to migrate across America were covered with hemp cloth. Early work jeans were made of hemp. Cannabis extract became popular in medicines during the 1800s.

Marijuana became popular as a recreational drug during Prohibition. It was especially associated with jazz clubs and was seen as a vice of minority groups. By the 1930s, growing public concern led to the passage of the Marijuana Tax Act of 1937, designed to end its availability as a drug by requiring a stamp to allow possession. This act had the side effect of outlawing hemp production; historians suggest this was the hidden goal parlayed by members of the developing synthetic-fiber industry. The stamp act later was ruled unconstitutional because the legal mandate to pay a tax required that people incriminate themselves and was thus a violation of Fifth Amendment rights. However, other federal laws and most state laws render it a crime to possess or distribute cannabis products, including marijuana (the leaves), hashish (the resin), and the essential oil. Cannabis was removed from the list of approved medical drugs in 1941.

In 1951, the Boggs Act incorrectly labeled marijuana as a narcotic. Several state laws punished possession with lengthy prison sentences. From 1955 to 1973, a person convicted for marijuana possession in Texas could have received a prison sentence of two years to life. In Utah, Georgia, Illinois, and Missouri, it was possible to be handed a life sentence for a second-possession charge. It also was possible to receive the death penalty in Georgia and Missouri for selling marijuana to a minor. In some countries, laws are very harsh. In Malaysia, selling any illegal drug is a capital offense, and in Singapore, possession of marijuana is punishable by hanging. As might be imagined, these countries do not have a large drug problem.

Marijuana now is illegal in almost every state, although penalties have been reduced in most for personal possession. Using and possessing small amounts of marijuana is legal only in Alaska and is a misdemeanor offense punishable by a small fine in several other states. Some states consider marijuana possession a felony offense punishable by several years in prison.

The FBI keeps statistics on drug arrests, and the records show that marijuana is a significant problem. From 1981 through 1986, distribution arrests totaled 417,188, and arrests for possession totaled 2,067,088. This brings the total number of marijuana-related arrests to nearly two and one-half million in our country just during those six years. Over the twenty-four-year period from 1965 through 1989, the total number of arrests for marijuana exceeded eight million. Approximately 400,000 people are arrested each year for marijuana possession. This drug is the only one with a lobby group: the National Organization to Reform Marijuana Laws (NORML). Including marijuana possession as a criminal act is a political controversy, but it is clear that an arrest record can be detrimental to a person's future.

Federal law classifies marijuana and its extracts as a Schedule I drug with high abuse potential and no accepted medical use. Its only legal use is research. Promising research results have been obtained using the drug to treat nausea and lack of appetite resulting from chemotherapy used in treating cancer. No claim is made that THC or marijuana itself is an anticancer drug, but it might reduce the unpleasant side effects of the anticancer drugs. Because marijuana tends to lower the pressure inside the eye, THC and marijuana experimentally has been used to treat glaucoma, an eye disease that can cause blindness. When used in low doses, it potentially relieves anxiety, distracts from mild pain, relaxes muscles, relieves menstrual cramps, helps control epilepsy, and stimulates the appetite. However, marijuana has not been approved for regular medical use; the aforementioned remedies often are based more on anecdote than research.

It should be noted that modern medicine uses only the active and effective ingredients from plants, not the raw leaf or resin that contains a mixture of dozens of chemicals. All that is prescribable is THC, the major active ingredient. Its trade name is Marinol, and it is approved only for the relief of chemotherapy-associated nausea. More research will determine if it is effective for other uses and whether marijuana also is safe enough for medical use.

## STATISTICS AND FACTS ABOUT CURRENT USE

In 1977, forty-three million Americans admitted to using marijuana at least on one occasion. Sixteen million of these Americans were current users. By 1981, about fifty million Americans had tried marijuana. In 1982, a national survey of households was conducted by the National Institute on Drug Abuse (NIDA). Some 64 percent of young adults reported that they had tried marijuana or hashish that year; 21 percent said they'd used it twenty or more days in the previous month. More disturbing, 27 percent of teenagers reported using marijuana: 6 percent said they used it almost daily.

Teenage use is probably the most disturbing aspect of marijuana use. Heavy use during adolescence raises several medical concerns; it also raises concerns about teenagers developing drug-oriented lifestyles that can lead to more serious problems. Fortunately, education appears to be having some effect on the popularity of the drug, even though marijuana is increasingly available. An annual NIDA-sponsored University of Michigan survey begun in 1975 of high school seniors found that 40 percent of those surveyed admitted to monthly use. This percentage increased to 51 percent by 1979 but since then steadily has dropped. The 1988 survey found monthly use among high school seniors at the 33-percent level. Approximately 3 percent of seniors reported daily use of marijuana. The decline in use appears solely due to education, for in 1988 some 87 percent of seniors said that they easily could purchase marijuana. However, 69 percent said that they would not use it even if it were legal.

The 1988 NIDA survey found that among nineteen-to-thirty-year-olds, 31 percent admitted to using marijuana in the past year, and 18 percent admitted to using marijuana at least once in the past month. This is a small decrease from the 1982 survey, but still shows that some thirty-seven million Americans reported using an illicit drug, usually marijuana, during the past year. Of these, eighteen million admitted to using marijuana within the month. Some experts have questioned these statistics, because they believe many people deny drug use in such government surveys out of fear of consequences for admitting use. Although exact figures are not known, marijuana appears to be the fourth most popular recreational drug in America today with an estimated thirty to forty million users. Its popularity only is surpassed by tobacco, caffeine, and alcohol.

## ORIGIN AND DISTRIBUTION

Cannabis products widely are available in many parts of the world. In fact, in some countries the recreational and religious use of marijuana and hashish is legal while alcohol is illegal. Cannabis plant fiber (hemp) is used today to make rope, twine, textiles, and quality bible paper. Materials made from hemp endure better than other commercially available fibers because of the oily resin. No THC is present in the aforementioned products because only the hemp fibers are used; also the manufacturing process removes all the flowers and the outer-leaf layer in which the THC is found. Smoking a hemp rope will not get you high—it only will make you cough.

Most of the U.S. marijuana supply used to come from Mexico and South America, and most hashish came from the Middle East or southwest Asia. However, marijuana smuggling has been targeted in America's "War on Drugs," so the price has increased and the drug now is considered a more valuable commodity. Also, less marijuana has been smuggled in; it is less cost-effective than cocaine or heroin because its greater bulk is more difficult to conceal. Due to smaller imports and rising prices, U.S. growers account for an increasing portion of the American supply. A recent estimate holds that one-fourth of U.S.-consumed marijuana is produced domestically. In fact, it is the largest cash crop in some states. Marijuana is estimated to be a $33 billion crop in the U.S. Although eradication efforts prevent one-fourth to one-third of the illegal crop from reaching the market, it is the country's most valuable cash crop.

Cannabis Sativa plants can grow in tropical regions to eighteen feet in height in three to five months. This "weed" has been found growing wild in several regions of the United States, probably due to prior cultivation for hemp fiber. Cannabis Indica is shorter and has less fiber but a higher resin content. It is cultivated only for its leaves, flower buds, and resin, which are used for their psychoactive effect. The third variety, Ruderalis, is considered low quality. These are all in the same specie, and hybrids can be made between these three varieties.

A developing trend is to grow hybrid varieties indoors under artificial lights. Several companies sell lights, watering mechanisms, special soils, carbon dioxide equipment, and other devices to supply indoor growers. Law enforcement officials have traced the sale of such equipment and have caught a number of indoor growers. Using specialized infrared detection equipment, police can detect the heat generated in an indoor greenhouse; they can detect the smell as well. Citizen information also has led to the arrest of many illegal growers. Even with these law enforcement efforts, indoor growing is an increasing problem.

### Composition

Cannabis contains 421 different chemicals: sixty-one are unique to this plant and four have some psychoactive property. The main psychoactive ingredient in marijuana is THC or delta-9-tetrahydrocannabinol, which first was isolated in the 1960s. When smoked, some of these ingredients turn into carcinogens, and slightly more of these dangerous chemicals are present in marijuana smoke than in tobacco smoke.

Marijuana can contain as little as one-half of 1 percent THC or as high as 8 percent THC for a high-quality seedless variety called sinsemilla. In recent years, selective breeding has produced stronger strains. However, most of the increase in quality isn't due to genetics but is a result of protecting the female plants from pollination by male plants. Hashish usually contains from 5 percent to 20 percent THC. The oil extract from cannabis usually contains around 20 percent THC, but can contain up to 50 percent. This oil usually is extracted from marijuana using alcohol as a solvent. The most common form of usage is the marijuana cigarette, called a joint, which contains the dried leafy matter and weighs about one gram. The marijuana supplied by NIDA for research contains 2 percent THC. However, most of the marijuana illicitly available contains more than 5 percent THC; so the NIDA marijuana is considered by users to be poor quality.

## Dosage and Pathway

The typical marijuana cigarette contains about 20 milligrams of THC. Government-grown marijuana cigarettes contain 2 percent THC and weigh one gram. In general, only half of the THC actually goes into smoke—the rest is destroyed by burning. Even so, smoked marijuana has about three times the potency of marijuana that is ingested. The effects of smoked marijuana or hashish begin one to five minutes after use, peaking in thirty minutes and lasting two to three hours. The effects of ingested marijuana or hashish take longer to manifest and also last longer. It is more difficult to regulate the dose when the drug is eaten, and people commonly ingest more than the preferred dose. It also is possible to vaporize to oil by heating without combustion. Vaporizing would limit lung damage and eliminate the damage of carbon monoxide poisoning but rarely is practiced by users.

Since THC is a vegetable oil, the drug is fat soluble. Most of the THC is broken down or metabolized by the body within a few hours, but the breakdown products are stored in the fat and only are released slowly to pass out through the urine and feces. THC can be detected in urine as long as one week after occasional use and over one month after stopping regular use. Detection is possible for as long as three months after heavy use ends.

## Effective Dose to Lethal Dose Ratio

No human death has been attributed directly to poisoning by an overdose of THC or cannabis products. It has been estimated that a lethal dose would require ingesting approximately seven pounds of flowering tops within a twenty-four-hour period. Experiments on mice and rats have shown that THC has to take up about one-thousandth of their body weight before it kills them. This means that about 40,000 times the ordinary dose is lethal. Therefore, cannabis qualifies as the least toxic psychoactive drug known. It should be cautioned, however, that because it is an illegal drug, the quality is not controlled. Other drugs such as PCP sometimes are mixed with marijuana. Danger also exists that herbicides such as paraquat might be mixed with the drugs, and the danger of contamination by insecticides is present as well. However, the greatest risk is probably to the lungs, where the danger to long-term health might rival tobacco.

## PHYSICAL EFFECTS

The most obvious physical effects of marijuana include red eyes and a dry mouth. This dryness might relate to the decrease in eye pressure. THC increases heart rate, which could be a dangerous side effect to heart patients. The appetite usually is stimulated. The speed at which eyes adjust to darkness also slows, which could impair night vision while driving.

Moderate-to-high doses of THC decrease the ability to quickly shift attention, which is probably the reason that driving skills are impaired under the influence. Short-term memory also is impaired, although fortunately this does not seem to be a permanent effect. While under the influence, brain waves slow and more alpha or relaxation waves are found. Many people become sleepy and a small number report diarrhea.

Several hormones are affected by THC. Some studies suggest that the level of the male sex hormone testosterone tends to decrease, which raises the possibility of a reduced sperm count in males who suffer from borderline fertility. Women can produce prolactin in less quantities, which means their milk production might be lowered if they are nursing.

### Difficult to Metabolize

THC is an oil and unlike alcohol cannot mix with the body's water. Alcohol leaves the body in one day. THC oil lodges in the fatty part of cells, and high doses might inhibit the passage of material into the cell centers. The concentration of oil in the cells builds each time a person uses the drug, since it takes several weeks for the body to cleanse itself of this oil. Daily users accumulate very high levels of this "gummy" THC or its metabolites. Although all cells contain fat, two areas of the body—the brain and the reproductive organs—contain high levels of fatty cells. This THC pyramiding might be responsible for the memory and reproductive problems associated with marijuana.

Several laboratory studies have found a connection between THC and a decreased immune response at the cellular level. However, this research has been conducted in test tubes using high doses. So far, an increase in colds or other diseases is not evident in users; further studies need to be conducted, though, as this is a possible danger.

In a 1976 study, marijuana produced quicker chest pain in cardiac patients than cigarette smoke. The increase in heart rate, although not a problem for most people, might be dangerous to heart patients.

Probably the most dangerous aspect of chronic marijuana use is its effect on the lungs. Hot marijuana smoke can irritate the lining of the lungs, producing scar tissue and bronchitis. As with tobacco use, there are more serious problems as time progresses—one problem might be cancer. To date this connection has not been made, but again, the possibility exists. It is probable that smoking marijuana and tobacco together greatly increases the risk of cancer. Marijuana smoke usually is inhaled through unfiltered cigarettes, and the smoke normally is retained for long periods of time. Several known cancer-causing agents are present in marijuana smoke, including the tarry carcinogens found in tobacco cigarettes. One study has isolated squamous metaplasia cells (precancerous cells) in marijuana smokers. Marijuana smoke contains one-and-one-fourth more known carcinogens than tobacco. Since marijuana smoke usually is held longer than cigarette smoke in the lungs, the danger inherent in smoking just one marijuana cigarette probably equals that of four tobacco cigarettes. Smoking higher potency marijuana (sinsemilla) to obtain the same THC dose would lower this risk. The NIDA drug-use survey suggests that marijuana users smoke less when they use higher potency marijuana. However, some marijuana users smoke the drug all day and probably risk the same diseases as a tobacco smoker.

## PSYCHOLOGICAL EFFECTS

Psychological effects depend on a number of factors, including the purity, dose, setting, and expectations of the user. In one study, those using marijuana alone were much more quiet and withdrawn than those using marijuana in a group.

In the 1930s when the drug was pronounced legal, increased aggressiveness and uncontrolled rages were effects attributed to marijuana users. However, research has not supported this claim. In fact, humans generally are less aggressive when they are under the influence of marijuana.

Some people claim that marijuana use aids in meditation and prayer, and some religious groups, such as Rastafarians, use marijuana as a religious sacrament.

Marijuana typically produces a feeling of euphoria and relaxation in most users. However, paranoia and intense fear has been reported among inexperienced users or with high doses. Effects such as perceptual distortions have led experts to classify this drug as a hallucinogen. These perceptual changes include an increase in awareness of bodily feelings, taste, hearing, and color vision. Sensitivity is not actually increased, but people might be more aware of sensations. Time distortions—in other words, events seem to happen more slowly or quickly than normal—are common.

Common cognitive impairments include decreases in ability to concentrate, reduced levels of judgment, increased reaction time, poor coordination, and lessened ability to perform complex tasks. These impairments might be ignored by some users who prefer to believe they can drive and concentrate better than they can while sober. However, several studies in California and Massachusetts have verified that marijuana use is associated with traffic deaths, although alcohol usually also is involved. The combined impairment from alcohol and marijuana especially is great. In one study using a flight simulator, pilots made seven times more serious errors while stoned on pot than while sober. In general, the effects of smoking two marijuana joints approximately equals being halfway to the legally drunk limit. The decrements in performance can last for hours after the high wears off.

Rarer, although possible, psychological effects can include more serious mental disturbances. Hallucinations, paranoia, confusion, panic attacks, anxiety, depression, and psychotic thinking all have been reported. Severe reactions are more likely to occur from larger doses and also are more probable when the drug is ingested. Novice and younger users are more vulnerable to these effects than older users, and the person's level of mental stability also can play a role.

## LONG-TERM EFFECTS

### Tolerance and Withdrawal

Marijuana use in high doses does result in tolerance to the drug: In order to experience the same effects over an extended period of time, the user must use a larger amount of marijuana. However, tolerance to marijuana does not increase as much as does tolerance to other drugs. When people use only small amounts, tolerance is rarely seen. One study indicated than brain-wave changes only occurred at high-level doses for experienced users, while changes could be seen at lower levels in novice users. Experienced users showed smaller brain-wave changes even when restricted from marijuana use for one, two, and three weeks. Brain wave changes would be toward slower frequencies (Alpha waves) indicating relaxation.

Some evidence suggests that cross-tolerance develops from marijuana to alcohol, although the level of cross-tolerance might not be very high.

Withdrawal effects sometimes occur with heavy users despite the generally accepted notion that marijuana only is psychologically addictive. The most common withdrawal effects are a mild headache and then an irritability that lasts one or two days. Rarer withdrawal effects include sweating, hot flashes, insomnia, hiccups, increased salivation, weight loss, brain-wave changes, depression, restlessness, a decrease in appetite, tremor, nausea, vomiting, and diarrhea. Some former heavy users say that they did not feel clear-headed until months after quitting.

### Harm to Lungs

Chronic marijuana use can cause a variety of problems to the lining of the lungs. Coughing and chest pains can result, proved in one study in which soldiers who smoked hashish over a six-month to two-year period showed more cases of bronchitis and asthma than those who did not smoke the drug. An additional factor in many of these cases was tobacco, which increases the risk. In a 1978 study, one joint of marijuana reduced lung capacity in the same measure as did smoking sixteen cigarettes. Another study indicates that marijuana smoke contains more benzanthracene, benzopyrene, and other tars than cigarette smoke. These substances are known cancer-causing agents. Marijuana smoke contains about the same amount of carbon monoxide and other irritants as tobacco smoke. Squamous metaplasia (precancerous) cells were identified in one study of marijuana smokers. In another study, lung cells exposed to marijuana smoke in a laboratory showed evidence of chromosome damage.

Although more research needs to be done, there is little doubt that smoking marijuana is damaging to the lungs. Because users breathe deeply and hold the smoke in longer than tobacco smokers, a reasonable estimate is that one marijuana cigarette is as harmful as four tobacco cigarettes.

### Decreased Sperm Count

One long-term study covering twenty years indicates that chronic smokers of hashish show a definite deterioration in the necessary protein that surrounds the chromosomal material in sperm cells. These findings suggest that chronic male smokers might have a decreased fertility level.

Other reports confirm that sperm count is directly reduced in heavy marijuana smokers. One study found significant reductions in the number of healthy sperm found in these heavy users. Effects are considered reversible if use ceases. One study found a 35 percent decrease in the male hormone testosterone three hours after subjects smoked one joint. In a novice user, the level returned to normal twelve hours after smoking; in a heavy user, return to normal took one week.

One study indicates that along with the decrease in the male sex hormone testosterone, breasts might enlarge in heavy users—especially in adolescents who still are developing sexually. Although these studies are not conclusive and other studies did not support this premise, it is reasonable to assume that heavy daily use of marijuana by adolescent males could interfere with normal sexual development.

### Female Reproductive System

One study found abnormal menstrual cycles occurred in 39 percent of marijuana users as compared to 12 percent of nonusers. In another study, pregnant marijuana smokers had a higher number than nonsmokers of stillbirths, miscarriages, and lower birth rates. Decreased levels of prolactin, a hormone responsible for milk production, also was noted in pregnant women.

The effect on women's reproductive systems might be worse than the effects on the reproductive systems of men. Men produce many sperm cells, but women produce a limited number of eggs.

THC has been shown to enter the fetus. It is possible that a pregnant woman may reduce sex hormone levels in a developing fetus, causing permanent changes in the hormone-sensitive sexual characteristics of the brain.

### Possible Reduced Immunity to Disease

Results are conflicting, but some studies suggest that marijuana smokers might be more prone to disease. In laboratory experiments in which living tissues were treated with THC, the disease-fighting cells emanating from these tissues were described as ill-formed and ineffective. This response hasn't been found in humans, but it is considered possible in heavy users and further research is needed.

### Flashbacks

Flashbacks generally have not been reported.

### Amotivational Syndrome

Many marijuana users are lethargic and unmotivated and exhibit a marked decrease in their level of ambition. Students sometimes begin to lose interest in their studies, career persons lose their drive, and a passive orientation to life can develop. Although this syndrome does not occur in all smokers, it appears that this is one of the more prevalent patterns among heavy daily users. This effect probably is due to a continuous marijuana intoxication. However, it is hard to say whether laziness is the result of marijuana smoking or whether people who are lazy tend to smoke marijuana. This effect is probably dose-related, as a longitudinal study of 1,380 UCLA undergraduates found no relation between use of marijuana and grade average. Although moderate use might not have an effect on motivation, continuous heavy use probably does because someone who abuses in this way constantly is stoned.

### Possible Mental Illness

Certain people who are predisposed to mental illness might become more disturbed after using this drug. Cannabis use was cited as a factor in some 10 percent of all patients admitted into mental hospitals in India. In Egypt, 30 percent of those admitted were cannabis users. Unfortunately, these studies did not compare these percentages with the extent of use in the population. It has been well-documented, however, that overdose can result in panic or states of anxiety, even in stable individuals.

### Possible Permanent Brain Damage

Whether marijuana use produces permanent brain damage still is an unanswered question. A 1977 study in India showed that eleven hashish users performed more poorly than nonsmokers on tests of mental abilities. A 1978 study might explain why. Three laboratory monkeys administered the equivalent of three joints of marijuana daily showed a clumping between nerve cells of waste material after six months of experimentation. This waste material probably slows or reduces communication between cells. Although it is reversible, this clogging of the space between nerve cells might well be responsible for memory lapses and the other mental abnormalities mentioned.

Reportedly, individuals who experience memory problems recover after quitting using marijuana. However, most users do not seem to experience such problems. Also, extensive long-term studies of chronic smokers in New York City by the La Guardia Commission, in India by the Indian Hemp Commission, in Costa Rica, and in Jamaica found little or no difference in memory problems between users and nonusers. The Jamaican study did find lower blood oxygen level among heavy users of marijuana and tobacco. A study in Costa Rica of eighty men who smoked an average of ten joints daily for twenty years found no organic brain damage or medical or psychological differences after these men had quit smoking for two days. The Costa Rican study also did not find a relationship between testosterone levels or immune system problems and the use of marijuana. However, studies of marijuana continue, and it is possible that detrimental effects will be found even in moderate users. Those people who use this drug are acting as experimental guinea pigs.

## PUBLIC OPINION AND LEGAL CONSEQUENCES

Most marijuana users who feel that marijuana is safe for adults still do not want their children to use this drug. The research on marijuana use identifies several dangers. Since this drug only legally can be used for research purposes, it is classified as a Schedule 1 drug under the Controlled Substances Act. Interstate trafficking even in small amounts of marijuana can carry a five-year sentence for the first offense and a ten-year sentence for the second offense. Larger amounts carry a federal penalty with those sentences as minimums. State laws vary greatly. Marijuana use completely is legal for personal use in Alaska; its use is considered a misdemeanor in some states and a felony offense in other states.

Drug use of any kind, including marijuana or alcohol, by inmates is prohibited by the Bureau of Prisons and all state systems. Using illegal drugs in prison is considered a most serious offense, and users face severe disciplinary actions.

Many Americans hold arrest records due to possessing or distributing marijuana. Since 1965, more than eight million Americans have received arrest records for marijuana. An arrest record can prevent people from obtaining desired jobs, which is certainly among the detrimental effects.

## REFERENCES

Dye, C. 1985. *Pot and personality: Old questions, new answers.* Phoenix: Do It Now Foundation.

Dye, C. 1985. *Pot: What's known, what's not.* Phoenix: Do It Now Foundation.

Hamilton, G. 1978. Marihuana: Peril or panacea. In *Drugs in perspective,* edited by W. P. Link, L. P. Miller, and B. Fisher. Rockville, Md.: National Institute on Drug Abuse, Division of Training.

Hever, J. 1990. *Hemp and the marijuana conspiracy.* Van Nuys, Cal.: Hemp Publishing.

Jones, H.C., and P.W. Lovinger. 1985. *The marijuana question and science's search for an answer.* New York: Dodd, Mead.

Marijuana—An update. 1988. *Journal of Psychoactive Drugs* 20 (1).

Mann, P. 1980. *Marijuana: The myth of harmlessness goes up in smoke.* Indianapolis: The Saturday Evening Post Society, Health Reprints.

Miranne, A. C. 1979. Marijuana use and achievement orientation of college students. *Journal of Health and Social Behavior* 20:194-99.

Parker, J. 1983. *Marijuana: A natural medicine?* Phoenix: Do It Now Foundation.

Peterson, R. C., ed. 1980. *Marijuana research findings: 1980.* Washington, D.C.: National Institute on Drug Abuse.

Satz, P., J. M. Fletcher, and L. S. Sutker. 1976. Neuropsychologic, intellectual, and personality correlates of chronic marijuana use in native Costa Ricans. *Annals of New York Academy of Sciences* 282:266-306.

# XII.
# HIV INFECTION AND AIDS

The Acquired Immune Deficiency Syndrome (AIDS) has become one of the top ten causes of death in the United States. It is projected that at the close of 1991, approximately 270,000 cases of AIDS will exist in the U.S. About 250,000 known AIDS cases exist, and about 100,000 people have died. Fewer people died in the Vietnam War. Fortunately, AIDS is preventable.

AIDS is a disease that destroys the body's ability to protect itself against infection. The AIDS virus invades and destroys the cells that recognize invading disease organisms. The function of these cells is to activate the body's ability to fight disease. Without them, our bodies cannot defend against attacks from bacteria and viruses. We are in a constant war against germs related to diseases including pneumonia and other illnesses, but our bodies normally are able to control those germs. If our immune system is weakened, these diseases can then develop and perhaps cause death.

AIDS is the terminal stage of HIV infection. The Human Immunodeficiency Virus (HIV) is carried from one person to another. Actually, the HIV virus is very frail when it is outside of the body, and the chances are good that it won't live long. This fact is supported by studies of many families who lived with an infected member and kissed the person, used the same silverware, and drank from the same glasses but were not infected.

## HISTORY

It is not clear exactly where and how the AIDS epidemic started and spread. This disease originally was traced to Africa, where a large percentage of people in certain villages are infected. Several theories have been popularized about where the disease came from, but no one really knows for sure. The most likely speculation is that the disease came from the African Green monkey and spread to humans. These monkeys, which are eaten by natives of that area, have been found to suffer from a similar virus. It might be that during the butchering process, blood entered humans who accidentally had cut themselves with the butchering tools.

## SYMPTOMS AND PROGRESSIVE NATURE

The destruction caused by HIV of the body's immune system is a slow, gradual process. Some people have died from AIDS infection as early as two years after the infection occurred. However, the average incubation time (from infection to the diagnosis of AIDS) is two-and-one-half to five years and can exceed ten years. This means that a person can feel healthy for many years but still infect other people if he or she engages in risky behaviors. People who are infected with HIV but haven't been diagnosed yet still are contagious. Of the approximately one-and-one-half to two million people in the United States who are infected with HIV, the vast majority do not have any physical problems related to the infection. A large percentage of these infected people are not aware that they are carriers. They look, work, play, and eat just like individuals who are not infected.

As the disease progresses in an apparently healthy person, he or she initially might not realize what is occurring. These people usually complain of unexplained weight loss, fevers that last for longer than a week, night sweats, weakness, and recurrent diarrhea. They might notice enlarging lymph glands in their neck, armpits, or groin. Some people will develop infections that cause white patches in their mouths. Others will notice whitish areas on the sides of their tongues. These complaints might last for weeks or months before they disappear, or these symptoms might never stop and instead without proper medical care they gradually will worsen. Just because a person has one or more of these problems doesn't necessarily mean that the person is HIV infected, since other diseases can cause similar problems.

As the HIV infection continues to progress, the individual's immune system becomes so weak that he or she risks developing an opportunistic infection. At this point, AIDS is diagnosed. The most common opportunistic infection is pneumocystis carinii pneumonia, which causes a cough and breathing trouble. Other diseases can infect the brain and cause severe headaches, confusion, memory loss, difficulty walking, and even coma. The eyes can be affected, and sometimes blindness occurs. The digestive tract can be invaded, resulting in severe diarrhea, high fevers, vomiting, and the inability to swallow without pain. The person might develop cancers. The most common is Kaposi's Sarcoma, a skin cancer.

As a person's defenses against disease become weak, diseases that easily would be fought off normally take the opportunity to attack throughout the body. These opportunistic diseases eventually cause the AIDS patient's death. Approximately 85 percent of AIDS patients die within four years after the AIDS diagnosis, although the period of survival varies greatly. Even though people are afraid of AIDS, the person with AIDS is at a much higher risk of contracting the diseases carried by noninfected people with whom he or she comes into contact.

## TRANSMISSION

Among the variety of bacteria and diseases, great differences exist in how easily they can be transmitted from one person to another. HIV is in a class of disease germs that are not transmitted easily and often are called sexually transmitted diseases (STDs) or blood-borne viruses or diseases. Hepatitis B and the deadlier hepatitis C are carried in body fluids, particularly in the blood. Syphilis is another blood-borne infection. All these sexually transmitted diseases are weak and can be transmitted only by intimate contact. You can't get syphilis or other venereal diseases from sitting on a toilet seat, even though some people claim this.

On the other hand, some airborne viruses can be transmitted easily from person to person by sneezes, coughs, telephones, and door handles, for example. These airborne viruses such as colds and the flu spread quickly through a population of people. Family members infected with cold or flu viruses invariably spread these diseases to other family members through casual contact.

The HIV virus is a fragile blood-borne virus. It is not airborne like the cold virus; if it were, we probably would have to isolate people with this disease. The HIV virus, which is the cause of AIDS, is found only within the body's fluids—particularly the blood and sexual fluids.

In order to transmit HIV infection, the body fluids from an infected person must enter the blood system of a healthy person. The AIDS virus cannot penetrate intact skin. However, these HIV-infected fluids must penetrate skin to spread the infection and even then, it apparently takes a large amount to cause infection because a healthy body easily can fight off a small invasion of viruses. HIV can be spread in several ways from one person to another, and these ways are called high-risk activities.

If a healthy person lived with a person suffering from a cold, hepatitis, syphilis, and AIDS, the healthy person probably would contract the cold but no other infection. We can rank the risk of contracting HIV infection based on knowledge gathered over nearly ten years of study. Some behaviors conducted with HIV-positive people are very risky, while other behaviors pose low risk or no risk at all. People can be totally risk-free from AIDS by acting in ways that are safe.

High-risk activities are those behaviors that increase the likelihood that the AIDS virus will be transmitted from one person to another. Since AIDS is a blood-borne virus, the following behaviors or actions must involve exchanging body fluids:

## Blood Transfusions

Before HIV and AIDS was recognized in 1981 as a health threat, a number of people, including children, were infected by the blood they received in hospitals to replace blood lost during operations or due to excessive bleeding. Approximately 1 percent of infections have occurred this way. Fortunately, tests were developed in 1985 to screen blood for HIV, and the blood supply now is considered safe.

It is fairly easy for the virus to reach an unborn baby, and this could be considered a risky blood transfusion if the pregnant mother-to-be is infected. Approximately 1 percent of HIV infections occur when mothers infect their babies. This can occur before delivery (intrauterine) or during delivery. Children born with the HIV virus sometimes progress into full-blown AIDS quickly and die very young.

## Intravenous (I.V.) Drug Abuse

Sharing dirty needles is the most risky behavior known and easily can result in transmitting HIV. The risk is not only for i.v. injectors, but also for those who inject drugs under their skin. For this reason, more than half the drug users who shoot drugs in certain metropolitan areas like New York City and parts of New Jersey and Puerto Rico are HIV positive. Other areas in which needle sharing is unusual were found to have low rates of HIV infection.

Using a new needle and syringe every time totally would protect a drug user from HIV infection. Cleaning needles and syringes with chlorine bleach or boiling them for half an hour in water greatly would lower the risk. Even the less effective measure of thoroughly cleaning the needle and syringe with tap water would help lower the risk. However, most addicts don't concern themselves with clean needles. Water, if anything, usually is the only cleaning solution used by i.v. drug users. Most of the time, people in a shooting gallery are concentrating on their withdrawal symptoms or on obtaining a high instead of thinking about infection. Some drug users rationalize this dangerous behavior by saying they have to die someday anyway. In certain cities like New York and Amsterdam in the Netherlands, volunteer groups or government agencies have provided free clean needles to addicts in exchange for dirty ones. Most localities argue that supplying clean needles only encourages drug abuse and have prevented distribution.

In prisons, the majority of inmates with HIV infection became infected by sharing i.v. drug needles on the street. Some inmates continue to shoot drugs while in prison, using an eye dropper and a stolen or broken needle to inject drugs. But these homemade "works" rarely are sterilized properly. Chlorine bleach or hydrogen peroxide often are not used, and few addicts use the prison alternative of cleaning with hot coffee. Also, needles are contraband items and very rare; therefore, the needles might be shared by many inmates.

Even with these problems and the high degree of security at a prison, heroin sometimes is smuggled into institutions by "mules" or inmates who swallow or insert into their body cavities balloons filled with drugs. They sometimes "double bag" the drugs and coat the sack with vaseline before swallowing it or inserting it into their rectum. Drugs can be smuggled into an institution in several other ways, even though people who are caught are punished. This demonstrates the strength of the craving for narcotics and other drugs and also the foolishness of some people. Overdoses (O.D.s) have occurred in prison due to the reduced tolerance levels to drugs, inmates have been punished and transferred, and some have received the probable death sentence of HIV infection because they decided to use dirty needles inside prisons.

### Drug Abuse

A second way that drugs can facilitate the spread of AIDS is through their psychological effects. Drugs tend to reduce inhibitions. Alcohol, cocaine, and other drugs can lower one's inhibitions about sex both inside and outside of prison. Remember the "old brain-new brain" model to which was referred in an earlier chapter? Generally speaking, drugs first dull the new brain or neocortex. The new brain houses judgment, morals, conscience, and other higher-level thinking processes. When a person becomes intoxicated, the old brain has an unfair advantage in directing behavior. The old brain houses the more primitive instincts and drives. The old brain is the source of rage, hunger and thirst, the sex drive, and other emotions. When inhibitions are lowered, the old brain becomes dominant and bad judgment can result. Hence, HIV-infected people might have sex while intoxicated with uninfected people—perhaps in a crack house—and the HIV infection spreads.

Prostituting oneself to get money for drugs or exchanging sex for drugs also spreads AIDS. The desire to get drugs results in behavior that normally might not occur.

Some drugs such as cocaine (in the early stages and at lower doses) reportedly increase sexual arousal. While this is not reported in long-term or heavy use, the social or occasional cocaine user potentially could give in to increased sexual arousal inspired by the drug.

A third way in which drug use might be related to AIDS is physical. The prolonged heavy use of alcohol evidently leads to a weaker immune system. Test-tube experiments suggest that marijuana might do the same at very large doses. Also, prolonged periods of stress, which might occur during a run on cocaine or amphetamines, could reduce the body's ability to fight disease. Thus, if the AIDS virus attacks a person who has an already weakened immune system, its advance might be more rapid than usual.

### Unprotected Anal Sex

A common method of spreading the AIDS virus is through unprotected sexual intercourse—especially anal intercourse—with an infected person. Sex involves exchanging body fluids, and unless a latex condom ("rubber") with a spermicide is used, the risk of transmission is high. Anal intercourse is the sex that carries the highest risk of HIV transmission. The anus has very thin walls and was not designed like the vagina for sexual penetration. Due largely to inadequate lubrication, anal intercourse can cause small tears in the rectum. Condoms also can tear because of this lack of lubrication. Sperm infected with the virus then can enter through these abrasions or small cuts. Data indicate that the receptive partner is at the higher risk. A study published in 1987 found that 98 percent of homosexual men who were infected had engaged in unprotected anal intercourse and had experienced anal bleeding.

In most prisons, condoms are not available because prison rules forbid any sexual contact. However, some inmates will break the rules. The more safety-conscious have used the fingers from latex gloves, lubricated with soapy water, as a substitute for condoms. Although the soap produces irritation, a petroleum-based lubricant will weaken the latex. Using this protection is safer than unprotected sex. However, it is not the same as using regular condoms with spermicide. The safest behavior, especially in prison, is abstaining from sexual activity.

### Unprotected Vaginal Sex

Anyone who has repeated anal or vaginal intercourse with an HIV-positive partner is at high risk for AIDS-virus infection. A 1988 study of the risk of heterosexual intercourse with a partner who tested positive for HIV infection found that condoms reduced the risk to one-tenth the risk of unprotected intercourse. One act of vaginal intercourse with no condom with an infected partner poses about a one-in-500 chance of infection. However, people usually don't have sex only once. The odds of infection after 500 sexual encounters with an infected person without the protection of a condom is estimated at two in three. Thus, the odds are high that a regular partner of an HIV-infected person will contract the infection if a condom is not used every time. Even then, a woman is not without risk. The odds are good that after 500 sexual acts with an infected partner even with the use of a condom, a one-in-eleven chance of transmission exists. It should be noted that these statistics factor in the 10 percent failure rate for the condom. If an infected person is very careful always to use a latex condom with spermicide and is very careful to keep it on the penis until withdrawing from the vagina, the risk is lower.

Although the risk of sexually transmitted infection is greater for women because it is they who receive contagious sperm cells during heterosexual intercourse, men also are at some risk. Studies in Africa, where the disease has existed for many years, indicate that both the female and the male partners might be at risk. Normally, vaginal fluid has few cells floating in it. However, if an infected woman is menstruating, blood and its HIV-infected immune system cells will be present in her vaginal fluid, which would increase the risk of infecting her male partner.

What increases the risk of sexual transmission of HIV the most are other sexually transmitted diseases. If a person has gonorrhea, syphilis, chlamydia, or genital herpes, many HIV- infected immune system cells will be present as the body tries to fight off these diseases. These HIV-containing immune system cells increase the risk of HIV transmission. These diseases also can create open sores and other skin problems that weaken the body's natural barrier to the virus.

### Moderate Risk Activities

Vaginal sex with the protection of a latex condom with spermicide is considered a moderate-risk behavior when one partner is HIV-infected. The risk associated with vaginal sex with a condom is considered low if the partner is not an i.v. drug user or a homosexual or bisexual male.

Oral sex also is a means by which to transmit the AIDS virus, but it is seen as lower risk. Probably because of digestive juices in the stomach and mouth and the thickness of the lining of the mouth, oral sex does not appear as potentially risky as anal and vaginal sex. Transmission of the disease by oral sex has been reported but is much less frequent than transmission through other forms of sex. Oral sex between women evidently is less risky than other forms of sex but still is viewed as a potential source of HIV infection.

In prisons, a slight chance of infection exists if shaving razors or toothbrushes are shared. Both of these hygiene instruments might collect blood and deposit this blood into the minor cuts or abrasions of an uninfected person. A greater chance for infection exists if a person is tattooed. Blood on the tip of an unsterilized tattoo needle potentially is infectious, and the skin is jabbed many times. The risk is lower than the risk from sharing needles to inject drugs. Hospital employees who have been stuck with contaminated needles have developed HIV infection in only about four out of 900 jabs. However, tattooing certainly is dangerous, because transmission from tatoo parlors has been reported.

Blood from an injured person such as someone hurt in an assault or accident also could be infectious. If this blood is contaminated, HIV could enter through broken skin, abrasions, or cuts to infect someone. Rubber gloves should be worn to prevent infected blood from entering the body through breaks in the skin. However, the risk from touching infected blood is very low unless the skin is cut or scratched deeply. Our skin normally can prevent HIV from entering our body. In an emergency in which someone is bleeding, normal first-aid procedures such as applying direct pressure with a cloth to a wound would pose minimal risks to the person offering help unless cuts are present on his or her hands. The "first-aid hero" later should wash all exposed skin thoroughly to further decrease this very low risk of infection. Of course, using gloves is recommended, and they should be available in first-aid kits.

## NONRISK BEHAVIORS FOR HIV INFECTION

It was mentioned earlier that AIDS is not caused by an airborne virus. Coughing, sneezing, shaking hands, drinking from the same cup, hugging, and other casual contact with infected people won't transmit this disease. This fact was proved even when infected children were touched, cleaned, and lived with for years by family members.

There are claims that this virus has been found in tears and sweat, although no evidence exists to support any assumption that contact with sweat or tears results in infection. The concentration of the virus in these substances is very small.

Unwarranted fear and even panic has arisen over situations in which infected people live with uninfected people. HIV-infected people should be treated with the same care as those who have hepatitis or venereal disease, which also could be fatal diseases. With all of these diseases, unless someone shares needles or has sex with the infected person, the roommate is in no danger.

The best evidence and research on the results of casual contact with HIV-infected people has come from studies of families in which one or more members are HIV-positive. More than 130,000 documented AIDS cases have been reported. None of these infections is the result of casual contact (*AIDS in Correctional Facilities: Issues and Options.* NIJ Publication, 1988 ed.:15). Additional evidence that supports the finding that AIDS is not spread through casual contact comes from seven separate studies. These studies involve examining 500 family members who shared beds, bathrooms, dishes, and even personal hygiene articles like razors and toothbrushes with the infected family members. The studies also cited affectionate kissing—even on the lips—between infected and noninfected. No extraordinary or unusual measures were taken by these family members to protect themselves during the routine and normal casual contact that usually is observed among family members. The findings were clear. No one caught AIDS, even after spending extended periods of time with these HIV-positive family members (*AIDS in Correctional Facilities: Issues and Options.* NIJ Publication, 1988 ed.:15).

Studies in schools provide the same evidence. In a French study, infected hemophiliac children had long-term casual contact with uninfected children. None of the uninfected children became HIV positive through casual contact (*Lancet,* September 13, 1986:598-601).

Three annual correctional studies by the National Institute of Justice have not found any cases in which AIDS has been transmitted through casual contact.

## Certain Body Fluids

Studies indicate that HIV is found in tears, saliva, and urine in very low concentrations and in blood, semen, and vaginal secretions (especially with the presence of other diseases) in higher concentrations.

In the study that found HIV in saliva, the saliva was drawn from the mouth in such a manner that it might have contained blood from the gums. Even so, in eighty-three samples of saliva from seropositive persons, only one could grow the virus under laboratory conditions (*New England Journal of Medicine,* December 19, 1985:1606). Although minimal risk is involved in kissing in which saliva is exchanged, no known cases of infection have occurred this way (*AIDS in Correctional Facilities: Issues and Options.* NIJ Publication, 1988 ed.:16). In one study, eighty-six families who had seropositive children who had bitten siblings showed no transmission of the AIDS virus because of the bite. In a separate study, an AIDS-infected person bit thirty health care workers, none of whom tested positive (*AIDS in Correctional Facilities: Issues and Options.* NIJ Publication, 1988 ed.:16). The risk of transmitting HIV from contaminated food or bites appears very low. Even if blood were introduced into food, it would have to be a sizable quantity, be freshly introduced, and somehow make it past strong stomach acids. No known cases of AIDS transmission through foods have been reported.

By some estimates, approximately a quart of urine or saliva would have to enter the blood stream of a healthy adult for infection to occur (*AIDS in Correctional Facilities: Issues and Options,* NIJ Publication, 1988 ed.:16). Based on these findings, we can conclude that saliva, urine, and tears are low-risk body fluids for HIV infection.

## Insects

Some people are concerned that a mosquito or some other type of insect such as head lice, fleas, or ticks might carry AIDS to an unsuspecting victim. In Belle Glade, Fla., an area with a high concentration of mosquitoes during certain parts of the year, researchers studied AIDS transmission. Their findings indicated that only high-risk behaviors—not insect bites—caused HIV transmission (*AIDS in Western Palm Beach County, Florida,* MMWR, 1986:609-12).

No known cases exist in which venereal or other sexually transmitted diseases like hepatitis have been carried by insects. The blood drawn by mosquitoes apparently does not sustain live HIV in their bodies. Furthermore, mosquitoes usually feed only once a day, which exceeds the estimated period of time HIV can live outside of the human body. The research therefore does not support any evidence to indicate that HIV can be spread by insects (*AIDS in Correctional Facilities: Issues and Options*, NIJ Publication, 1988 ed.:17).

## AIDS IN CORRECTIONS

People live with AIDS in prison just as people live with AIDS outside of prison. Outside of prison, HIV-positive people work in many different kinds of jobs—even in food service or in health care settings. Hepatitis, HIV, sexually transmitted diseases, tuberculosis, and other infections usually are not screened by employers. Your child's babysitter, your grocer, and your barber could be HIV-positive and you wouldn't necessarily know it.

Greater control actually exists in prisons. We can limit who works in the kitchen and who works in the hospital, even though the risks of transmission are minimal through routine job functions. Since HIV is treated as any other blood-carried disease, normal precautions should be taken with everyone because HIV status rarely is known. Blood never should be touched without using latex gloves, unless it is an emergency situation. Even then, the precautions previously mentioned should be used. Strong cleaning fluids like bleach should be used to clean blood from floors and other surfaces. Tattooing and sharing needles both are high-risk activities and strictly are prohibited by prison officials. Unprotected homosexual contact is a high-risk activity, and all sexual behavior is prohibited. Simply living with an HIV-infected person is not a high-risk activity.

The fear and prejudice against HIV-positive people is based on ignorance and fear. When someone is told they are HIV-positive, most fear for their own health and become paranoid about who knows they're infected. Many HIV-positive inmates were prejudiced against HIV-positive people until they found out they themselves were positive. As one inmate put it, "I used to believe we should treat HIV people differently, until I became one myself. Now all I want is to be treated like everyone else."

## TREATMENT AND VACCINES

Several medical authorities have proposed some promising treatments for HIV infection and for AIDS. Dr. Jonas Salk, who discovered the polio vaccine, presented his research findings at the 1989 World AIDS Conference. The Johns Hopkins Medical School and other institutions have conducted research on vaccines and treatments, and much money is being spent on these projects. Dr. John Rossi of California's Bechman Research Institute has been working on a vaccine using the science of genetics (ribosomes). His test-tube experiments have been positive, as his drug in experiments has stopped the reproduction of HIV by disrupting RNA, the cell substance that HIV needs to copy itself. Meanwhile, unusual treatments for AIDS such "Compound Q" derived from the Chinese cucumber root are being studied (*Richmond Times Dispatch*, March 11, 1990). Despite these efforts, scientists do not expect to produce a vaccine for several years, if ever. HIV is a retrovirus like the common cold. The virus can change form, and one cure might not work on other strains.

To date, the most effective treatment for HIV infection is the drug Azidoithymide or AZT, which is manufactured by the Burroughs Wellcome Company. This medication inhibits the spread of HIV within the body by interfering with the virus's ability to reproduce. Some people are afflicted with side effects from AZT, including anemia and other blood-related problems. AZT has extended the lives of some people for many years. For others, AZT has not been beneficial.

Medical researchers have learned a lot about how the body's immune system works due to the great increase of research related to the fight against the HIV epidemic. New drugs and treatments can be expected over the next few years, but of course the most effective protection is prevention.

## SUMMARY

The HIV virus can be spread only by sexual contact, exchanging body fluids by such acts as sharing needles, or perinatally from mother to baby. Consequently, education is the key to containing this illness and stopping the spread. Casual sex is a high-risk activity unless prophylactics and spermicides are used. Monogamous relationships in which partners remain sexually faithful to one another protect against HIV infection. Drug abuse also can spread AIDS, because drugs reduce inhibitions about sex, because sex sometimes is offered in exchange for drugs, and because sharing needles to inject drugs can spread AIDS, hepatitis, and other infections. It appears that many people will die because they use poor judgment and fail to take precautions. While the discovery of an AIDS vaccine is possible, no guarantee exists now of a cure or of a preventive vaccination. The only reliable defense against AIDS is to avoid high-risk behaviors. In that case, a person doesn't need to worry about becoming infected with this disease.

## REFERENCES

Darrow et al. 1987. Risk factors for human immunodeficiency virus (HIV) infections in men. *American Journal of Public Health* 77 (4 April).

Hurst, N., and S. B. Hulley. Preventing the heterosexual spread of AIDS. *Journal of the American Medical Association* 259 (22 April).

National Institute of Justice. 1988. *AIDS in correctional facilities: Issues and options.* 3d ed. Washington, D.C.: GPO.

# XIII.
# THE IMPACT OF DRUG AND ALCOHOL ABUSE ON THE FAMILY

Seven million children live in homes in which one or both parents are alcoholics. Twenty-one million adults grew up in families disrupted by alcoholism. These adults are four times more likely than the average adult to become substance abusers themselves.

Alcoholism is an illness that affects the entire family. It seals off the alcoholic and isolates the family members from each other and from others outside the family. Even though the problems are enormous, the issues are avoided, denied, overlooked, or masked. Every member of the family is affected by the drinking person, and every family member plays an important role in the alcoholic's drinking.

Because of family loyalty, love, or convenience, family members sometimes act in ways that enable alcoholics to continue drinking. Spouses might drive intoxicated partners home, call bosses to make excuses for their partners' absences from work, and take on additional responsibilities. Sometimes children will become overburdened to keep peace at home. The older children sometimes become caretakers for the younger ones. Resentment builds toward the alcoholic parent who thrusts the child into premature adult roles.

## EFFECTS ON THE FAMILY

The way alcoholics think and behave not only is harmful to themselves, it is harmful to their family members as well. The emotional upset caused by the alcoholic's drinking behavior makes everyone miserable and creates an unhealthy climate that strains the relationship that holds a family together.

The following unhealthy feelings commonly are experienced in an alcoholic family:

1. *Suspicion:* Family members begin to believe the alcoholic is lying or manipulating them. This leads to accusations, arguments, and conflicts. Unpredictability leads to inconsistent parenting.

2. *Fear:* Family members become afraid of the alcoholic's mood swings and the anger that sometimes erupts into violent episodes. Children in substance-abusing families never know what to expect.

3. *Disappointment:* The alcoholic often disappoints his or her family by breaking promises. Children soon learn not to trust adults. This also greatly affects a child's sense of self-worth. The child might feel that the adult discounts the child's emotions or personal value.

4. *Resentment:* As the alcoholic's behavior places more and more demands on other family members, they become resentful and angry toward the alcoholic. This is acted out in a variety of ways.

5. *Isolation:* Family members become alienated from each other and from most people outside the family. They are unable to invite friends over because of the possibility that their alcoholic family member might show up drunk and make a scene.

## ROLES IN THE FAMILY

Children can adopt several roles in response to the turmoil caused by substance abuse in their family. Three examples of family roles will be discussed.

### Model Number 1 (Gerald T. Rogers)*

Brian, who is "the responsible child," has taken on the parental responsibilities that his parents have abdicated. He has become "pseudomature." That is, he appears to be mature but he has not had the opportunity to emotionally grow and thrive in a normal way. He takes care of his younger siblings and even reminds his parents that it is time to go to work when he should be out playing ball and enjoying relationships with his peers. This type of person often grows up to become a "driven" workaholic because he does not know how to enjoy life. Some people believe that the responsible child or "leader" becomes either rigidly intolerant of those with alcohol problems or highly prone toward alcoholism him or herself, as he or she attempts to deal with repressed anger over this lost childhood.

Terry, "the rebellious child," is acting out his anger and resentment of his father's drinking and the problems it is causing. He is drawing the family's attentions away from the alcoholic, and the family begins to blame him for all the conflicts and problems. Without intervention, he is likely to begin taking his father's beer from the refrigerator. His rebelliousness can lead to drug experimentation and abuse. He might try marijuana or even crack. He is likely to have a full-blown addiction by the age of fifteen.

Lisa is described as the "quiet child," who does not cause problems for the family but who has many problems of her own. She is dominated by fear and turns to fantasy and withdrawal in order to cope with the family turmoil. She is afraid and feels neglected by her parents. She needs attention and love but her parents are unable to meet her needs because of their own problems. Without help, Lisa is likely to grow up and develop an addiction of her own. She might turn to drugs to fill her emptiness, or she might marry someone similar to her alcoholic father to unconsciously try to save him. Fearful children might try to redeem themselves as adults as a result of self-blame over parental problems.

As adult children of alcoholics or drug abusers, these people might marry or unite with a substance abuser and relive this traumatic childhood period by enabling an alcoholic who has the same traits as their alcoholic parents did. Also as adults, children of alcoholics feel more comfortable with the familiar and tend to marry into similar relationships. This might be due to learning or to self-blame over a parental alcohol problem. Repeated marriages to alcoholics who sometimes are abusive commonly occurs as the cycle repeats itself. A learned helplessness and illogical dependency predominate as the adult child feels torn between the pain of family addiction and loyalty to his or her spouse who, through addiction, becomes a master manipulator. These children are prone to codependency.

The mother in this family is developing her own alcohol problem as she moves more deeply into the role of an enabler. She initially covers for the father's drinking and takes the entire responsibility for the children. As the father manipulates her into his own addiction, she becomes codependent with him, relinquishing her role as parent and adding pressure to Brian, who assumes the parental role.

The father follows the disease progression typical of many addictions. He moves into heavy and compulsive use and correspondingly drives his family into further disruption as a consequence. He neglects his children who want to be loved and supported and shows an increasing rage toward them. He lies to his kids by promising to take them out, then he manipulates his spouse to go drinking with him. He spends more and more of his money on his addiction, resorting to his wife's paycheck to support his own habit. When a school counselor intervenes to stop the spiraling cycle of disruption at school, he becomes resentful and angry rather than face his addiction. He is in total denial over the problems he has created.

*These roles are illustrated in the film, *Soft is the Heart of a Child*.

### Model Number 2 (Virginia Satir)

This model depicts numerous roles that family members can take. Generally, these roles can vary from family to family, and shifts to different roles can occur.

The Enabler is usually the spouse, but in a sense, the entire family is an enabler to some extent. Enablers help an alcoholic or drug abuser continue their habit. They pay bills, make excuses, and slow the inevitable hitting bottom that most compulsive users will experience. Enablers sometimes had alcoholic parents themselves and feel like they are being loyal to the family and keeping the family together by doing what they do. They can be very dependent emotionally, have a martyr complex, and have poor interpersonal skills that also require treatment. In essence, they are codependent.

The Hero or Responsible Child usually is a child who tries to do everything right or perfect, believing this might help improve the family situation. Heroes make good grades and do things perfectly and in doing so avoid further family friction and alleviate in their own minds any sense of guilt over family problems. These children attempt to protect the family from outside intervention because of the shame and embarrassment.

The Scapegoat is a child who frequently gets into trouble. It is convenient to blame this child for whatever goes wrong in the family. By being inept or vulnerable, this child diverts attention from the parent who is actually the problem. This child might have problems at school and generally demands attention through problem behavior. The Scapegoat provides an effective diversion from problems in the alcoholic parent by making him or herself look worse. He or she also is prone toward substance abuse.

The Rebel is a very angry and defiant child who has learned to satisfy his or her own emotional needs through impulsive or aggressive behavior. The rebel basically cultivates antisocial behavior and can get into legal problems beginning at a very young age. He or she often expresses anger directly toward authority figures who he or she mistrusts. The Rebel seeks to gain self-fulfillment through material and "ego-boosting" activities. Because of the Rebel's hatred of authority and the rejection of social values, he or she can develop criminal thinking patterns and behavior. These children tend to behave impulsively and have little tolerance for frustration.

The Lost Child is a withdrawn and fearful child who tries to reduce family tension by being very quiet. This child seldom complains, even if he or she receives unfair treatment compared to the other children. The Lost Child tends to withdraw from the family and entertains him or herself for hours with simple toys or simple diversions. These children use fantasy extensively to escape the pain present in the family and turn to older siblings, teachers, neighbors, or others outside the home for support when needed.

The Mascot or Clown child is the "family jester." He or she uses humor as a defense against problems in the family. The Mascot or Clown diverts attention by being funny, cute, or adorable. These children fill their own need for family attention by putting on a show that everyone, including the drug-dependent parent, can enjoy. These children know how to make a joke just at the right moment to break up a tense situation and divert focus away from the real problem.

### Model Number 3 (Claudia Black)*

This model portrays a more recent understanding of how dependent family members relate to one another.

The Responsible Child assumes the role of parent because of the irresponsible behavior of the drug-abusing parent. The responsible child sacrifices his or her ability to "feel" by becoming a "good soldier" for the family's sake. They have the burden of parenthood thrust on them from a very young age and have intense amounts of repressed anger over being robbed by their parents of their childhood. They make good workers but have poor interpersonal and emotional development. The responsible child has difficulty establishing meaningful relationships later in life because of problems trusting and developing intimacy.

The Adjuster is highly adaptable. These children accept everything unconditionally. They have a fatalistic orientation toward life and might become passive or dependent as adults. They blindly follow without questioning and accept the fact that they are in a disturbed situation.

The Placater is depicted as a sensitive child who blames him or herself if everyone in the family is not happy. This child tries to soothe hurt feelings and comfort those in pain. The Placater works hard to make his or her family perfect but never achieves this goal. These people tend to subordinate their own needs and wants. Consequently, they often struggle with asserting themselves and frequently repress their feelings or withdraw from stress rather than express their needs.

Acting Out is the aforementioned rebel. Anger toward authority, a sense of entitlement, and antisocial behavior are common. Problems in school, frequent punishment, and defying authority mark this child's future. This child is prone to drug and alcohol abuse as a form of rebellion and impulsiveness. He or she typically is viewed as being self-centered and having an attitude of entitlement in life.

*This model is illustrated in the film *Roles*.

### Summary of Models

Experts generally agree that these roles develop. In reality, however, we often see a blending of these roles in a disturbed family in which alcohol or drugs cause this disruption. Much of what we know about the roles family members take has come to us recently from the people who have been affected by alcoholism. Children of alcoholics who have grown up under these circumstances have identified distinctive patterns of behavior that they and their siblings developed. By learning about these patterns, people are able to understand why adult children of alcoholics behave the way they do and can begin to make some positive changes.

## HELP FOR THE NONALCOHOLICS IN THE FAMILY

Plenty of help is available for the family when they are ready to accept it. Sources are listed in the telephone book under the heading "alcoholism information and treatment." Some examples of treatment sources for families are licensed psychologists, substance-abuse counselors, and other mental-health professionals who are experienced and well-trained to assist dependent and/or codependent families in overcoming problems. The following self-help groups also are an important part of recovery:

> Al-Anon Family Group Hdqtrs.
> PO Box 862, Midtown Station
> New York, NY 10018
> 212/302-7240

> Alateen Family Group Hdqtrs.
> Box 182, Madison Square Garden
> New York, NY 10159-0182
> 212/683-1771

Al-Anon and Alateen are a worldwide network of support groups for family and friends. The program is adopted from Alcoholics Anonymous and therefore participation is confidential and cost-free.

> Children of Alcoholics Foundation
> 200 Park Ave., 31st Fl.
> New York, NY 10166
> 212/351-2680

Adult Children of Alcoholics groups help people overcome self-defeating thought and behavior that once developed as a child.

Wives Self-Help Foundation
Smylie Times Bldg., Ste. 205
8001 Roosevelt Blvd.
Philadelphia, PA 19152

## SUMMARY

Drug abuse, including alcoholism, is a family disease. The damage can last into adulthood when adult children relive the trauma in hurtful ways. The roles that develop seem to be a natural response to the imbalance caused by the addicted parent. Though these roles vary in families, they generally have included the "Responsible Child," also described as the "Hero or Leader," who inherits the early burden of parenthood and tends to be a rigid perfectionist in later life. There is also an "Acting Out" role, also described as the "Rebel," who draws attention by being disruptive and defying authority. A "Placater" also might develop. This child learns to calm parents, smile superficially, and subordinate his or her own needs. Fear often underlies this child's behavior. Children of Alcoholics (COAs) have a greater incidence of alcohol and drug abuse and often repeat the cycle of addiction, which is passed from one generation to the next.

## REFERENCES

*Alcohol and the family.* Daly City, Cal.: Krames.

Black, C. 1988. *It will never happen to me.* Center City, Minn.: Hazelden.

Black, C. *My dad loves me, my dad has a disease.* Center City, Minn.: Hazelden.

Black, C. *The stamp game.* Center City, Minn.: Hazelden.

*Cocaine and the family: What you can do.* Daly City, Cal.: Krames.

*Everything you need to know about chemical dependence.* 1990. Minneapolis: Johnson Institute.

# XIV.
# *RELAPSE PREVENTION*

Relapse prevention might well be the most important objective of an inmate after release. Maintaining sobriety potentially could prevent the deterioration of health, improve relationships with loved ones, allow the inmate to keep his or her freedom in society, and very well even save his or her life. In this chapter, we will examine how relapse begins and look at the factors that led to addiction the first time around. We also will examine vulnerabilities or areas of weakness—those times when inmates are most likely to again abuse drugs—and look at alternatives to this abuse.

Relapse prevention involves breaking old patterns that increase the likelihood of drug abuse and starting new patterns of behavior that are incompatible with substance abuse. This chapter will be divided into two major sections: the first involves relapse prevention during incarceration and the second addresses relapse issues in the community.

## RELAPSE PREVENTION WHILE INCARCERATED

### *Knowing the Rules*

Drugs are available in almost every prison. Inmates know who to see and how to get the drugs. A minority of inmates in most prisons use drugs. Marijuana and alcohol seem to be preferred, although cocaine and heroin might be increasing in popularity because of the shorter period of detection as compared to marijuana. "Home brew" or rotted fruit juice contains a maximum of 14 percent alcohol and usually tastes bad, but it is used more than seems reasonable in this strict environment.

Urine surveillance programs are a deterrent. Inmates are aware that disciplinary action will be taken against those whose urine tests positive for drugs. Inmates should be reminded in a matter-of-fact way about the consequences of drug or alcohol abuse in prison. Inmates should know that regardless of their personal philosophy about drugs, these sanctions are real and probably would be a consequence of drug abuse.

Inmates should know that when someone risks his or her freedom (whether this risk results in delayed release, loss of good time, or segregation) over a desire to get high, then a problem does exist.

The BOP disciplinary rules, for example, place the use of illegal drugs in the category of greatest severity—the same category in which assault is considered. The possible penalties are up to sixty days segregation in addition to loss of all good time and a disciplinary transfer. Even those sentenced under the new guidelines can be prevented from gaining fifty-four days a year of good time.

Alcohol use is considered a high-category offense. Penalties can include loss of half of all good time, thirty days in segregation, and a disciplinary transfer. An inmate who refuses to take a urine or Breathalyzer test faces similar punishment. Bringing drugs into the institution can lead to both BOP penalties and an additional sentence from the court.

### Health Can Be Affected

Drug abuse has caused immense health problems. The education portion of this manual focused on the types of health problems resulting from drug or alcohol abuse. Inmates may be able to offer personal examples about how their health or the health of a friend or relative has been affected by substance abuse.

### Peer Pressure

Peer pressure is the influence associates exert on a person's behavior. Peer pressure occurs when people make decisions aimed at pleasing others rather than themselves. Both negative and positive peer pressure occur in prison. Pressure to use drugs is negative peer pressure because drug use conflicts with the values of health, safety, and freedom. Certain individuals will give in to this pressure from others to use drugs. Peer pressure tactics include:

- Persistently asking someone to use drugs

- Ignoring someone who doesn't use drugs

- Insulting someone who doesn't use drugs (calling him or her a snitch, for example)

- Glorifying drug abuse and the effects of intoxication

- Creating a subculture that protects abusers

It takes a strong individual to stand up to peer pressure. Human beings are social creatures. We crave acceptance and recognition. Sometimes we are willing to sacrifice our health and ignore our better judgment to gain this acceptance. Peer pressure is the social reward-and-punishment system that others exert on an individual to make him or her do something. Think about how you might have felt as a child when your friends laughed at you for wearing "funny" clothes. Most people try to avoid embarrassment and gain recognition and acceptance. A type of negative peer pressure occurs when a group of people you seek to join won't accept you until you start using drugs.

The influence might be very subtle. The change could be as simple as the way people talk to you or how often you are recognized. The desire for acceptance is what drives many into these drug abuse groups, since rejection or criticism is scarce as long as everyone can continue to get high. Soon, the drug becomes everyone's best friend.

In many prevention programs in schools, the following four-step procedure to counteract peer pressure is taught:

1. Ask questions when you are unsure about the motives of your associate. ("Why do you want me to risk my release?")

2. Identify rules. ("Man, that's a 100-level shot!")

3. Identify sanctions. ("I'm not trying to do any more time or get a disciplinary transfer.")

4. Offer an alternative activity. ("I'm going to work out. Do you want to come?")

### Drug Substitutes

Most drug abusers and alcoholics do not experience the same degree of craving in prison (after detoxification) that they experience outside. Although numerous exceptions to this observation exist, keeping clean and sober generally is easier in prison. Drug availability is limited, and users can't "get it like they want it." Sometimes, however, users switch to legal drugs. It is not so unusual to see a former drug abuser drinking ten cups of coffee a day. The slang term "dope fiend sweet" describes the massive amount of sugar used in coffee or tea to obtain the desired effect. While coffee, tea, and cigarettes aren't as strong as some drugs, they too can be abused.

It's not so unusual to see inmates who excessively use these substances start the same abuse pattern they began on the street. Excessive use of caffeine and nicotine could lead to sleep problems, and the inmate can find him or herself complaining to the hospital about nervousness and insomnia. Some ask for medication and actually believe that sedatives or tranquilizers are their only recourse. The cycle of abuse already is beginning again. When drugs—legal or illegal—are viewed as a way to solve problems, relapse prevention has failed, and the inmate has tricked him or herself back to abuse.

### Treatment Available During Incarceration

A variety of treatment activities are available to inmates while they are incarcerated. A drug education class is only one of many constructive activities in which inmates will participate.

In some institutions, the inmate might be able to continue drug treatment in a comprehensive program. These programs are several months in length, unit-based, and involve daily programming averaging two to three hours. In these programs, the participant is able to address, in detail, treatment issues identified specifically for him or her. This drug education class might serve as a stimulus to the inmate to become interested in more intense programming.

The majority of institutions also offer the inmate the opportunity to participate either in Alcoholics Anonymous or Narcotics Anonymous. These groups, based on the twelve-step philosophy, offer an opportunity for long-term intervention and ongoing lifestyle assessment. One of the advantages is the continuity of programming, which would be available to the inmate when he or she is released to the community. Virtually no community in this country exists that does not offer some form of twelve-step counseling.

In any given institution, the mental health unit might offer courses in relaxation, stress management, communications, assertiveness, family relations, anger management, positive mental attitude, or some type of cognitive/behavioral therapy (such as rational behavior therapy). All of these group activities effectively can complement efforts to prevent relapse.

The Rational Behavioral Therapy (RBT) approach developed by Dr. Maxie Maultsby particularly is relevant to specific aspects of relapse prevention. The RBT approach focuses on the relationship between thoughts and feelings. In such a group, the participant learns to identify the self-talk that might contribute to feelings of anger, depression, guilt, or boredom—feelings that might increase the likelihood of drug abuse. One of the most important aspects of Maultsby's approach involves understanding habit formation and change. The chapter called "Emotional Reeducation Process" in his book *Help Yourself to Happiness* is highly relevant to understanding the concept of craving.

The basic point is that whenever we attempt to break an old habit, we likely will go through a period in which we experience a sense of discomfort. This feeling, which Maultsby calls "cognitive-emotive dissonance," is predictable and understandable based on known principles of conditioning. To break old habits, we must accept this temporary discomfort and learn to act with our heads rather than our gut. Important techniques can be learned that lessen the affects of cognitive-emotive dissonance. Specifically, through positive affirmations (self-statements) and imagery we mentally can rehearse habit change.

### Other Motivation Programs

Numerous other positive activities are available within the institution. The programs offered through the chaplain's office, education, vocational training, and recreation all can provide constructive alternatives.

### Addressing the Four A's While Incarcerated

Each individual who participates in a drug abuse prevention class should generate a personal plan related to the following elements: alternative activities, associates, aftercare, and abstinence.

What constructive activities within the institution will inmates choose for themselves? Who are the associates with whom they will choose to spend most of their time? Who will they avoid? What types of institutional aftercare activities (such as the programs beyond the drug education class) will they choose while still incarcerated? Finally, how does the issue of abstinence relate to them while they still are incarcerated? Do they believe it is acceptable to occasionally have a drink or engage in illegal drug use while incarcerated? How are they going to manage the use of legal substances such as caffeine, nicotine, and high levels of sugar while in prison? How can regular affirmation and imagery prepare them for the streets?

## RELAPSE ISSUES IN THE COMMUNITY

### Drug Use Shortly After Release

It is not unusual for inmates to get drunk or high the first day out of prison. Inmates who never touched drugs while "down" find something with which to get high shortly after release. In actuality, this behavior might have been caused by recurrent thoughts about drugs or alcohol while still in prison. Several inmates who abused drugs shortly after release reported after their parole was revoked they'd thought about getting high for months or years prior to release. The seed is planted early, and the following excuses can accompany this behavior:

1.  "I owe it to myself, because I've been straight for so long."

2.  "I owe it to myself, because I've been 'down' so long."

3.  "I owe it to myself, because these people gave me the shaft."

4.  "I just want to see if I can handle it now that I'm clean."

5.  "I want to test it to see if it's good before I sell it."

6.  "I have a long bus ride and need something to steady my nerves."

7.  "I really had it rough, so now I deserve to celebrate."

### Drug Use at the Halfway House

Some inmates will use drugs at their halfway house believing they can "beat" the urine surveillance. Several methods of timing drug use and flushing the system can be tried to continue abuse undetected. These attempts often simply delay the inevitable violation and return to prison that will follow either while in the halfway house or while on parole.

Inmates should be aware of the way a positive urinalysis will be treated at a halfway house. In the federal system, for example, a Code 100 incident report is written, the U.S. Marshal Service is notified, and the inmate is picked up for return to custody. These halfway house failures and early parole violators often report a sense of intense depression and frustration since they essentially must begin again. The parole board must retard their release. The inmate, his or her family, his or her employer, and friends again must put everything "on hold." Trust in the individual again is violated. The violation/halfway house failure often hurts more than the initial sentence.

### Drug Use After Release to the Community

Drugs and alcohol obviously are everywhere. They cannot be escaped or completely avoided. Chances are great that someone an inmate knows is using drugs. What makes the situation even more difficult is that many inmates have family members and close friends or associates who again will expose them to drugs. Most inmates return to the same neighborhoods in which they know where drugs are and who uses them. An inmate will have a reputation when he or she returns to the street; he or she either will live up to that reputation or change. The same factors will be present in the community that existed before the inmate was incarcerated. Parties, places, and people will need to be avoided in order to increase the likelihood of success.

In a recent study of several hundred relapse episodes obtained from clients with a variety of problem behaviors such as drinking, smoking, heroin addiction, compulsive gambling, and overeating, researchers identified six primary high-risk situations. Three of these situations are associated with almost three-quarters of all the relapses reported.

1.  Escape from Negative Emotional States (35 percent of all relapses in the sample): situations in which the individual experiences a negative (or unpleasant) emotional state, mood, or feeling such as frustration, anger, anxiety, depression, or boredom prior to or at the time the first lapse occurs.

2.  Social Pressure (20 percent of the relapses): situations in which the individual responds to the influence of someone else or a group of people who exert pressure on the individual to engage in the prohibited behavior. Social pressure either is direct (interpersonal contact with verbal persuasion) or indirect (being in the presence of others who are engaging in the same target behavior even though no direct pressure is involved, for example).

3.  Interpersonal Conflict (16 percent of the relapses): situations involving an ongoing or relatively recent conflict associated with any interpersonal relationship, such as marriage, friendship, family members, or employer-employee relations. Arguments and interpersonal confrontations occur frequently in this category.

4.  Desire for Positive Emotional States (12 percent of the relapses): situations in which the individual engages in the prohibited behavior to increase feelings of pleasure, celebration, sexual excitement, freedom, and other positive-affective states.

5.  Escape from Negative Physical States (12 percent of the relapses): situations involving unpleasant or painful physical or physiological reactions. Includes physical states such as withdrawal symptoms and cravings specifically associated with prior drug use. This category also includes physical states not associated with prior drug use such as pain, illness, injury, fatigue, trauma, and other physical disorders.

6.  Testing Personal Control (5 percent of the relapses): situations in which the individual engages in the prohibited behavior to "test" the effects of treatment or a commitment to abstinence, including tests of "willpower." This category also includes testing one's ability to engage in controlled or moderate use and to "just try it once" to see what happens.

### Relapse Prevention Strategies

If the individual can execute an effective cognitive or behavioral coping response in the high-risk situation (he or she assertively counteracts social pressures, for example), the probability of relapse decreases significantly. The individual who copes successfully with the situation is likely to experience a sense of mastery or control. Successfully mastering one problem situation often is associated with expecting to be able to cope successfully with the next challenging event. As the individual is able to cope effectively with more and more high-risk situations, perception of control increases cumulatively. The probability of relapse then decreases.

What happens if an individual is not able to cope successfully with a high-risk situation? It might be that the person never has acquired the coping skills involved or that the appropriate response has been inhibited by fear or anxiety. Or, perhaps the individual fails to recognize the risk involved and respond before it's too late.

Whatever the reason, if a coping response is not performed, the person is likely to experience a decrease in self-efficacy frequently coupled with a sense of helplessness and a tendency to give in passively to the situation. As self-efficacy decreases in the precipitating high-risk situation, one's expectations for coping successfully with subsequent problem situations also begin to drop. If the situation also involves the temptation to engage in the prohibited behavior to cope with the stress involved, the stage is set for a probable relapse.

The combination of being unable to cope effectively in a high-risk situation with positive outcome expectancies for the effects of the drug greatly increases the probability that an initial lapse will occur. At this point, unless a last-minute coping response or sudden change of circumstance occurs, the individual might cross over the border from abstinence. Whether or not this first lapse is followed by a total relapse depends largely on the individual's perceptions of the "cause" of the lapse and the reactions associated with its occurrence.

### Community Problems and Abuse

A number of inmates will pass the first several hurdles in prison, the halfway house, and the first part of their release only to find that their lives aren't working out as planned. These people might find they aren't being promoted fast enough in their job, that their spouse or loved one is putting pressure on them to produce financially or emotionally, or other problems. Marital problems, separations, infidelity, work difficulties, disease, unemployment, boredom, and financial pressure are a few factors that are a part of life. Crises can cause a bad attitude toward life and toward sobriety. During a crisis or period of intense pressure, abuse is more likely, and drugs might be used to provide a temporary escape from pressure.

### Peer Pressure in the Community

In the community, inmates might find that family members are using drugs, friends are using drugs, and even their boss might be using drugs. If they go out on a date, their date might offer them drugs. Peer pressure to use will be present in the community.

Many well-intentioned inmates have succumbed to this pressure and returned to drug abuse. They find they easily can refuse at first, but they weaken later. The probability of relapse is high. Depending on the population studied, more than half of those people who are trying to recover from drug or alcohol abuse will relapse.

Statistics indicate that more than half of those who quit alcohol or drug abuse will relapse within the first year. Inmates can stay out of that group if they are prepared to handle certain situations.

### The Cost of Addiction

Most people who use drugs don't think about the cost. Cost can be measured in terms of emotional pain, family disruption, and financial loss. Thinking about these losses can be useful if it would help prevent addiction and relapse.

### Treatment Alternatives in the Community

At first, many people use drugs as a form of recreation, escape, spiritual fulfillment, etc. These motives are not necessarily bad, but drugs usually are a poor means to an end. The key to prevention is to find alternative ways to cope with problems or to fulfill desires. Learning to solve problems, to relax, to manage anger, to think before taking action, and to resolve family problems are important issues in drug abuse prevention.

Probably the most widely available treatment resources in the community are self-help groups. In the February 5, 1990, issue of *Newsweek* magazine, statistics indicate that approximately 500,000 support group meetings are held each week in the United States. These meetings are attended by approximately fifteen million Americans.

The primary self-help group is, of course, Alcoholics Anonymous. About 1.7 million Americans regularly attend these groups. The twelve-step treatment approach in the "Anonymous" groups aren't appropriate for everyone. They involve discussing a "higher power" and the spiritual nature of humans. Alcoholics Anonymous views its members as participating in a fellowship that provides assistance in dealing with the disease of alcoholism. The first step in the self-help process is recognizing that one is an alcoholic and admitting to personal powerlessness over one's drinking. AA groups meet on a regular basis in every area of the country. These groups involve little or no cost. Al-Anon can provide support for relatives and friends.

Individual and other group counseling also is available through private practitioners and local community mental health services. Depending on the area in which the inmate is released, a vast range of resources is available. Mental health centers can provide a number of additional needed treatment options such as family or vocational counseling. For those individuals who have military backgrounds, the Veteran's Administration might present an excellent treatment alternative. Contact with a VA representative prior to release might be helpful.

Inpatient treatment programs should be discussed. Private or community hospital-based inpatient programs typically might range from fourteen to sixty days. A relatively standard inpatient program might be about one month in length. Although the treatment philosophies vary, many in-patient programs follow the disease model and strongly encourage the twelve-step living promoted in the "Anonymous" groups.

One intense type of inpatient setting that might warrant specific discussion is the therapeutic community. The therapeutic community (TC) models vary in terms of specific lengths of stay and treatment approach. The common element of virtually all TCs is a highly structured, generally sheltered setting in which there is a long-term and intense focus on issues involving substance abuse.

A final treatment option that deserves discussion involves various medications that can be prescribed to help people deal with drug abuse problems. For decades, alcoholics have been prescribed Antabuse to deter the use of alcohol. This drug, of course, makes the user extremely ill if he or she ignores the inherent warning and ingests alcohol. Some inmates might have participated in methadone maintenance programs. Although such programs might have peaked in the mid-1970s, today tens of thousands of narcotic addicts still attempt to deal with their abuse problems, at least in part, by using this longer-acting, synthetic narcotic substance.

Recently, a number of cases of "breakthroughs" against cocaine use have been described. For example, a few researchers report that in prescribing various anti-depressant drugs called tricyclics, the cravings for cocaine significantly diminish. Other investigators have reported that by prescribing bromocriptine, which potentiates the action of the neurotransmitter dopamine, cravings can be diminished significantly. Some researchers have combined antidepressants with amino acids L-tryptophan and L-tyrosine in yet another treatment approached purported to block cocaine euphoria and reduce craving. At this point, the medical search for a cocaine "cure" is in the early stages, and reports of success need further validation. Inmates should know that these substances at best aid in modifying a destructive lifestyle and are not a total answer.

## REFERENCES

(see also Chapter II)

Cohen, S. *The substance abuse problems: New issues for the 1980s.* Vol. 2. New York: The Haworth Press.

Gold, Mark S. 1984. *800-Cocaine.* New York: Bantam Books.

Judson, H. F. 1975. *Heroin addiction.* New York: Random House.

National Institute on Drug Abuse. April 1986. *Cocaine use in America.* Prevention Networks (ADM 86-1433).

Ray, O. *Drugs, society, and human behavior.* 3d ed. New York: The Haworth Press.

# XV.
# SPECIALS NEEDS POPULATIONS

Correctional populations are societies within society—a microcosm of the world in which we live. They are composed of diverse groups of individuals having a unique culture, heritage, and background. Effective substance abuse treatment programs consider these distinctive attributes, which accompany many addicts and drug abusers, for a variety of reasons.

First, the knowledge base concerning the important role of social and psychological influences on the development and maintenance of addictive/abusive behavior has grown dramatically over the past two decades. It is clear from the available scientific evidence that an individual's peer group, family, educational background, and personal associates have a significant role in determining whether or not an individual will abuse drugs or alcohol. By better understanding all factors that motivate particular individuals to abuse drugs or alcohol, including cultural and environmental influences, programs may be more effectively designed to enhance the possibility of successful treatment outcome.

Secondly, while the ideal manner in which to undertake treatment may be to conduct comprehensive individual assessments and design a treatment plan based exclusively on individual needs, the limited availability of highly qualified treatment professionals and supportive budgets may make this approach unrealistic. Knowledge of specific populations enable the limited number of treatment professionals that work within the criminal justice system to design treatment programs with group treatment protocols that target the needs most commonly observed in those groups.

Some of the special offender group populations that often necessitate specialized programming include women, pregnant women, HIV-positive offenders, the older offender, the mentally ill, and members of diverse racial groups and ethnic minorities. The latter category consists of blacks, Hispanics, Native Americans, and Asian-Americans, as well as individuals who cite membership in and identify with other unique ethnic groups. This brief delineation is by no means exhaustive nor reflective of the much broader cultural diversity that exists in society and the criminal justice system. A brief review of some of the special needs that have been identified for some of the special populations indicated follows.

## WOMEN

Women who abuse drugs and alcohol, until relatively recently, have received minimal attention (Fellios 1989). Doshan and Bursh (1982) indicated that research on the special problems of women who abuse drugs and effective treatment strategies was in an embryonic stage. This is supported by research findings from the National Institute on Drug Abuse that despite concerted efforts during the early part of the past decade, only twenty-five women-oriented community-based substance abuse treatment programs, serving 547 women, could be located (Beschner and Thompson 1981). Over the past decade, however, much has occurred to increase public concern and attention. Concern brought about by the medical profession with regard to fetal alcohol syndrome (FAS), as well as children born to crack-addicted mothers, has helped increase awareness and concern (Fellios 1989).

Unfortunately, there is even more limited research in the area of specific treatment modalities for women offenders. Some of the more common findings for female alcohol and drug abusers in the general population, particularly the physiological and medical consequences, are likely to be equally valid with regard to the criminal justice population. These include the following:

1.  Women who are characterized as alcoholic are remarkably heterogeneous.

2.  The greatest number of alcohol-related problems were reported by women aged eighteen to twenty and unemployed women looking for work (Wilsnack and Beckman 1984).

3.  Women appear to be more prone to some of the complicating medical consequences of heavy drinking than men (Gombert and Lisansky 1984).

4.  All grades of liver damage may develop more rapidly in women (Saunders, Davis, and Williams 1981).

5.  Heavy drinkers have more gynecological problems (Wilsnack, Klassen, and Wilsnack 1984), neurological changes reflected in computerized tomographic (CT) scans (Jacobson 1986), and increased risk of breast cancer when compared to nondrinkers (Schatzkin et al. 1987). Hence, women in need of substance abuse treatment are more likely to have chronic medical problems that require special attention.

Women also face different psychological and sociological factors than their male counterparts. Changing roles and work ethics are reflected in the number of women leaving the household to work and dealing with the stresses and pressures of the work world. Significant pressures often develop when women feel they must choose between homemaker/mother and work. Often, women who become divorced have no choice but to work in support of their children. Some research (Rathod & Thompson 1971) indicates that female alcoholics are more likely to be divorced and the single head of a household. Such women are often unskilled, work full-time at menial jobs, with wages at or below the poverty level, and live in constant financial crisis. They may have the added burden of raising children virtually alone as well as handling all the domestic tasks and responsibilities inherent to running a household. Such pressures are often tremendous, and one can readily understand how some of them may resort to alcohol or drug use to cope with the stress of such a lifestyle. Women substance abusers tend to have higher levels of personal distress, depression, and anxiety and lower levels of self-esteem when compared to male substance abusers (Beschner and Thompson 1984). Many women entering treatment are often victims of physical and sexual abuse, the consequences of which may be emotionally devastating.

A menu of program options should be available to assist women with the unique pressures that they face. Among these options should be support groups that confront the high levels of denial, negativism, helplessness, and hopelessness many substance abusing women feel. Wellness education groups, which share information particularly applicable to females, are encouraged. Groups designed to enhance self-esteem and skills building efforts—skills needed to face and overcome the problems confronting them on release—are required. Groups designed to empower women, to encourage them to feel that they are not helpless and not in a hopeless situation are seen as instrumental in facilitating change. They can benefit from learning that they control a great deal of their world by making changes in their lifestyles, including healthier forms of living and coping with stressful events.

Supportive family members, if available, should be incorporated into the treatment regimen. Reintegrating women offenders into a supportive community on release, by networking with available treatment services for follow-up care and maintenance, is of paramount importance. Newly acquired skills and the fragile new sense of self-esteem may be easily undermined and victimized if not encouraged by a nurturing supportive environment.

## PREGNANT OFFENDERS

Pregnant offenders with substance abuse problems represent a very special population for treatment consideration. These offenders should be a treatment priority for every system, not only for the offender's personal well-being but the well-being of the unborn child. Generations of children continue to be born who are adversely affected, often in devastating manner, by the consequences of the addictive behavior of the mother. In 1988, at least 375,000 babies were born addicted in the United States (Rua 1990). Many children born to addicted women are afflicted with fetal alcohol syndrome (FAS), cocaine addiction, and Human Immunodeficiency Virus (HIV) infection.

Intravenous drug use is the primary cause of AIDS transmission involving pediatric cases. Recent data from the Centers for Disease Control indicate that approximately three-fourths of perinatal AIDS case are children whose mothers either used drugs intravenously or were the sexual partners of IV drug uscrs (Rua 1990). We have yet to fully realize and appreciate the long-term personal tragedies of the individuals involved. In the face of such tragedy, it seems almost impertinent to mention the ccnsequences to our medical, educational, and social services systems in fiscal terms, but the costs are staggering and will continue to mount.

Highly specialized programs need to be made available to these offenders. These include appropriate medical and prenatal services along with all services from the therapeutic milieu indicated above for women offenders. Additional support services addressing issues of mother-child bonding, child development and child care, health, and safety should be addressed. Therapists should be skilled in dealing with separation issues that these incarcerated women deal with when away from their children. Additional issues involving guilt and dysphoria produced from both psychogenic factors and biogenic factors (postpartum and drug withdrawal) should be given special attention. Consideration should be given to enrolling the children who are born under these circumstances into infant stimulation programs, with the goal of mitigating some of the damage that they may have received during the prenatal period. Needless to say, these infants will require high levels of attention from medical, psychological, and educational specialists from birth.

## AIDS AND HIV-POSITIVE POPULATIONS

Currently, there are more than 100,000 cases of Acquired Immune Deficiency Syndrome in the United States. There are an additional one-and-one-half million individuals who are projected to be carriers of the AIDS virus according to the Centers for Disease Control. More than 50,000 deaths have been attributed to AIDS or AIDS-related complications, with that number projected to exceed 250,000 by 1992. Despite the fact that homosexual men have accounted for more than 60 percent of all United States AIDS cases, the incidence of cases among intravenous drug users is growing rapidly. More than 30 percent of all persons with AIDS are found among intravenous drug users (RYA 1990), one of the most rapidly growing groups of individuals afflicted with the disease.

Many individuals who are HIV-positive and who later develop AIDS are found within the criminal justice system. Since 1981, AIDS has been the leading cause of death in New York State Prisons (New York State Health Department 1989) and the leading cause of death for New York City males aged thirty to fifty-nine and New York City females aged one to nine and thirty to thirty-nine. Within the Federal Bureau of Prisons, the majority of HIV-positive inmates are black (61.2 percent) despite the fact that black males comprise only about 29.5 percent of the overall federal prison population (Federal Bureau of Prisons 1989). Approximately 61 percent of those inmates testing positive for the AIDS virus in the Bureau of Prisons listed intravenous drug use as a risk factor.

Perhaps no issue more readily underscores the need to find effective intervention and treatment strategies with members of the drug-abusing population than that of AIDS. Treatment and educational programs must be developed to deal with the complications associated with seropositive and AIDS patients in the criminal justice setting that parallel those services available in the community. This includes providing specialized diagnostic, screening, and supportive individual and group services, when appropriate, to offenders who demonstrate a homosexual orientation and lifestyle, as well as offenders who have used drugs intravenously. The type and frequency of medical services required of this population are substantially greater than general population inmates.

## OLDER OFFENDERS

The elderly often manifest substance abuse problems due to a variety of psychosocial and biological reasons, particularly abuse of licit drugs and alcohol. Lawson (1989) points out that the aging process alters the manner in which drugs are absorbed and distributed, metabolized, and excreted. They have decreased tolerance, more clinical and toxic side effects, and increased physical illnesses and complaints. Impairment in the senses, loss or impairment of some body functions, and sensory impairment associated with aging are common to this population as well.

Additionally, the bereavement associated with loss of family, friends, and spouse are often difficult to deal with. Retirement, loneliness, depression, isolation, and loss or substantial reduction in income are powerful stressors associated with later life. Suicide occurs at significantly higher levels for the elderly than in the general population.

Treatment programs should be encouraged to focus on the development of realistic goals presented in active and supportive groups. Themes that the therapist should be prepared to deal with include death and dying, grief, depression, loneliness, isolation, abandonment, existential or "meaning of life" issues, physical and/or mental deterioration, helplessness, and uselessness. It is also suggested that groups that provide wellness and fitness activities should be offered in addition to the more traditional informational/experiential groups. Positive attitudes expressed through dynamic, highly motivated therapists are likely to generate enthusiastic responses from this population.

## THE MENTALLY ILL (Dually-diagnosed)

There is little question that many substance abusers often present with substantial levels of psychiatric impairment. Mentally ill offenders should be evaluated for the possible role of substance abuse in their behavioral disorders. The use of drugs other than those often prescribed in treating psychiatric disorders can result in a number of potentially serious, if not fatal, interactions. Unfortunately, efforts by the mentally ill offender at "self-medication" to deal with symptoms of their illnesses, such as stress, anger, depression, and other negative feelings, or symptoms of psychosis (e.g., visual or auditory hallucinations) are commonplace.

Clearly, diagnostic expertise in properly differentiating this population and arranging effective treatment strategies is essential. A close working relationship with medical professionals is essential in managing the mentally ill offender. Techniques may include contracting with the client for abstinence, education as to the nature of the mental illness, explanation of the dangers of using drugs other than those prescribed for psychiatric reasons, the development of alternative coping skills, availability of support networks, and an interdisciplinary approach to case management.

## RACIAL AND ETHNIC MINORITIES

Blacks, Hispanics, and Native Americans are frequently over-represented in the criminal justice system when compared to their membership in the general population. For a variety of reasons that appear to be largely psychosocial in origin, members of these minority cultures are often at greater risk for developing substance abuse problems than members of the general population as a whole. Special efforts must be made to better understand the origins of these factors and attempts made to foster understanding of the cultural diversity that leads to the development of more effective treatment strategies for these populations.

It is highly unlikely that any treatment modality that does not take into consideration the role of social and cultural backgrounds will be effective. This may be particularly true for members of minority cultures. Effective communication must be established before any meaningful interventions can begin. The use of therapists who are fluent in the clients' native language is required. Over 50 percent of the Hispanic population in this country speaks Spanish exclusively or as their preferred language (Eden and Aguilar 1989).

Therapists who share the primary cultural characteristics of the target population may also facilitate the therapeutic process and serve as positive role models for group members. It is also highly likely that more homogeneous groups may be helpful in the treatment process, as they may promote more ready identification, cohesiveness, and self-disclosure by group members.

There is clearly a paucity of information that evaluates the sociological and psychological risk factors of individuals to substance abuse from an intracultural perspective. Further, the psychological dynamics of the relationship between minority cultures and the dominant culture in the development of substance abuse have yet to begin to be fully explicated. Such investigations are vital if we are to better understand all components of the multivariate etiology of addiction.

## REFERENCES

Dugger, R. 1990. *Comprehensive substance abuse treatment program.* Tallahassee, Fla.: Florida Department of Corrections.

Eden, S., and R. Aguilar. 1989. The Hispanic chemically dependent client: Considerations for diagnosis and treatment. In *Alcoholism and substance abuse in special populations,* G. W. Lawson & A. W. Lawson, eds. Rockville, Md.: Aspen.

Federal Bureau of Prisons. 1989. *HIV infection among Bureau of Prisons inmates.* Research Bulletin, Washington, D.C.: Office of Research and Evaluation.

Fellios, P. 1989. Alcoholism in women: Causes, treatment, and prevention. In *Alcoholism and substance abuse in special populations,* G. W. Lawson & A. W. Lawson, eds. Rockville, Md.: Aspen.

Gomberg, E., and J. Lisansky. 1984. Antecedents of alcohol problems in women. In *Alcohol problems in women,* S. C. Wilsnack & L. J. Beckman, eds. New York: Guilford.

Jacobson, R. 1986. Female alcoholics: A controlled CT brain scan and clinical study. *British Journal of Addiction* 81:661-669.

Lawson, A. 1989. Substance abuse problems of the elderly: Consideration for treatment and prevention. In *Alcoholism and substance abuse in special populations,* G. W. Lawson & A. W. Lawson, eds. Rockville, Md.: Aspen.

New York State Health Department. 1989. *AIDS in New York state.* Albany.

Rathod, J., and I. Thompson. 1971. Women alcoholics: A clinical study. *Quarterly Journal of Studies on Alcohol* 32:45-52.

Rua, J. 1990. Treatment works: The tragic cost of underestimating treatment in the "Drug War." Washington, D.C.: National Association of State Alcohol and Drug Abuse Directors.

Saunders, J., M. Davis, and R. Williams. 1981. do women develop alcoholic liver disease more readily than men? *British Medical Journal* 282:1141-1143.

Schatzkin, A., D. Y. Jones, R. N. Hoover, P. R. Taylor, L. A. Brinton, R. G. Ziegler, E. B. Harvey, C. L. Carter, L. M. Licitra, M. C. Dufour et al. 1987. Alcohol consumption and breast cancer in the epidemiologic follow-up study of the first national health and nutrition examination survey. *New England Journal of Medicine* 316:1169-1173.

Wilsnack, S., and L. Beckman, eds. 1984. *Alcohol problems in women.* New York: Guilford.

Wilsnack, S., A. Klassen, and R. Wilsnack. 1984. Drinking and reproductive dysfunction among women in a 1981 national survey. *Alcoholism: Clinical & Experimental Research* 8:451-458.

# Appendix A
# *TRUE/FALSE STUDY QUESTIONS AND ANSWERS*

The following questions may be used in practice sessions, as review material, or can be included as part of the program at the discretion of the instructor. One way to use them is to complete a chapter, and then ask students to discuss the questions as a group. If kept confidential, these questions may be used as a final exam, although multiple choice questions are generally better.

## CHAPTER III

### TRUE OR FALSE

1. _____ Most people who have an addiction tend to deny this problem to others.

2. _____ Psychological addictions are easier to break than physical ones.

3. _____ Drug and alcohol abuse has a tendency to run in families.

4. _____ Illegal drugs can be used safely by the majority of people.

5. _____ If people completely can stop using drugs for a year, they have proved that they have no drug problem.

6. _____ Treatment for drug abuse usually succeeds the first time a person gets help.

7. _____ Occasional use of any drug is safe once a physical addiction has been overcome.

8. _____ The first step in overcoming a psychological addiction is to acknowledge to oneself that there is a problem.

9. _____ One's addiction can be contagious since others also might be influenced to use drugs to fit in or be accepted.

10. _____ Becoming irritable, craving, then looking for drugs is best described as a physical addiction.

11. _____ If a person relapses, this proves that he or she is going to be an active addict for the rest of his or her life.

12. _____ The majority of people who experiment with addictive drugs become addicts.

## CHAPTER IV

### TRUE OR FALSE

1. _____ There are two types of drugs, psychoactive and nonpsychoactive.

2. _____ Nonpsychoactive drugs affect moods, behaviors, and perceptions.

3. _____ Psychoactive drugs include substances that have stimulant, depressant, and anticancer properties.

4. _____ The sedative/hypnotics or general depressants include the barbiturates, alcohol, and cocaine.

5. _____ Cocaine is classed in the same category as nicotine.

6. _____ Cocaine is second only to alcohol as the most abused drug.

7. _____ Tolerance increases over time for all psychoactive drugs.

8. _____ Synergism means that drugs combined or taken together have less of an effect than if taken separately.

9. _____ Valium is a stimulant.

10. _____ A placebo will work if the user believes it will.

11. _____ Nonpsychoactive drugs sold over the counter, such as aspirin and Tylenol, are not dangerous.

12. _____ Legal drugs kill more people than illegal drugs.

## CHAPTER V

### TRUE OR FALSE

1. _____ Methanol (wood alcohol) is drinkable alcohol.

2. _____ Ethanol, which can be used as a gasoline additive, is drinkable alcohol.

3. _____ Most alcohol is eliminated through the kidneys.

4. _____ Alcohol is a toxic waste product or excretion of yeast.

5. _____ Alcohol is a liquid and therefore is very low in calories.

6. _____ Sedatives and alcohol safely can be used together, since one drug has no effect on the other.

7. _____ Withdrawal from alcohol is more dangerous than withdrawal from heroin.

8. _____ One beer has less alcohol than a shot of whiskey.

9. _____ Cirrhosis of the liver usually is reversible once drinking stops.

10. _____ Three-quarters of all murders involve the use of alcohol.

11. _____ Sniffing solvent inhalants such as paint thinners, butane, gasoline, and glue fumes cause intoxication similar to alcohol.

12. _____ Sniffing solvents is no more dangerous than drinking alcohol.

## CHAPTER VI

### TRUE OR FALSE

1. _____ Narcotics originated from a plant cultivated by Native Americans in the Andes Mountains.

2. _____ Heroin is a natural narcotic found in raw opium.

3. _____ "Analgesic" means painkiller.

4. _____ Dilaudid, Demerol, Talwin, Percodan, and Methadone are all synthetic narcotics.

5. _____ Morphine can be extracted from morning glory seeds.

6. _____ Quaaludes, Librium, Ativan, Xanax, and Tranxene are all synthetic narcotics.

7. _____ Constipation and cough suppression are two side effects of narcotic use.

8. _____ Heroin legally is prescribed in England.

9. _____ Physical dependence develops toward every narcotic analgesic.

10. _____ Dirty needles are responsible for the spread of AIDS, hepatitis, endocarditis, and encephalitis.

11. _____ Heroin is much more addicting than the other narcotics.

12. _____ Shooting or smoking narcotics is more addictive than snorting.

## CHAPTER VII

### TRUE OR FALSE

1. _____ Stimulants have legitimate medical uses.

2. _____ A period of calm often is associated with stimulant withdrawal.

3. _____ Amphetamines have been legally used by soldiers in wartime.

4. _____ Amphetamines can be detected in the urine for up to two days.

5. _____ Smoking amphetamines is not possible.

6. _____ Coffee and amphetamines are both in the same class of drugs.

7. _____ Stimulants increase the appetite for food.

8. _____ Amphetamines are safer to use than cocaine.

9. _____ Coffee and nicotine are classified as weak stimulants.

10. _____ Dextroamphetamines and methamphetamines also are weak stimulants.

11. _____ Amphetamines don't cause paranoia like cocaine.

12. _____ Amphetamines are the best way to lose weight.

**CHAPTER VIII**

## TRUE OR FALSE

1. _____ Cocaine is classified medically as a narcotic.

2. _____ Severe depression often is associated with cocaine withdrawal.

3. _____ Paranoid reactions nearly always occur after long-term heavy use of cocaine and amphetamines.

4. _____ Mixing cocaine with heroin cancels the effects of both drugs.

5. _____ Smoking cocaine is safer than snorting.

6. _____ "Crack" is cocaine hydrochloride.

7. _____ Stimulants mask natural drives such as hunger.

8. _____ Death can result during the first use of cocaine.

9. _____ Coffee and tobacco affect the heart like cocaine.

10. _____ Chewing coca leaves has most of the detrimental effects of cocaine.

11. _____ Truly pure cocaine does not irritate the nose.

12. _____ Crack cocaine gives more doses for the money than powder.

## CHAPTER IX

### TRUE OR FALSE

1. _____ Tobacco is addictive, like heroin.

2. _____ Tobacco can be snorted intranasally.

3. _____ Nicotine is a prime cause of cancer.

4. _____ Chewing tobacco does not cause cancer.

5. _____ Tobacco medically is classed as a stimulant, as is cocaine.

6. _____ Tobacco use can make penile erections difficult.

7. _____ Cigarette use will not harm a baby while it is safe in the womb.

8. _____ Most adult cigarette smokers started smoking before they started high school.

9. _____ Emphysema is reversible if a person stops smoking.

10. _____ Nicotine leaves the brain within half an hour.

11. _____ The skin of people who use tobacco is more wrinkled than of those who don't.

12. _____ People who chew tobacco are safe from heart and artery problems.

**CHAPTER X**

## TRUE OR FALSE

1. _____ LSD slows down most bodily processes.

2. _____ LSD makes most people more easily influenced by suggestion.

3. _____ Psilocybin comes from a cactus.

4. _____ Not only does PCP cause numbness, but depending on the dose it also acts as a disinhibitor, depressant, and hallucinogen.

5. _____ PCP presently is used as an anesthetic in surgery.

6. _____ MDA and MDMA are both depressants and hallucinogens.

7. _____ Tolerance develops to mescaline.

8. _____ Peyote, a cactus containing mescaline, is used legally by Native Americans.

9. _____ A person under the influence of PCP is more likely to produce a "blank stare" than is a person under the influence of LSD.

10. _____ PCP makes a person under the influence more sensitive to pain.

11. _____ PCP is associated with irrational violence.

12. _____ A person under the influence of LSD can see colored patterns with his or her eyes closed.

## CHAPTER XI

### TRUE OR FALSE

1. _____ Cannabis, the plant marijuana comes from, was used for rope, cloth, and paper in the past.

2. _____ Marijuana contains less cancer-causing tar than an equal amount of tobacco.

3. _____ The active ingredient in marijuana is medically classified as a narcotic.

4. _____ Marijuana or its active ingredients are used to treat cancerous tumors.

5. _____ Hashish has the same active ingredient as marijuana.

6. _____ Evidence exists that heavy marijuana use lowers the level of testosterone, the male sex hormone.

7. _____ Marijuana can be eaten but is less potent that way.

8. _____ Marijuana use and increased aggressiveness go together.

9. _____ While stoned on marijuana, a person has less ability to remember things.

10. _____ Marijuana will help a drunk person drive better.

11. _____ Most youths who experiment with marijuana will become addicted to cocaine or heroin.

12. _____ Before modern medicine, marijuana was used to treat menstrual cramps in women.

## CHAPTER XII

### TRUE OR FALSE

1. _____ It is safe to share razors, needles, or tattoo equipment with others.

2. _____ AIDS can be cured with a medicine called AZT.

3. _____ Casual contact such as shaking hands can transmit the AIDS virus.

4. _____ Pregnant women with the AIDS virus can transmit this disease to their unborn babies.

5. _____ I.V. drug use is one of the most common ways that AIDS is spread.

6. _____ People with AIDS usually die from pneumonia or some other disease rather than AIDS itself.

7. _____ Homosexuals and drug users are the only people who get AIDS.

8. _____ A study at Johns Hopkins Medical Center has proved that a complete blood transfusion will eliminate the AIDS virus from the body.

9. _____ The HIV virus has been found in saliva and tears.

10. _____ A person with AIDS is in more danger of catching a disease from other people than others are of catching AIDS from him or her.

11. _____ The HIV-antibody test will detect all people who are infected with HIV.

12. _____ Unprotected anal sex is much more dangerous than protected vaginal sex.

## CHAPTER XIII

### TRUE OR FALSE

1. _____ The alcoholic parent doesn't hurt anyone but himself or herself.

2. _____ Children show no ill effects of a parental drug/alcohol problem.

3. _____ The child who becomes rebellious often turns to drug or alcohol abuse prior to adulthood.

4. _____ Nonalcoholic members of the family can find support through Al-Anon and Alateen.

5. _____ ACOA groups are for Adult Children of Alcoholics.

6. _____ An alcoholic or drug-addicted parent still can be a good parent.

7. _____ An enabler is a helpful person who unknowingly prolongs the addiction by saving the abuser from the consequences of his or her behavior.

8. _____ Children who are raised by alcoholic or drug-abusing parents have no higher risk of abusing alcohol or drugs themselves in the future.

9. _____ The eldest child is usually the most fearful and meek, since he or she is exposed to the parental problem first.

10. _____ Physical abuse is no more frequent in alcoholic families than nonalcoholic families.

11. _____ Alcoholism tends to run in families.

12. _____ When sober, alcoholics and drug addicts usually are very close to their children emotionally.

## CHAPTER XIV

### TRUE OR FALSE

1. _____ Once a physical addiction is over, elements associated with drug use do not produce an emotional reaction in a person.

2. _____ It is a good idea to test one's ability to resist temptation by sitting in a bar and drinking nothing but soda.

3. _____ Cravings for cocaine can be induced by seeing sugar.

4. _____ A recovered addict should avoid any excitement or pleasure in order to prevent a relapse.

5. _____ A relapse into addiction takes less time than the original addiction.

6. _____ A relapse means that a person is a hopeless failure.

7. _____ The justice system is sympathetic toward addicts who don't steal.

8. _____ Our society is becoming more tolerant of casual drug use.

9. _____ People need ways to escape from emotional pressures.

10. _____ In the prison system, the use of drugs is considered as serious as assault.

11. _____ Hanging out with drug-using buddies has no relationship with relapse.

12. _____ Once a person has been an addict, that person cannot take the chance of having any fun.

## ANSWERS TO SAMPLE CHAPTER QUESTIONS (TRUE/FALSE)

| | | | | | | | | | | | | | |
|---|---|---|---|---|---|---|---|---|---|---|---|---|---|
| | | | | | | **CHAPTER** | | | | | | | |
| | III | IV | V | VI | VII | VIII | IX | X | XI | XII | XIII | XIV | |
| **Item** | | | | | | | | | | | | | |
| 1. | T | T | F | F | F | F | T | F | T | F | F | F |
| 2. | F | F | T | F | T | T | T | T | F | F | F | F |
| 3. | T | F | F | T | F | T | F | F | F | F | T | T |
| 4. | F | F | T | T | T | F | F | T | F | T | T | F |
| 5. | F | T | F | F | F | F | T | F | T | T | T | T |
| 6. | F | F | F | F | T | F | T | F | T | T | F | F |
| 7. | F | T | T | T | T | T | F | T | T | F | T | F |
| 8. | T | F | F | T | F | T | T | T | F | F | F | F |
| 9. | T | F | F | T | T | T | F | T | T | T | F | T |
| 10. | F | T | T | T | F | F | T | F | F | T | F | T |
| 11. | F | F | T | F | F | F | T | T | F | F | T | F |
| 12. | F | T | F | T | F | F | F | T | T | T | F | F |

## TRUE-FALSE ANSWER EXPLANATIONS

### Chapter III

1.　T　　People often feel shame at their addiction and hide their problem.

2.　F　　Physical addictions end within weeks as the body gets back in balance, but memories and desires can last a lifetime.

3.　T　　Genetics may play a role; more importantly people often repeat what they have learned as a child.

4.　F　　Most illegal drugs are illegal due to being dangerous.

5.　F　　A person who has been addicted is in danger of quick relapse into addiction if drugs are used again.

6.　F　　Many people fail several times before success.

7.  F    Occasional use may lead to total relapse.

8.  T    A person must desire to change to be successful.

9.  T    Most people who try drugs do so at the urging of friends.

10. F    These are symptoms of psychological addiction.

11. F    A person can relapse, then be successful on his or her next try. A belief in hopelessness is dangerous.

12. F    Most people who experiment with drugs satisfy their curiosity and quit, and some use without becoming addicted. People with no goals or other sources of happiness or with emotional problems easily become trapped into addiction.

## Chapter IV

1.  T    Penicillin and aspirin are drugs, but do not affect the mind.

2.  F    Psychoactive drugs have these effects.

3.  F    Anticancer drugs are not psychoactive.

4.  F    Cocaine is a stimulant drug, not a sedative.

5.  T    Tobacco and nicotine, its active ingredient, is a stimulant.

6.  F    Marijuana is more popular than cocaine; prescription tranquilizers are also abused more often.

7.  T    This may not be true for low doses of marijuana or caffeine, but tolerance develops when higher doses are used.

8.  F    Synergism means that effects are more than additive.

9.  F     Valium is a sedative that reduces anxiety.

10. T     The placebo effect refers to expectations producing psychological changes.

11. F     Overdoses of over-the-counter painkillers kill hundreds each year.

12. T     Illegal drugs are responsible for less than 1/100th of the deaths that tobacco, alcohol, and other legal drugs cause.

## Chapter V

1.  F     Methyl alcohol (methanol) is poisonous.

2.  T     Drinking alcohol can be used as a fuel when pure.

3.  F     The liver detoxifies 95 percent of the alcohol in the blood.

4.  T     Alcohol can be called "yeast urine," as it is a waste product when yeast eats sugar.

5.  F     Alcohol is high in calories, but contains no nutrients.

6.  F     Alcohol combined with other sedatives can kill.

7.  T     Heroin withdrawal is painful but not dangerous, while abrupt withdrawal from constant alcohol use can cause psychosis and even death.

8.  F     They contain the same amount of alcohol; the beer is more dilute but larger.

9.  F     Cirrhosis (scarring of the liver) is permanent.

10. T     Alcohol reduces fears (inhibitions) about consequences of behavior.

11. T     All solvents that dissolve oil will produce intoxication of brain cells.

12. F     Our bodies cannot detoxify other solvents as well as we can alcohol and so death may result.

### Chapter VI

1. F     Although cocaine is termed a narcotic by some laws, it is actually a stimulant.

2. F     Morphine is the strong narcotic found in the opium poppy, while heroin is diacetyl-morphine, a semisynthetic derivative.

3. T     Look at any aspirin bottle.

4. T     They are all narcotics made by chemists.

5. F     Morphine comes from opium poppies.

6. F     None of them are narcotics, rather they are sedatives.

7. T     During withdrawal the opposite will occur (diarrhea).

8. T     Heroin is preferred due to having fewer side effects than the weaker narcotics.

9. T     All narcotics have similar effects, and all are addictive.

10. T     Needles push diseases past our main defense: our skin.

11. F     All narcotics are addicting when used in doses that produce the same effects.

12. T     The more rapidly drugs enter the brain the more addictive.

## Chapter VII

1. T   Amphetamines are used to prevent narcolepsy, a condition in which people fall asleep without warning. Ritalin is used to help children with attention deficit disorder.

2. T   Stimulants drain bodily resources, and people are exhausted after excessive use.

3. T   The German Blitzkrieg in World War II involved soldiers overwhelming defenders by fighting constantly for days. Amphetamines kept these men awake and also increased aggressiveness. Amphetamines have been used in more recent wars as well.

4. F   Amphetamine use can be detected in the urine for two weeks after last use.

5. F   "Ice" is methamphetamine in large crystals. It can be smoked, which often produces long-lasting paranoia.

6. T   Both are stimulants, although amphetamines are stronger.

7. F   Stimulants decrease hunger, which is why "speed freaks" become so thin.

8. F   Amphetamines last much longer in the system, so the body suffers from stress longer.

9. T   Enough caffeine can produce similar effects as amphetamine, but with more side effects. Nicotine (tobacco) is a weaker central nervous system stimulant, but has strong cardiovascular effects.

10. F   They are among the strongest and longest-lasting stimulants.

11. F   Amphetamines can produce a longer-lasting paranoia.

12. F   Weight loss by use of amphetamines usually returns. Only a permanent change in eating and exercise habits produces long-lasting change.

## Chapter VIII

1.  F      Cocaine is medically classified as a stimulant.

2.  T      Cocaine drains our natural pleasure chemicals, making pleasure more difficult to experience. Also, people often have guilt feelings about what they did to stay high.

3.  T      Heavy use of stimulants drains people of pleasant motivations, leaves our most primitive emotion: fear. Paranoia is defined as unreasonable fear.

4.  F      "Speedballs" combine but do not cancel the effects of heroin and cocaine.

5.  F      Smoking crack (cocaine base) allows dangerous amounts of cocaine to enter the bloodstream. Snorting may burn holes in the nose, but limits the amount absorbed into the system.

6.  F      Rock or crack cocaine is cocaine base, like it is found in the plant. Powder cocaine is a water-soluble salt, cocaine hydrochloride.

7.  T      People on cocaine or "speed" feel no hunger.

8.  T      Some people have heart attacks on the first use. This is quite rare, but can happen in people who have blood vessels going to the heart that spasm easily or whose heart goes into spasms easily.

9.  T      All stimulants speed up the heartrate and raise blood pressure.

10. F      There are few, if any, detrimental effects when coca leaves are chewed, as the leaves contain only 1 to 2 percent cocaine and also vitamins. Secondly, the cocaine is absorbed slowly so that only moderate doses reach the brain.

11. F      Even pure cocaine is an irritant that also constricts blood vessels and can kill the skin inside the nose. Because it also blocks pain in that area, the damage might not be felt immediately.

12.  F    Crack cocaine, in convenient doses, is a marketing ploy to make more money for dealers. It usually costs more per dose than powder.

## Chapter IX

1.  T    Many heroin addicts have said that quitting tobacco was more difficult than quitting heroin.

2.  T    Snuff was a popular way to take tobacco before cigarettes became so popular.

3.  F    Nicotine is implicated in heart and circulatory diseases, but not in cancer. Other ingredients, the half-burned "tars" can cause cancer.

4.  F    Prolonged irritation where the wad touches will kill skin cells. These dead cells may eventually be replaced by out-of-control cancer cells.

5.  T    Tobacco raises blood pressure like cocaine.

6.  T    Nine-tenths of men who complain of erection problems smoke tobacco, and most are helped by stopping smoking.

7.  F    Low birthweight is frequent in babies of women who smoke.

8.  T    The majority start by age fourteen.

9.  F    Emphysema is a permanent scarring of the lungs.

10. T    Nicotine is water-soluble and leaves the brain quickly, making an addict desire another smoke.

11. T    Poor circulation in smokers ages the skin quickly.

12. F    Chewing tobacco will probably save a person from lung cancer, but not from cardiovascular disease.

## Chapter X

1.  F     LSD acts as a mild stimulant, as the calming of sleep is impossible.

2.  T     LSD weakens the sensory filtering system, making a person more aware of sensations and thoughts, but less able to ignore and reject ideas.

3.  F     Psilocybin comes from a mushroom; mescaline is found in a cactus.

4.  T     PCP has a range of effects depending on dose. Small doses are similar to alcohol, but with larger doses comes loss of sensation, confusion, and visual hallucinations.

5.  F     PCP caused too many problems and is no longer being used for surgery.

6.  F     They are both variants of amphetamines and are classed as hallucinogenic stimulants.

7.  T     If used often, more mescaline is needed to induce the same effect.

8.  T     Members of the Native American Church can legally use peyote as a traditional religious sacrament.

9.  T     PCP reduces awareness and puts people into a stupor, while LSD increases awareness.

10. F     PCP eliminates awareness of pain, and people have been known to tear muscles and break bones without feeling it until the PCP wears off. Even gunshots do not have the usual effect of producing a state of shock.

11. T     Although violence on PCP is rare, when it does occur the person becomes totally berserk and very dangerous. The person is psychotic and irrational and cannot be controlled with normal pain compliance holds.

12. T     LSD allows awareness of normally unconscious mental processes. These can include awareness of the brain's visual processing system activity. In contrast to PCP, these visions are not true hallucinations because a person remains aware that they are drug-induced.

## Chapter XI

1. T　Cannabis, better known as hemp in the past, was the preferred source for rope fiber before synthetics. In colonial America farmers were required by law to grow hemp. The covered wagons that moved West had hemp cloth covers. The first drafts of our Constitution were written on hemp paper.

2. F　All plants contain chemicals that, when burned, produce "tars" that can cause cancer. Marijuana smoke contains less of some tars than tobacco, but more of others.

3. F　Tetra-hydro-cannabinol (THC for short) is a weak hallucinogen with sedative properties. It is medically classified as a narcotic, which affects the body's endorphin pain-relieving system.

4. F　THC, under the trade name of Marinol, is used to relieve nausea produced by other drugs used to fight cancers. Some people smoke marijuana for the same reason, although without a prescription. However, THC or marijuana does not fight cancer itself.

5. T　Hashish, the dried resin scraped off marijuana, contains a higher concentration of THC, the active ingredient.

6. T　High doses of THC temporarily lower the level of not only the male sex hormone, but also female sex hormones.

7. T　When eaten, it takes three times as much marijuana to have the same effect as when smoked. However, smoking irritates the lungs and is especially bad for people with asthma.

8. F　People tend to relax and become lazy on marijuana, rather than aggressive.

9. T　High doses of marijuana interfere with quick memory retrieval, and forgetting the topic of conversation is common.

10. F　Although small doses of marijuana may cause a drunk driver to slow down, the additional problems with memory and reduced scanning add

to the danger. Driving while intoxicated endangers others in addition to the driver.

11.    F      Most people who experiment with drugs do not progress to addiction. However, this experimentation and the association with illegal drug dealers raises their risk of becoming addicted.

12.    T      Marijuana, usually called hemp in the past, was a widely used remedy for cramps before modern medicine.

## Chapter XII

1.    F      Undried blood on a razor blade could possibly transmit the AIDS virus. Tattooing and especially shared i.v. needles have caused many to become infected when the equipment was not properly sterilized.

2.    F      AZT can slow the progression of AIDS, but is not a cure.

3.    F      Shaking hands, hugging, sharing food, and other nonsexual activities are not risky behaviors for the spread of the AIDS virus, which is mainly present in blood and sexual fluids.

4.    T      Approximately half of the babies born to HIV-infected mothers are infected. Breast milk has also been shown to have transmitted the disease in a few cases.

5.    T      Sharing intravenous hypodermic needles is by far the most risky behavior one can do regarding AIDS.

6.    T      AIDS itself does not usually kill, because the loss of the immune system allows diseases that are normally fought off to become deadly.

7.    F      The AIDS virus can be transmitted by blood transfusions and by male-female sex.

8.    F      At present there is no known way to remove all the AIDS virus from the body, although many medical studies are presently being conducted.

9.  T    Small amounts of the virus have been found in saliva and tears. However, there is no proven case of transmission from these fluids. This is because there are so few found in these fluids and also because the virus dies when it contacts the oxygen in air.

10. T    Giving others the AIDS virus requires sexual or blood exchange, while many other diseases can be transmitted by simply coughing.

11. F    A person may not show positive when tested until several months after infection. Most infected people test positive after three months, and one can be certain of a true negative after six months.

12. T    The anus does not have the natural sexual lubrication that the vagina has, and so rubbing can damage the skin more, sometimes making places that sperm and the AIDS virus can enter the body. AIDS transmission can occur with regular male-female intercourse, and a latex condom will reduce the danger. However, there is still some risk when an infected person has sex with another person.

## Chapter XIII

1.  F    The spouse and children of an alcoholic almost always are hurt emotionally if not physically.

2.  F    Children of abusers often have long-lasting emotional problems.

3.  T    Use of alcohol or drugs is often a way to demonstrate a rebellious attitude.

4.  T    Al-Anon and Alateen are designed to help families and teenagers who have been affected by an alcoholic parent.

5.  T    There are support groups for adults to discuss and deal with the lingering effects of growing up in an alcoholic family.

6.  F    If truly addicted, the drug becomes such a focus that children are neglected.

7.   T      For example, an "enabler" might call the worksite of a spouse to explain that the spouse is sick to cover up the fact that he or she is drunk or hungover.

8.   F      Children of parents who abuse alcohol or other drugs are four times more likely to develop a problem if they use.

9.   F      The eldest child often has to take on the role that an abusing parent neglects.

10.   F      Family violence is much higher in alcoholic families. Alcohol abuse appears to promote negative emotions and primitive aggression in many people.

11.   T      There is a genetic factor in that even children raised apart from their alcoholic parents are at more risk than other children. However, most of the problem appears to be passed down the generations due to learning.

12.   F      Most alcoholics or drug addicts have personal problems that they attempt to ignore by remaining intoxicated. They often lack the relaxed and loving social skills that create emotional closeness with their children.

## Chapter XIV

1.   F      A psychological addiction refers to strong cravings or desires that can be stimulated by observing drug-related activities or equipment. Memories associated with drugs can last a lifetime.

2.   F      Putting oneself in a tempting situation is a risky game to play.

3.   T      Even snow has been reported to stimulate cravings for cocaine.

4.   F      People need to have fun. A successful recovery must include finding a variety of pleasurable but not damaging things to do for fun.

5.  T    People easily and quickly fall back into old habits. Even the body can learn to become addicted, as physical addiction to narcotics occurs quicker than the first time.

6.  F    Relapse is common when a person is struggling to overcome an addiction. One should not give up after a failure but learn from it and try again.

7.  F    Society is presently very punitive toward users of illegal drugs. Lengthy incarceration, fines, loss of jobs, and the taking of houses, cars, and other belongings is part of the "zero tolerance" philosophy, even for simple users.

8.  F    The average citizen who does not use drugs blames much of the violence and ills of society on drug users.

9.  T    Everyone has pressures, but drug abuse is a poor way to deal with them. Temporary escape is necessary at times, and movies, books, walks, art, talking to friends, playing with pets, and many other methods exist to "get away" for a while. However, one should not make escape a way of life, as problems cannot be solved unless they are faced.

10. T    The federal prison system considers the use of illegal drugs as serious as assault. This is because the smuggling and payment for drugs can lead to violence.

11. F    Drug abuse is a lifestyle, and if a recovering addict leads much of that lifestyle and associates with people who use, the danger of relapse is high.

12. F    Pleasure is an important part of life. Learning to have fun while sober is necessary for full recovery.

# Appendix B
# *RECOMMENDED FILMS*

Many film companies will offer discounts for bulk orders. Check to see if you can order all your films at one time to receive lower prices, especially since many distributors (FMS and Coronet/MTI, in particular) carry the same films.

## Chapters II and III: OVERVIEW OF DRUGS AND ADDICTION/ THERORETICAL PERSPECTIVES

*A Matter of Balance.* Kinetic Films, 255 Delaware Ave., Ste. 340, Buffalo, NY 14202; 716/856-7631.

*And Then I'll Stop...* Pyramid Films, P.O. Box 1048, Santa Monica, CA 90406; 800/421-2304. Sophisticated cartoon.

*Brother Earl's Street Talk* and *What Problem.* Gerald T. Rogers Productions, 5215 Old Orchard Rd., Ste. 990, Skokie, IL 60077; 800/227-9100. Also sold by FMS. Lively speaker—disease concept.

*Drug Dependency: The Early Warning Signs.* AIMS Instructional Media Services Inc., 6901 Woodley Ave., Van Nuys, CA; 800/367-2467.

*Drug Profiles: The Physical and Mental Aspects.* AIMS Instructional Media Services Inc., 6901 Woodley Ave., Van Nuys, CA; 800/367-2467.

*Eight Hour Substance Abuse Program in Spanish (or English).* Pride Inc., 2715 Australian Ave., West Palm Beach, FL; 800/543-6909. Includes nine videos and a 300-page manual. A lecture format in the medical model/disease concept format. The 1990 cost is $1,295.

*It's Not My Problem.* (John Bradshaw) Pyramid Films, P.O. Box 1048, Santa Monica, CA 90406; 800/421-2304.

*How to Sabotage Your Treatment.* Gerald T. Rogers Productions. 800/227-9100. Shows common problems clients have in accepting treatment.

*Psychoactive Drugs.* Pyramid Films, 1537 14th St., Box 1048, Santa Monica, CA 90406.

*Medical Aspects of Mind-Altering Drugs.* FMS Productions, P.O. Box 337, 1029 Cindy Ln., Carpinteria, CA 93013; 800/421-4609.

*One Out of Ten.* Southerby Productions, 1709 E. 28th St., Long Beach, CA 90806.

*The Feeling Chart.* FMS Productions, P.O. Box 337, 1029 Cindy Ln., Carpinteria, CA 93013; 800/421-4609

*Shame and Addiction.* (John Bradshaw) FMS Productions, P.O. Box 337, 1029 Cindy Ln., Carpinteria, CA 93013; 800/421-4609.

*Second Half.* (Thomas Henderson) FMS Productions, P.O. Box 337, 1029 Cindy Ln., Carpenteria, CA 93013; 800/421-4609.

*Uppers, Downers, All Arounders.* Kinetic Films. 225 Delaware Ave., Ste. 340, Buffalo, NY 14202; 716/856-7631.

## Chapter V: ALCOHOL AND OTHER SEDATIVES

*Adult Children of Alcoholics: Choices for Growth.* Human Services Institute, P.O. Box 14610, Dept. A0123, Bradenton, FL 34280-4610.

*Alcoholism and the Family.* FMS Productions, P.O. Box 4428, E. Montecito St., Ste. F, Santa Barbara, CA 93140; 800/421-4609.

*Alcohol and Human Physiology.* AIMS Instructional Media Services, 6901 Woodley Ave., Van Nuys, CA 91406-4878; 800/367-2467.

*Children of Alcoholics.* Coronet/MTI Films, 420 Academy Dr., Northbrook, IL 60062; 800/621-2131.

*Chalk Talk.* (Father Martin) FMS Productions, P.O. Box 337, 1029 Cindy Ln., Carpinteria, CA 93013; 800/421-4609.

*Cruel Spirits. Alcohol and Violence.* Coronet/MTI Films, 420 Academy Dr., Northbrook, IL 60062; 800/621-2131.

*From Now On.* Gerald T. Rogers Productions, 5225 Old Orchard Rd., Ste. 23, Skokie, IL 60077; 312/967-8080.

*Drunk and Deadly.* Pyramid Films, P.O. Box 1048, Santa Monica, CA 90406; 800/421-2304. DUI film.

*Guidelines.* (Father Martin) FMS Productions, P.O. Box 337, 1029 Cindy Ln., Carpinteria, CA 93013; 800/421-4609.

*I'll Quit Tomorrow.* Johnson Institute, 510 N. 1st Ave., Minneapolis, MN 55403-1607; 800/231-5165.

*Three Headed Dragon.* FMS Productions, P.O. Box 337, 1029 Cindy Ln., Carpenteria, CA 93013; 800/421-4609. Concentrates on thinking, feeling, and behaving.

*Twelve Steps: The Video.* Gerald T. Rogers Productions, 5225 Old Orchard Rd., Ste. 23, Skokie, IL 60077; 312/967-8080.

## Chapter VI: NARCOTIC ANALGESICS

*Dead is Dead.* AIMS Instructional Media Services Inc., 6901 Woodley Ave., Van Nuys, CA; 800/367-2467.

*Heroin and Human Physiology.* AIMS Instructional Media Services, 6901 Woodley Ave., Van Nuys, CA 91406-4878; 800/367-2467.

*From Opium to Heroin.* FMS Productions, P.O. Box 337, 1029 Cindy Ln., Carpinteria, CA 93013.

*Scag.* Britannica Films, 425 N. Michigan Ave., Chicago, IL 60611; 800/558-6968.

*Wall of Denial.* Kindred Publishing, 815 N. Salisipuedes St., Suite 2, Santa Barbara, CA 93103; 800/727-8858.

## Chapter VIII: COCAINE AND CRACK

*Cocaine, Beyond the Looking Glass.* The Hazelden Foundation, Pleasant Valley Rd., Box 176, Center City, MN 55012-0176.

*Cocaine Blues.* Pyramid Films, P.O. Box 1048, Santa Monica, CA 90406; 800/421-2304. Older film.

*Cocaine Diary.* Coronet/MTI Films, 420 Academy Dr., Northbrook, IL 60062; 312/940-1260 or 800/621-2131.

*Cocaine Country.* Films Incorporated, 5547 N. Ravenswood, Chicago, IL 60640-1199; 312/878-2600, ext. 43.

*Cocaine, The End of the Line.* AIMS Instructional Media Services Inc., 6901 Woodley Ave., Van Nuys, CA 91406-4878; 800/367-2467.

*Cocaine and Human Physiology.* AIMS Instructional Media Services Inc., 6901 Woodley Ave., Van Nuys, CA 91406-4878; 800/367-2467.

*Cocaine Pain.* Coronet/MTI Films, 420 Academy Dr., Northbrook, IL 60062; 312/940-1260 or 800/621-2131.

*Cocaine Trail.* Coronet/MTI Films, 420 Academy Dr., Northbrook, IL 60062; 312/940-1260 or 800/621-2131.

*Haight-Ashbury Cocaine Film.* FMS Productions, P.O. Box 337, 1029 Cindy Ln., Carpinteria, CA 93013; 800/421-4609.

*Smokeable Cocaine.* MTI/Coronet or FMS Productions, P.O. Box 337, 1029 Cindy Ln., Carpinteria, CA 93013; 800/421-4609. Recommended film.

*Straight Talk on Crack/Cocaine.* Pride Inc., 2715 Australian Ave., West Palm Beach, FL 33407; 800/543-6909. Film series and program on cocaine.

## Chapter IX: TOBACCO

*Medical Aspects of Tobacco.* FMS Productions, P.O. Box 337, 1029 Cindy Ln., Carpinteria, CA 93013; 800/421-4609.

*Smoking: How to Stop.* Pyramid Film and Video, Box 1048, Santa Monica, CA 90406; 800/421-2304. (1977)

*Smoking: A Report on the Nation's Habit.* Journal Films, 930 Pitner Ave., Evanston, IL 60202; 800/323-5448. (1982)

*Smoking: Games Smokers Play.* Document Associates/The Cinema Guild, 1697 Broadway, Ste. 802, New York, NY 10019; 212/246-5522.

## Chapter X: HALLUCINOGENS

*Angel Death.* FMS Productions, P.O. Box 337, 1029 Cindy Ln., Carpinteria, CA 93013; 800/421-4609. Sold by MTI also.

## Chapter XI: CANNABIS (MARIJUANA)

*Hemp for Victory.* H.E.M.P., 5632 Van Nuys Blvd., Van Nuys, CA 91401. 1942 USDA film on hemp history.

*Marijuana.* (Dr. Olms-1990) FMS Productions, P.O. Box 337, 1029 Cindy Ln., Carpinteria, CA 93013; 800/421-4609.

*Marihuana and Human Physiology.* AIMS Instructional Media Services, 6901 Woodley, Van Nuys, CA 91406-4878; 800/367-2467.

*Waking Up From Dope.* Athena Productions, 22458 Ventura Blvd., Ste. E, Woodland Hills, CA 91364; 818/880-6370.

## Chapter XIII: THE IMPACT OF ALCOHOL AND DRUG ABUSE ON THE FAMILY

*A Letter to Dad.* Gerald T. Rogers Productions, 5215 Old Orchard Rd., Ste. 990, Skokie, IL 60077; 800/227-9100 or 708/967-8080. (60 mins.)

*Alcohol and the Family.* (Father Martin) FMS Productions, P.O. Box 337, 1029 Cindy Ln., Carpinteria, CA 93013; 800/421-4609.

*Children of Alcoholics.* MTI/Coronet Video, 420 Academy Dr., Northbrook, IL 60062; 312/940-1260 or 800/621-2131.

*Children of Denial.* "Roles," "Recovery," and "Child's View." MAC Publishing, 5005 E. 39th Ave., Denver, CO 80207; 303/331-0148. Four separate videos, based on the work of Claudia Black.

*Ernie Larson Series II.* Kinetic Films, 255 Delaware Ave., Buffalo, NY 14202; 716/856-7631.

*Healing the Family Within.* (Robert Subby) Concept Media, P.O. Box 19542, Irvine, CA 92713; 800/233-7078 or 714/660-0727. Five videos on codependency also available.

*Inheriting Alcoholism.* Coronet/MTI Films, 420 Academy Dr., Northbrook, IL 60062; 312/940-1260 or 800/621-2131.

*Lots of Kids Like Us.* Kinetic Inc., 255 Delaware Ave., Ste. 340, Buffalo, NY 14202; 716/856-7631.

*My Father's Son.* Gerald T. Rogers Productions, 5225 Old Orchard Rd., Ste. 23, Skokie, IL 60077; 312/967-8088.

*Pieces of Silence.* (Robert Subby) Concept Media, P.O. Box 19542, Irvine, CA 92713; 800/233-7078 or 714/660-0727.

*Soft is the Heart of a Child.* Operation Cork, 8939 Villa La Jolla, Ste. 203, San Diego, CA 92037; 619/452-5716.

*The What and Why of Codependency.* Concept Media, P.O. Box 19542, Irvine, CA 92713; 800/233-7078 or 714/660-0727.

## Chapter XIV: RELAPSE PREVENTION

*Breaking the Chains.* Kinetic Films, 255 Delaware Ave., Ste. 340, Buffalo, NY 14202; 716/856-7631.

*Recovery Series I and II—Ernie Larsen.* Kinetic Films, 225 Delaware Ave., Ste. 340, Buffalo, NY 14202; 716/856-7631. Twelve-step approach.

*Together: Families in Recovery.* Gerald T. Rogers Productions, 5215 Old Orchard Rd., Ste. 990, Skokie, IL 60077; 800/227-9100.

*Twelve Steps, The Video.* Gerald T. Rogers Productions. 800/227-9100. Explains each step through dramatization.

*What Can I Do Today?* Pyramid Films, P.O. Box 1048, Santa Monica, CA 90406; 800/421-2304. Twelve-step.

# Appendix C
# *RECOMMENDED RESOURCES*

AA World Services
P.O. Box 459, Grand Central Station
New York, NY 10163
212/686-1100

Al-Anon Family Group Hdqtrs.
P.O. Box 862, Midtown Station
New York, NY 10018
212/302-7240

Alateen
P.O. Box 182, Madison Square Garden
New York, NY 10159-0182
212/683-1771

Alcoholism Center for Women
1147 S. Alvarado St.
Los Angeles, CA 90006

Alcoholism in the Black Community
ABC Addiction Services
East Orange General Hospital
300 Central Ave.
East Orange, NJ 07019

American Atheist Addiction
Recovery Group
2344 S. Broadway
Denver, CO 80210
303/722-1525

American Council for Drug Education
204 Monroe St., #110
Rockville, MD 20850
301/294-0600

Batterers Anonymous
1269 Northeast St.
San Bernardino, CA 92405
714/383-2972

Channing L. Bete Co.
South Deerfield, MA 01373
413/665-7611
*Numerous pamphlets, easily understood.*

Cocaine Anonymous (CA)
712 Wilshire Blvd., Ste. 149
Santa Monica, CA 90401
213/553-8306

Drugs Anonymous
P.O. Box 473, Ansonia Station
New York, NY 10023
212/874-0700

Drug Enforcement Administration
FTS Number 633-1469
*They will supply up to 100 copies of a free color booklet titled "Drugs of Abuse." If this excellent DEA summary of drug types and their effects is used in class, be sure to tell students that alcohol is included with the sedatives and that caffeine and tobacco are included with the stimulants.*

Drug Policy Foundation
4801 Massachusetts Ave., N.W.,
Suite 400
Washington, DC 20016-2087
800/388-3784

Families Anonymous
P.O. Box 528
Van Nuys, CA 91408
818/989-7841

Families in Action
National Drug Information
3845 N. Druid Hills Rd., #300
Decatur, GA 30033
404/325-5799

The Haworth Press
10 Alice St.
Binghamton, NY 13904-9908
800/3-Haworth
*Numerous books, journals, and pamphlets.*
*Addictions model.*

Hazelden
Box 11
Center City, MN 55012
800/328-9000
*Numerous books, pamphlets, and training*
*programs. Medical model.*

Health Edco, Inc.
P.O. Box 21207
Waco, TX 76702
800/433-2677
*Displays, diseased body specimens, models.*

International Council on Alcohol and the
Addictions
33 Russell St.
Toronto, Ontario
M4S 2S1 Canada
416/595-6033

The Johnson Institute
510 N. 1st Ave.
Minneapolis, MN 55403-1607
800/231-5165
In Minnesota: 800/247-0484
*Numerous books, pamphlets, and training*
*programs. Disease model.*

Krames Communication
312 90th St.
Daly City, CA 94015-1898
(800) 228-8347
*Colorful pamphlets, simple to understand;*
*good family material.*

National Self-Help Clearinghouse
33 West 42nd St., Room 1206 A
New York, NY 10036
612/840-7607

NCADI Publications Catalogue
P.O. Box 2345
Rockville, MD 20852
301/468-2600
*Many books and pamphlets and free*
*publications and videos.*

NarAnon
P.O. Box 2562
Palo Verdes, CA 90274
213/547-5800

Narcotics Anonymous
P.O. Box 9999
Van Nuys, CA 91409
818/780-3951

National Association of Alcoholism &
Drug Abuse Counselors
3717 Columbia Pike, #300
Arlington, VA 20004
703/920-4644

National Institute of Drug Abuse
5600 Fishers Lane
Rockville, MD 20857
301/443-1644

NORML
1636 R St., N.W.
Washington, DC 20009
202/483-5500

Potsmokers Anonymous
316 E. Third St.
New York, NY 10009
212/254-5810

U.S. Public Health Service
AIDS Hotline 800/342-2437
*Free pamphlets about AIDS, etc., in*
*several languages.*

# Appendix D
## *SUGGESTED INTAKE LECTURE*

### What is addiction?

Addiction is an irresistible compulsion to use drugs at increasing frequency even in the face of serious physical and/or psychological effects. This use eventually leads to the extreme disruption of personal values and life.

### What does addiction include?

1. Increased tolerance. You need more of the drug more often to get the same effect.

2. Withdrawal. You become physically ill or experience severe discomfort and irritability when you stop taking the drug.

3. Deterioration in family relationships. You pull further away from your family and friends because you believe they will not approve of your drug use.

4. Job performance suffers. You begin to call in sick, and the quality of your work deteriorates.

5. Illegal activities appear. You sell drugs or begin to associate with those who are criminally inclined. You end up in prison.

6. Your physical and mental health deteriorates. You develop medical or psychological problems directly or indirectly related to your use.

### What can be done?

1. Intensive self-evaluation. One needs to be honest with him or herself. If you have a problem, the first step is to be strong enough to recognize it and admit it to yourself.

2. Ask for help. Seek treatment through the drug abuse program at the institution. Your attitude is crucial in how much you will gain from treatment. You must want change and be willing to work toward your recovery.

3. Attend "self-help" groups. Once released, attend AA or NA to continue to arrest your addiction. Most addiction counselors agree that you can never be cured of an addiction. Your addiction to drugs only can be arrested. The cravings and desire to use drugs might return occasionally. Regular attendance in self-help groups will help ensure that you will refrain from drug abuse once released.

4.  Seek help if you have a relapse. Chances are good that if you go back to drugs, you only will sink deeper into addiction without some type of intervention. Let family members help. Most people who go back to drugs begin to shut out the world around them when they need to do the opposite.

5.  Remember the problems that arose as a result of your past drug abuse. Drug users sometimes forget the pain and suffering they have experienced from their past abuse. Think about what drug abuse did to your values, health, and family.

6.  Remember that addiction can lead to legal complications. The new federal sentencing guidelines do not offer the opportunity for parole and hence more actual prison time probably will be served for drug-related crimes.

## What we expect from you if you decide to enter treatment here:

1.  That you attend and participate in every group session you enroll in.

2.  That you will complete all outside assignments as requested.

3.  That you will accept responsibility for your decisions and accept the consequences.

4.  That you refrain from abusing drugs.

## What you can expect from the program:

1.  A presentation of the mental and physical effects of drugs and alcohol.

2.  The opportunity to better understand your own personality and what motivates you.

3.  The opportunity to examine how your abuse has affected your family.

4.  The opportunity to change if you desire.

5.  Increased knowledge about personal vulnerabilities, which can help you prevent relapse.

# Appendix E
# *THE TWELVE STEPS*

We admitted that we were powerless over our addiction, that our lives had become unmanageable.

We came to believe that a power greater than ourselves could restore us to sanity.

We made a decision to turn our lives over to the care of God as we understood Him.

We made a searching and fearless inventory of ourselves.

We admitted to ourselves, to God, and to another human being the exact nature of our wrongs.

We were entirely ready to have God remove all these defects of character.

We humbly asked Him to remove our shortcomings.

We made a list of all the persons we had harmed and became willing to make amends to them all.

We made direct amends to such people wherever possible, except when to do so would injure them or others.

We continued to take a personal inventory and when we were wrong promptly admitted it.

We sought through prayer and meditation to improve our conscious contact with God as we understood Him, praying only for knowledge of His will for us and the power to carry that out.

Having had a spiritual awakening as a result of these steps, we tried to carry this message to addicts and to practice these principles in all our affairs.

# Appendix F
# LESSON PLAN OUTLINES

## Chapter I: INTRODUCTION

**PURPOSE:**

To provide an overview of the referral, screening, and basic level of programming in a comprehensive drug education program.

**OBJECTIVES:**

1. To understand how and why people become addicted to a drug by examining the different dynamics of the primary addict, the primary criminal, and the cultural addict.

2. To understand the effects continued abuse can have on one's health and life.

3. To understand how difficult and complicated it can be to treat an addiction.

4. To understand that treatment can be successful.

5. To convey the message that treatment programs are available during incarceration and while in the community.

6. In small groups, to develop a sense of trust and cohesion.

**TIME FRAME**

Two hours

**EXERCISES AND TEACHING TOOLS:**

1. Use a "name game" to help introduce group members to one another.

   • Have members pick a word that describes their personality that begins with the first letter of their first name, such as Gregarious George, "Jeffin" John, Action Allen, or Energetic Emily, for example. Next, ask each member to repeat the "slang" names of those who previously have introduced themselves.

   • Have members pick their favorite food and repeat it before their first name. For example: Hamburger George, Pizza John, Fried Chicken Allen, Steak Emily. Next, ask each member to repeat the "slang" names of those who previously have introduced themselves.

2.  Value Clarification Exercises

    -   Divide the group into smaller groups of three or four people. Ask each group to list in order from most dangerous to least dangerous the following drugs and to explain their reasons for their choices: marijuana, PCP, cocaine, alcohol, caffeine, heroin, tobacco. (Provide pencils and paper.)

    -   Redivide the small groups and ask them to rank order the following from most offensive to least offensive and have each group discuss their reasons for their decisions: an alcoholic mother who physically abuses her only child; a heroin addict who stays high all of the time and must resort to burglary to support his habit; a married executive with five children who loses everything because of his addiction to cocaine; a young teenager who smokes PCP daily and murders an elderly woman while high.

    -   Ask each member of the group how he or she would think, feel, and react if he or she found out that one of his or her children (age fifteen) was using marijuana.

    -   Ask each group member how he or she would react in thoughts, feelings, and actions if he or she found out the identity of the person who sold one of his or her children some PCP, which resulted in the psychiatric hospitalization of this child for one month.

## Chapter III: EXPLAINING ADDICTION

**PURPOSE:**

To provide an understanding of the progressive nature of addictions and the accompanying denial system that hinders effective treatment.

**OBJECTIVES:**

1.  To identify three reasons for drug abuse.

2.  To understand the difference between psychological and physical addiction.

3.  To understand that the body has a natural balance (homeostasis) and that drug abuse disrupts this balance.

4.  To understand the disease concept of addiction, including the effects on family.

5.  To understand the progressive nature of addiction.

**TIME FRAME:**

Two hours

**EXERCISES AND TEACHING TOOLS:**

1.  Have group members draw a picture of an addict or discuss what an addict looks and acts like. Be sure to list on the chalkboard or flipchart the terms used to describe an addict. Most people draw or describe the extreme, although an addict could be anybody and could look and act like anyone. People do not need to be "laying in an alley" to be an addict.

2.  Review the list of "triggers" of craving completed earlier.

3.  Ask members for personal examples of withdrawal experiences.

4.  Have group members add up all the money that they collectively have spent on drugs and alcohol in their entire lives. Add the total dollar amount on a flipchart or a chalkboard. This shows—by using money as a measure—the amount of interest and commitment group members have had toward drugs and alcohol.

5.  Have each group member list the specific impact drugs or alcohol have had on family, school, personal freedom, etc. This sensitizes group members to the effects of drugs or alcohol on their daily lives.

6.  Show the following films:
    *I'll Quit Tomorrow*
    *Drug Dependency: The Early Warning Signs*

## Chapter IV: A GENERAL OVERVIEW OF DRUGS
## AND DRUG ABUSE TERMINOLOGY

**PURPOSE:**

To provide an overview of the drug classifications and to introduce some common terminology.

**OBJECTIVES:**

1. To be able to identify five classes of drugs.

2. To understand the basic differences between these drug classes.

3. To understand generally how drugs affect the brain.

4. To understand what is meant by "synergism, antagonism, and potentiation."

5. To identify at least two dangerous drug combinations.

**TIME FRAME:**

Two hours

## Chapter V: ALCOHOL AND OTHER SEDATIVES

**PURPOSE:**

To present the effects of alcohol and other sedatives on the physical, psychological, and social well-being of users.

**OBJECTIVES:**

1. To identify at least three physical problems that can develop as a result of using alcohol and other sedatives.

2. To state three areas of psychological functioning that are affected by alcohol and other sedatives.

3. To be able to explain the family disease concept.

4. To understand the legal implications relating to the use and abuse of alcohol and other sedatives.

**TIME FRAME:**

Three hours

**EXERCISES AND TEACHING TOOLS:**

1. To illustrate why larger people often can drink more, a large and a small glass or jar of water can be used. Place one drop of food coloring in the big jar and one drop in the small jar. The food coloring does not color the water in the large jar as much. The drops show how one drink is dispersed through the blood system. Blood-alcohol content (BAC) therefore takes into account body size.

2. Show cirrhotic liver specimen and alcoholism folding display or models of affected body tissues sold by HEI, P.O. Box 21207, Waco, TX 76702; 800/433-2677.

3. Use pamphlets published by the following organizations:

   - AA World Services
     P.O. Box 459
     Grand Central Station
     New York, NY 10153
     212/686-1100

   - Al-Anon Family Group Headquarters
     P.O. Box 862
     Midtown Station
     New York, NY 10018
     212/302-7240

- Krames Communications
  312 90th Street
  Daly City, CA 94015-1898
  415/994-8800

- Channing L. Bete Co.
  South Deerfield, MA 01373
  413/665-7611

- NIDA
  5600 Fishers Lane
  Rockville, MD 20857
  301/443-1644

- Hazelden Foundation
  Box 11
  Center City, MN 55012
  800/328-9000

- Wisconsin Clearinghouse
  Dept. BC
  P.O. Box 1468
  Madison, WI 53701
  800/262-6243

- The Johnson Institute
  10700 Olson Memorial Highway
  Minneapolis, MN 55441-6199
  612/544-4165

What would you say about a disease
A disease that takes thousands of lives each year
Causes more deaths in youth
Costs billions of dollars a year to treat
Results in billions of dollars in lost productivity
Splits more families
Ruins more marriages
Kills more police than anything else,
and there is treatment available which most persons afflicted fail to use?

G.J.P.

## Chapter VI: NARCOTIC ANALGESICS: THE OPIATES

**PURPOSE:**

To develop an awareness of the effects of natural, semisynthetic, and synthetic narcotic analgesics on the body and mind and to understand the addictive properties of these drugs.

**OBJECTIVES:**

1. To identify three historical events related to narcotic use in America.

2. To understand three physiological effects of narcotic use.

3. To understand three psychological effects of narcotic use.

4. To identify three diseases that can result from using narcotics illicitly.

5. To understand the difference between medical and recreational use.

**TIME FRAME:**

Two hours (not including films)

**EXERCISES AND TEACHING TOOLS:**

1. Use the folding display on drug abuse sold by HEI, P.O. Box 21207, Waco, TX 76702.

2. Show the following films: *From Opium to Heroin* by FMS Productions and *Dead is Dead* by AIMS Media.

3. Ask each student to develop a list of elements that trigger thoughts about or cravings for the drug. Discuss with the students the true/false sample questions.

## Chapter VII: AMPHETAMINES AND OTHER STIMULANTS

**PURPOSE:**

To discuss the hazardous effects (psychological and medical) of amphetamine and other stimulant abuse. There is a potential trend away from cocaine abuse toward amphetamine abuse. Other types of stimulants as well as a description of look-alike stimulants are examined. A description of "ice" is included.

**OBJECTIVES:**

1. To describe the addictive properties of amphetamines and other stimulants.

2. To provide insight into stimulants of different strength levels and their dependence-producing properties.

3. To describe the psychological and medical consequences of stimulant abuse.

4. To outline treatment strategies for stimulant abuse.

**TIME FRAME:**

Two to two-and-one-half hours

## Chapter VIII: COCAINE

**PURPOSE:**

To discuss the hazardous effects (psychological and medical) stemming from the abuse of cocaine. Treatment strategies for cocaine abuse are outlined. A special section on "crack" cocaine is included. Although cocaine is classified as a stimulant, it is such a problem that an entire chapter is devoted to it.

**OBJECTIVES:**

1. To describe the addictive properties of cocaine.

2. To provide a self-assessment to determine whether one is addicted to cocaine.

3. To describe the psychological and medical consequences of cocaine abuse.

4. To outline treatment strategies for cocaine abuse.

5. To discuss the physical and psychological hazards of crack cocaine.

**TIME FRAME:**

Two to two-and-one-half hours (excluding films)

**EXERCISES AND TEACHING TOOLS:**

1. Administer Cocaine Addiction Survey found in Dr. Mark Gold's book *800-COCAINE.*

2. *Straight Talk on "Crack"/Cocaine* is a self-contained nine-video program (lecture format) specifically designed for use with inmates in treatment for crack/cocaine abuse. The program can expand this section into a forty-five-day program geared specifically to cocaine addiction (the 1990 price is $1,500). Available from Pride, Inc., 2715 Australian Ave., West Palm Beach, FL 33407; 800/543-6909.

## Chapter IX: TOBACCO

**PURPOSE:**

To develop an awareness of the mental and physical effects of tobacco products, whether they're smoked, chewed, or taken intranasally.

**OBJECTIVES:**

1. To identify four historical phases in the history of tobacco use: use by Native Americans, popularization around the world, economic importance to the development of America, and recent decline in use due to medical concerns.

2. To understand physiological effects, such as constricting blood vessels—increased blood pressure; paralyzation of lung cilia; tar and carbon monoxide; lung and throat irritation; and the role in impotence.

3. To understand psychological effects, including initial dizziness and lightheadedness; unusual combination of tranquilizing and stimulant properties; and addictive properties.

4. To understand the medical dangers of tobacco, such as bronchitis; emphysema; lung, mouth and throat cancer; the higher risk of heart attack; risk to fetuses.

**TIME FRAME:**

One-and-one-half hours

**EXERCISES AND TEACHING TOOLS:**

1. Show glass-encased sample of lung damaged by smoking sold by Spenco Medical Corporation, P.O. Box 8113, Waco, TX 76710.

2. Demonstration of tar sample taken from cigarette into "smoking doll" sold by Health Edco, Waco, TX 76702.

## Chapter X: HALLUCINOGENS

**PURPOSE:**

To present information on the psychoactive substances called hallucinogens.

**OBJECTIVES:**

1. Describe the general effects of drugs in the hallucinogens drug class, sometimes called psychedelics or mind-expanders.

2. Identify at least five drugs classified as hallucinogens.

3. Recall factual information about the names, history, origin, forms, dosage, path in the body, and effects while under the influence of LSD, psilocybin, mescaline, and PCP.

4. Describe at least two adverse effects of intoxication of LSD, psilocybin, mescaline, and PCP.

5. Describe at least two adverse long-term effects of psilocybin, mescaline, and PCP.

**TIME FRAME:**

Two hours

**EXERCISES AND TEACHING TOOLS:**

1. Before presenting the information on intoxicating effects of each drug, ask class members who have used the drug describe their experiences.

2. Assign homework in which drug X could be any of the hallucinogens: Ask, "What could you do naturally to produce experiences similar to the intoxicating effects of drug X?"

3. At the end of the lesson, ask class members to address this question: "In your opinion, which of the drugs we have discussed is the most harmful and why?"

4. Conduct a contest similar to the old "College Bowl." Divide the class into two teams. Ask the members of each team, in sequence, a question about the hallucinogens. Score points for correct answers.

## Chapter XI: CANNABIS (MARIJUANA)

**PURPOSE:**

To understand the mental and physical effects and the potential dangers of cannabis products.

**OBJECTIVES:**

1. To understand that cannabis products include marijuana, hashish, the oil extract, and the active ingredient THC.

2. To know that cannabis has an ancient history of use for hemp fiber and for medicinal, religious, and recreational purposes.

3. To know that its legality varies by nation and state, with acceptance in some areas, severe penalties in others.

4. To know that it is the most popular illegal drug in the United States; one-sixth of working-age adults regularly use it.

5. To learn the physical effects, including red eyes, increased heart rate, and impaired night-vision recovery.

6. To learn the mental effects, including impaired short-term memory, increased awareness of sensations, time distortions, and interference with complex tasks such as driving.

7. To become aware of possible medical problems such as lung damage, hormone reduction, and risk to unborn children.

8. To become aware of fear about the possibility of brain damage—that use is experimental and is not medically risk-free.

9. To appreciate the severe penalties for possession and distribution of the drug due to its prohibition.

**TIME FRAME:**

Two hours

**EXERCISES/TEACHING TOOLS:**

1. Ask group members to discuss ways they have behaved foolishly while stoned.

2. Display lung damaged by tobacco and discuss the similar danger potential of marijuana.

## Chapter XII: HIV INFECTION AND AIDS

**PURPOSE:**

To provide an overview of the human immunodeficiency virus (AIDS) and its effects; to understand the routes of infection and high-risk activities with specific emphasis on drug abuse.

**OBJECTIVES:**

1. To give a clear definition of AIDS.

2. To know at least three ways in which the AIDS virus can be transmitted.

3. To understand the progressive nature of the disorder.

4. To understand the physical symptoms associated with the disorder.

5. To understand how people diagnosed as HIV-positive are not contagious in terms of casual contact.

6. To learn that HIV-positive people should be treated humanely and fairly.

7. To learn that other diseases can be transmitted sexually and by sharing needles.

**TIME FRAME:**

Two hours

**EXERCISES AND TEACHING TOOLS:**

1. Ask group members if they know anyone who has AIDS or is HIV-positive. If they do, ask them how they reacted when they learned that information about the person.

2. Ask group members to describe how they would relate to news that their best friend is HIV-positive. Would this affect their relationship?

3. Ask members what they would do if they found that a family member had become infected through drug abuse with HIV. How would they feel about hugging, kissing, or sharing a glass of water with that person?

4. Ask members how they would react to news that they are HIV-positive. How would they like to be treated by others?

5. Show the following films:

   - *Needle Talk*
     *Bad Way to Die*
        by N.Y. State films (N.Y. Department of Corrections); 212/285-4632

- *Not A Game: Sexually Transmitted Diseases*
  *Nova: Can AIDS Be Stopped?*
    by Coronet/MTI Films; 800/621-2131

- *AIDS: Everything You Should Know*
    by AIMS Films; 800/367-2467

- *AIDS: The Facts*
    by Health Edco; 800/443-2677

- *About AIDS*
  *Young People and AIDS*
    by E. Channing L. Bete Co., Inc.; 800/628-7733

6. Use the following handouts/display materials/books:

- *Facts About AIDS*
  *AIDS Prevention Guide*
  *AIDS and You*
    available in a variety of languages from U.S. Public Health Service
    AIDS Hotline; 800/342-2437; 800/458-5231 (bulk orders)

- *AIDS: What You Don't Know Can Kill You*
  Flip chart: *How Does AIDS Kill?*
  Folding display: *AIDS*
  Teaching guide: *Teaching AIDS: A Teacher's Guide*
  Display model: *Sexually Transmitted Diseases,*
    available in English and Spanish from Health Edco; 800/443-2677

- Booklet: *AIDS*
    (available in English and Spanish)
  Brochure: *Understanding and Preventing AIDS*
    (available in English and Spanish)
  *Safer Sex*
  *Understanding Safer Sex*
  *The Love Bugs*
    from Krames Communications; 800/228-8347

- *About AIDS*
  *AIDS Information for Inmates*
    from Channing L. Bete Co., Inc.; 800/628-7733

- *Children, Parents, and AIDS*
  *Teenagers and AIDS*
  *Women, Sex, and AIDS*
  *Your Job and AIDS*
  *HIV Infection and Workers in Health Care Settings*
  *Drugs, Sex, and AIDS*
  *HIV Infection and AIDS*
  *School Systems and AIDS*
  *Men, Sex, and AIDS*

*Emergency and Public Workers and AIDS*
from The American Red Cross

- *AIDS in Correctional Facilities: Issues and Options*
*AIDS and the Law Enforcement Officer*
from the National Institute of Justice

- *About AIDS and IV Drug Abuse*
*What Gay and Bisexual Men Should Know About AIDS*
*About Protecting Yourself From AIDS*
from the Virginia Department of Health and other state health departments

## Chapter XIII: THE IMPACT OF DRUG AND ALCOHOL ABUSE ON THE FAMILY

### PURPOSE:

To teach coping skills related to alcohol use in a family setting; to provide an understanding of the effects of drug and alcohol abuse on family members; to review possible behavior patterns of the drug abuser's or alcoholic's children, which develop in response to parental substance abuse; and to understand that long-term emotional effects can develop in adult children of alcoholics and drug abusers.

### OBJECTIVES:

1. To identify three specific behavior patterns or roles that children commonly develop in alcoholic/drug abusing families.

2. To understand the relationship of early dysfunctional patterns to problems in adulthood.

3. To learn sources of help for the nonaddicted members of the family.

### TIME FRAME:

Education program, film *Soft is the Heart of a Child*, and discussion: two hours

Counseling version—*Children of Denial* and supporting films/books/manual based on the work of Claudia Black: Twelve hours

### EXERCISES AND TEACHING TOOLS:

1. Show the 26-minute videotape, *Soft is the Heart of a Child*

   - Use a flipchart or blackboard to list the names and the behavioral descriptions of the family members portrayed in the video. Divide the group and ask each smaller group to list on paper the names of the characters in the video. Then ask them to discuss the behavior of each character and determine which character had the most problems. Ask the small groups to share their perceptions and list their responses under the names of the characters on the board. Ask participants to predict what each child will be like as an adult.

2. Use the pamphlet titled "Alcoholism in the Family" to discuss the feelings that are common in the alcoholic family and observed in the video.

3. Ask participants to read the book, *It Will Never Happen to Me* by Claudia Black. *My Dad Loves Me, My Dad Has a Disease* and *Repeat After Me, The Stamp Game* by Claudia Black also are recommended. (All by Hazelden Educational Materials, Box 11, Pleasant Valley Rd., Center City, MN 55012; tel. 800/328-9000 (in Minnesota dial 800/257-0070). Relate how these roles can be similar to those adopted by children who grow up in homes where parents are dependent on other drugs such as cocaine.

4. Have group members form small groups to define what a healthy family is, what the proper roles of parents should be, and what level of communication and emotional expressiveness is normal.

5. Show these suggested films:

- *Alcohol, Children, and the Family* and *Adult Children of Alcoholics* are films that feature Dr. Cermack, chairman of the National Association for Children of Alcoholics. (AIMS Media, 6901 Woodley Ave., Van Nuys, CA; 800/367-2467)

- *Alcoholism and the Family*. (FMS Productions, P.O. Box 4428, 520 E. Montecito St., Ste. F, Santa Barbara, CA 93140; 800/421-4609)

- *Children of Alcoholics,* a 30-minute film from the perspective of a seventeen-year-old daughter and twelve-year-old son in an alcoholic family (MTI/Coronet Films, 108 Wilmot Rd., Deerfield, IL 60015; 800/421-4609.) Other MTI films such as *Inheriting Alcoholism, In the Shadow* series, *Codependents, Lots of Kids Like Us, Scared, Sad and Mad,* and *Families of Alcoholics* also might be useful.

- *Children of Denial* (28 minutes) is based on the work of Claudia Black. (MAC Publishing, 5005 E. 39th Ave., Denver, CO 80207; 303/331-0148.) Three other films titled *Roles, The Recovery Process,* and *Child's View* and a guide for treatment specialists that supports the film *Children of Denial* can be purchased as a package to expand this group into a twelve-hour program.

- *Codependency,* a five-video series program, includes:
  *The What and Why of Codependency*—22 minutes
  *Characteristics of Codependents*—23 minutes
  *The Path to Recovery*—20 minutes
  *Healing the Family Within*—44 minutes
  *Pieces of Silence*—56 minutes

- These films and accompanying material can expand the presentation of this chapter to ten hours. (Concept Media, P.O. Box 19542, Irvine, CA 92713; 800/233-3078 or 714/660-0727)

- *Soft is the Heart of a Child;* recommended film—clearly depicts roles of children in an alcoholic family, (Gerald T. Rogers Productions, 5225 Old Orchard Rd., Ste. 23, Skokie, IL 60077; 312/967-8080)

- *My Father's Son,* also produced by Gerald T. Rogers Productions, shows the familial link, enabling, and effects on children and might also be useful.

6. Distribute these recommended pamphlets:

- *Alcoholism in the Family*
  *Cocaine in the Family*
     Available from Krames Communication, 312 90th Street, Daly City, CA 94015-1898; 800/228-8347